How to Win in Small Claims Court in California

HOW TO WIN
IN SMALL
CLAIMS COURT
IN CALIFORNIA

with forms

Royce Orleans Hurst
Mark Warda
Attorneys at Law

Sphinx Publishing
A Division of Sourcebooks, Inc.
Naperville, IL • Clearwater, FL

First Edition, 1998

Published by: **Sphinx® Publishing: A Division of Sourcebooks, Inc.®**

Naperville Office	Clearwater Office
P.O. Box 372	P.O. Box 25
Naperville, Illinois 60566	Clearwater, Florida 33757
(630) 961-3900	(727) 587-0999
Fax: 630-961-2168	Fax: 727-586-5088

Interior Design and Production: Shannon E. Harrington, Sourcebooks, Inc.

This publication is designed to provide accurate and authoritative information in regard to the subject matter covered. It is sold with the understanding that the publisher is not engaged in rendering legal, accounting, or other professional service. If legal advice or other expert assistance is required, the services of a competent professional person should be sought.

From a Declaration of Principles Jointly Adopted by a Committee of the American Bar Association and a Committee of Publishers and Associations

Library of Congress Cataloging-in-Publication Data
Hurst, Royce Orleans.
    How to win in small claims court in California / Royce Orleans
Hurst, Mark Warda.—1st ed.
        p.   cm.
    Includes index.
    ISBN 1-57071-358-8 (pbk.)
    1. Small claims courts—California—Popular works.   I. Warda,
Mark.   II. Title.
KFC976.Z9H87   1998
347.794'04—dc21   98-14287
                                                              CIP

Printed and bound in the United States of America.

Paperback — 10 9 8 7 6 5 4 3 2 1

DEDICATION

To Hyman Wolfson, JD, CPA, M.B.A.

1920-1996

My law and mediation partner, my father, my friend

Royce Orleans Hurst

CONTENTS

Using Self-Help Law Books

Whenever you shop for a product or service, you are faced with various levels of quality and price. In deciding what product or service to buy, you make a cost/value analysis on the basis of your willingness to pay and the quality you desire.

When buying a car, you decide whether you want transportation, comfort, status, or sex appeal. Accordingly, you decide among such choices as a Neon, a Lincoln, a Rolls Royce, or a Porsche. Before making a decision, you usually weigh the merits of each option against the cost.

When you get a headache, you can take a pain reliever (such as aspirin) or visit a medical specialist for a neurological examination. Given this choice, most people, of course, take a pain reliever, since it costs only pennies, whereas a medical examination costs hundreds of dollars and takes a lot of time. This is usually a logical choice because rarely is anything more than a pain reliever needed for a headache. But in some cases, a headache may indicate a brain tumor, and failing to see a specialist right away can result in complications. Should everyone with a headache go to a specialist? Of course not, but people treating their own illnesses must realize that they are betting on the basis of their cost/value analysis of the situation, they are taking the most logical option.

The same cost/value analysis must be made in deciding to do one's own legal work. Many legal situations are very straight forward, requiring a simple form and no complicated analysis. Anyone with a little intelligence and a book of instructions can handle the matter without outside help.

But there is always the chance that complications are involved that only an attorney would notice. To simplify the law into a book like this, several legal cases often must be condensed into a single sentence or paragraph. Otherwise, the book would be several hundred pages long and too complicated for most people. However, this simplification necessarily leaves out many details and nuances that would apply to special or unusual situations. Also, there are many ways to interpret most legal questions. Your case may come before a judge who disagrees with the analysis of our authors.

Therefore, in deciding to use a self-help law book and to do your own legal work, you must realize that you are making a cost/value analysis and deciding that the chance your case will not turn out to your satisfaction is outweighed by the money you will save in doing it yourself. Most people handling their own simple legal matters never have a problem, but occasionally people find that it ended up costing them more to have an attorney straighten out the situation than it would have if they had hired an attorney in the beginning. Keep this in mind while handling your case, and be sure to consult an attorney if you feel you might need further guidance.

INTRODUCTION

California's small claims system provides a useful, simplified procedure for suing people or businesses that have caused you to suffer damages. Many claims are too small to warrant the services of an attorney but too big to ignore.

Simply filing a small claims case often gets results from people who know they owe money but haven't gotten around to paying it. Being brought before a judge is not something people look forward to, and sometimes being served with the claim brings an immediate check. On the other hand, going through the whole case and winning a judgment may be useless if a person has no money and there is nothing for you to collect.

California has several procedures for collecting judgments that are not often used because people either don't know about them or they think they are too complicated. One of them allows you to send a *keeper* to the losing party's business to collect money from the cash register. Another procedure forces the losing party to appear in court for a judgment debtor exam where you can ask questions about the losing party's assets. This book will explain how to use those procedures. You can be sure that the prospect of revealing all of their assets will cause many people to pay up!

While the small claims court was designed to make it possible to take court action without the expense of an attorney, legal advice can be very valuable in determining whether or not to sue, or if you are the defendant, what claims or defense to present. If you need legal advice, there are many attorneys who offer free or low cost consultations in the hope that you will hire them now or in the future. Most county bar associations can refer you to an attorney who will give you an initial consultation for a reasonable fee.

Before filing your case it is advisable to read this entire book. Sometimes information relating to the end of the process is important in planning the initial steps, or a decision made in the beginning may affect the procedures towards the end.

It is also useful to keep in mind the many alternatives available to resolving civil disputes. Increasingly popular is the process of mediation, where a neutral person assists the parties in reaching a resolution of the issues. It is a cooperative process where both sides get a chance to talk things out with the help of a person who has skills in interpersonal relationships. This procedure has many advantages over litigation in situations where you want to maintain a relationship, such as your landlord, your neighbor, your employer, or your best friend. You can decide to mediate at any time during the process, including the day of the hearing, or after judgment to work out a payment plan. Some courts even require the parties to try mediation and have mediators waiting in the courtroom on the days hearings are set. (Information regarding how to find a mediator is in appendix H.)

Author's Notes

Fresh out of law school in 1979, I was hired by the City Attorney's Office of a major city in California to defend cases brought against the city by its residents and visitors who fell on its sidewalks, clashed with its police, collided with its vehicles and light standards, and rented its facilities. As a prerequisite to filing a lawsuit against most governmental agencies, a claim must be served in which the government is put on notice of a potential lawsuit. In the four years I worked for the city, not once did I see a claim for damages approved; not even a claim made by an elderly woman who fell over a tree stump and asked for $1.89 to replace her torn nylons.

Some of the toughest cases to win were the small claims appeals. These were cases that had been won by the plaintiffs in small claims court, appealed by the city and then assigned to attorneys. I was at a clear disadvantage. While I had several dozen cases in my caseload, and not a lot of time to devote to each case, the small claims plaintiffs were knowledgeable on the applicable law, dedicated, well-prepared, and determined to win, much more so than the lawyers who they sometimes hired to take over the appeal.

More out of curiosity than anything else, I started attending small claims sessions to see if my opponents were extraordinary in any way. What I found was an array of litigants. Some strode into court confidently, carrying blow-ups of photos of intersections. Others looked like they could barely drag themselves out of bed, making every mistake possible. This I expected. What was troubling were the easily preventable mistakes in preparation that could have easily been avoided if the parties had only known the peculiarities of the rules and statutes of the small claims court. This book is meant to be a guide for those who don't know the first thing about presenting or defending a small claims case. It is also my hope that it will serve as a reference for more sophisticated parties who need only occasional help or guidance.

I have now become a full time mediator, helping people and organizations in the task of creative problem-solving so that they can move past the win-lose model towards a solution which results in a "win-win" for all. Although not every case can be resolved by mediation, many disputes can, resulting in real satisfaction.

The best advice I ever got as an attorney was to prepare every case as though it is going to trial. In California, only five percent of civil cases actually do. So I'm passing this advice on to you. The better prepared you are to try your case, the stronger you will be in negotiation or mediation, whether you attempt one of these processes voluntarily or by directive of the court.

Royce Orleans Hurst

June 1, 1998

INTRODUCTION TO SMALL CLAIMS COURT

1

WHAT IS SMALL CLAIMS COURT?

Small claims court is a forum where people with "small" disputes can have a judge, a commissioner, or an attorney acting as a temporary judge decide their legal rights. It is usually located in a courtroom set aside in the municipal court. The parties cannot be represented by an attorney in California although attorneys can represent themselves if they are bringing or defending a claim. The rules of procedure are simplified so that cases can be heard within forty days of filing, or seventy days, if the defendant lives out of the county where you are filing the initial paperwork. It is important to note that some counties have local rules and procedures that must be followed in addition to the more general state rules.

HOW MUCH CAN YOU SUE FOR?

The small claims court has *jurisdiction* of up to $5,000, meaning that $5,000 is the upper limit of a judgment that can be granted by the court, not including costs fees and interest. But there is an exception to the limit if you file more than two small claims actions in one year. The limit for the third and every other case you file for the rest of the year will be $2,500. There is no limit on the number of claims where you can ask for $2,500 or less. Even if the judge deciding your case thinks you should recover $10,000, the law limits the amount you can recover to $5,000. This is a vast improvement over the $2,500 limit that was in place until a few years ago.

TYPES OF CASES   The most common kind of case involves a request for money, such as when someone damages your property and refuses to pay for it or your landlord refuses to return your security deposit. Small claims actions for unlawful consumer practices are filed against almost every kind of commercial establishment, including banks, auto towing companies, property management firms, department stores, furniture rental companies and auto tune-up franchises. Suits proliferate against governmental entities such as school districts, cities, counties and the State of California since they rarely pay legitimate claims made against them. It is important to know that a suit against the government (e.g. a city vehicle crashed into your motorcycle) requires special claims procedures within specific time periods. Local merchants sue customers for wrongful "stop payment" orders where the damages include the amount of the check and up to $1,500 in penalties under California's bad check statute.

There are very few lawyers who will take on a personal injury lawsuit where the damages are under $5,000 because it simply is not cost-effective for them. On the other hand, injured people with $3,000 or $4,000 in damages rarely want to pay contingency fees (often amounting to over $1,000). As a result, many personal injury suits are heard in small claims court.

There have been efforts in the state legislature to raise the amount you can sue for in auto accident cases to $10,000. So far, these efforts have failed, probably because of the strong consumer attorney lobby. But personal injury suits are not limited to auto accidents. You can sue when you've suffered injury as a result of a product that did not operate the way it was supposed to, such as a chair that did not hold a normal person's weight. You can also sue if you are injured when someone pulls a chair out from under you as a prank. If they didn't mean to injure you, this is an example of *negligence*. Another example of negligence is the situation where a store owner fails to clean up spilled liquids within a reasonable time. Or your neighbor's dog may have taken a bite out of a member of your family because the dog was not properly restrained. The dog's owner is negligent for his failure to restrain the dog. Even if a dog never bit anyone before, you can sue the owner in small claims court under the theory of *strict liability*. (There is no such thing as a free bite.) Other examples of potential liability include a property owner's lax security resulting in unnecessary exposure to criminal activity or the failure of restaurant employees to wash their hands after using the lavatory resulting in food poisoning. The possibilities of negligent behavior are endless.

You can sue when the terms of a contract are breached and you suffer damages as a result. (The blinds you ordered for your windows were measured incorrectly and are six inches too short.) You can bring an action when an intentional act of someone caused you harm. For example your neighbor punched you in the face causing a broken tooth or ordered their dog to attack you.

Can You Ask for Remedies Other Than Money?

The small claims court also hears *equitable actions*. These are special kinds of cases where the plaintiff requests that the judge order someone to do something other than pay money. Some examples of equitable actions are:

SPECIFIC
PERFORMANCE

In some cases money is not an adequate remedy. For example, suppose you purchased an oil painting to be delivered on Saturday. If the seller refuses to deliver the painting, you could sue him for *specific performance* which means you ask the judge to force him to deliver the painting to you.

RESCISSION   If a deal was made under a *mistaken* assumption or under duress you could sue for rescission of the contract. Rescission is discussed in chapter 6.

RESTITUTION   If you were the seller of an oil painting, and the buyer obtained possession without paying for it, you could ask for *restitution*, meaning it would be returned to you. Getting an item back is often better than getting a money judgment that will never be paid.

REFORMATION   Where a written agreement does not express the true understanding of the parties, a court can reform the contract to express their intent. For example, if you sign a receipt to sell a 1988 auto to your neighbor and accidentally write 1998, you probably won't have to deliver a 1998 car to him. If he sued for that you could ask the judge to *reform* the contract to reflect the correct date.

NUISANCE   Another special kind of case is a *nuisance* action. Loud music from the apartment upstairs is a private nuisance if it only bothers you. Another example is your neighbor's cat that uses your daughter's sandbox as a litter box. But if several people in a particular neighborhood are subject to the same nuisance, such as noxious fumes from a factory or a house where drugs are sold, it is a *public nuisance*. This is an example of the type of situation where consulting a lawyer for advice makes financial sense since the cost can be spread among several people.

HOW DOES THE PROCEDURE WORK?

When you file a claim, you are the *plaintiff* and the persons or company you are suing is the *defendant*.

Filling out the claim is fairly simple. You then hand over the claim to the court clerk who checks it for accuracy and directs you to the cashier to pay.

The clerk will then assign a time and date for the hearing. Be sure to find out whether the court has night or Saturday sessions if you prefer them. If some days are better for you than others, be sure to let the clerk know. You can also file your claim by mail but very few people take the chance since a careless mistake will result in the claim being sent back to you unfiled.

After the case is filed, it is up to you to make sure the defendants get served properly and that your witnesses show up promptly on the date of the hearing. It is up to you to prepare your case and present it to the judge. If you fail to appear for your own case, the judge can decide it against you. If you are inclined to forget to show up at important engagements, make sure you have asked your family members to keep reminding you of the date and have at least one of them plan to go with you.

After your case has been heard, the court will usually make its decision within three weeks of the hearing. You will receive the judgment in the mail, which starts the time period running for an appeal. After the appeal period is over, formal collection procedures can begin.

Do You Need an Attorney?

Small claims court was designed for people who do not plan to use an attorney. In fact, attorneys are normally not permitted in small claims court in California. However, if the amount of money in dispute is substantial, or the law is confusing to you, you may wish to obtain a consultation with an attorney just to make sure you are on the right track.

Cases with a value of more than $5,000 are often filed in small claims court despite the monetary limits. In situations where the attorneys' fees would cost more than the portion of the claim in excess of $5,000, it may make sense to take advantage of the benefits of small claims court. For example, if the contractor you hired to build your swimming pool refused to finish the job, and you paid another contractor $7,200 to do the work, the $5,000 you could win in small claims court still leaves you $2,200 short. If an attorney tells you that he would charge you only $1,500 to represent you in municipal court, it seems that you would still come out ahead by $750 by using the attorney. However, it costs $86 to $93 to file a case in municipal court, $66 to $73 more than you would pay in small claims court, so now you are only ahead by approximately $675. If the lawyer plans to take depositions, subpoena records, or hire an expert, that $675 may not be enough to cover the costs of litigation.

Another important issue to consider is whether the type of lawsuit allows the winner to collect attorney's fees. Even simple one-page contracts sometimes have an attorney's fee paragraph hidden in the small print. Since no attorneys are permitted in small claims court, neither party will be required to pay the other's lawyer.

There is no way of guaranteeing a result. If you file the claim in small claims court and lose, you'll probably wonder if you would have won if you had hired an attorney to pursue the case in municipal court. On the other hand, if the attorney loses in municipal court, you may be responsible for your opponents attorney fees as well as your own. In that case, you will surely regret not having filed the case in small claims court. In fact, even though lawyers are allowed to represent parties during the appeal of a small claims act the hiring of an attorney is usually not cost-effective and few do so.

WHERE ELSE CAN YOU GET HELP?

It is important to remember that the court clerks are not attorneys and are prohibited from giving legal advice. Nevertheless, they are often excellent sources of information regarding the preparation of forms and the procedures adopted by the local courts. You should always listen carefully to the advice of the clerk. They have the "inside track" on the preferences and nuances of their particular courts. Some clerks have worked at the courthouse for so many years that they are more knowledgeable than most attorneys and judges on small claims matters. Be polite and don't argue with them. Astute attorneys know that a court clerk can be your best friend or your worst enemy. They can put your case on the top of the pile or on the bottom. They can direct your case to the judge who takes all day to hear two cases or to the judge who will get you in and out of the court in less than an hour. Even if you are only going to the courthouse to pick up a form, don't let the clerk see you looking unkempt. They may take it as a sign of disrespect for the court and they will remember.

Under California Code of Civil Procedure §116.940 all counties are required to provide advice on small claims court. The person providing this advice is called the *small claims advisor* and may be available in person or by telephone. Smaller counties may share an adviser with other counties. Appendix F contains the name, address and telephone number, where available, of the advisor for each county.

WHAT TYPES OF LOSSES CAN YOU RECOVER?

As a general rule, you can only recover actual out-of-pocket losses directly relating to the subject matter of the case. For example, if you are suing a dry cleaner for ruining a dress, you can sue for the replacement value of the dress (depending on whether it was brand new or retrieved from your mother's closet because clothes from the 1950s look really cool). If you are suing an auto mechanic for improperly repairing your car, you can sue for the cost of repairs if they do not exceed the value of the car. If you loaned money that hasn't been repaid, you may be entitled to interest as well as the principal of the loan. In a personal injury case, you are entitled to a whole range of damages including pain and suffering, economic loss and future medical treatment.

You generally can't recover for the fact that you missed a day of work because you didn't have the dress or car. Nor can you recover lost wages for time you spend in court or your travel costs to court, even if you had to fly in from out-of-state or drive a long distance.

In some situations, under specific statutes you may be entitled to recover penalties and punitive damages.

If you are the prevailing party, meaning you won on a significant issue in the case, you probably will be awarded your costs of the suit. These include your filing fee, sheriff's fee and witness fees. It is up to you to decide if it is worth spending $100 in costs to win a $50 case since you would be entitled to $150 if you win.

As discussed in the next chapter, you should ask for as much as possible within the small claims court in order to improve your negotiating position (even if you know you will not be granted everything in court), but as a practical matter, you usually won't get much more than out-of-pocket losses.

TERMINOLOGY

While the court system strives to make small claims court as simple as possible, there are still legal terms that are used to describe many forms and procedures. These are defined in the glossary in the back of this book.

BEFORE YOU SUE 2

SHOULD YOU SUE?

Before you file a case in small claims court, you should first analyze whether it is worth your time and effort to go through the whole process. Even though a trial in small claims court is much quicker and easier than a case in municipal or superior court, you will have to spend a lot of time preparing your case, filing the correct forms and collecting the judgment. Maybe you want to file a case because you are upset about something, but a trial can be an emotionally draining experience, even if you win. It will be even more upsetting if you lose, especially if you end up paying damages to the other side. Most cases settle out of court because you can never predict what result you will get in court. No matter how right you are, or how strong your case is, the court can rule the other way for any number of reasons.

You should almost always attempt to resolve the dispute before filing the case. In fact, the law governing small claims procedures requires you to ask the other side to pay the amount owed before you file the lawsuit. The reason for this rule is that many people come to court and say they haven't paid the amount owed simply because they were never asked! It is a good practice to make the request in writing and keep a copy of it to present to the court as evidence that you have tried to resolve the matter.

DO YOU HAVE A CASE?

In order to win a lawsuit against someone, you must be able to prove they are liable under some acceptable legal theory. In many instances, a person who has clearly suffered a loss may not be able to win their case because the law doesn't place the liability on another person. Before filing your case you must find a legal theory that will allow you to win. Some cases are easy. If a person did something intentionally (like hitting you in the jaw) or failed to do something that was legally required (like pay back a loan) then you have a clear case.

Sometimes you must use a more complicated theory, such as negligence or implied warranty. In cases like these you will only win if the facts of your case fit into the legal definitions. If you are struck by lightning while walking at an amusement park, the owners will probably not be liable because the courts consider lightning an "act of God" and not the legal responsibility of the landowner. (A person once tried to sue God for an act of God. He served the papers on a local church as an "agent of God." But the court said that the church was not legally able to accept service of process for God so the court "did not have jurisdiction over the defendant.")

For another example, imagine you have leased a house from a landlord. When you signed the lease, you agreed to take care of minor maintenance and the landlord agreed to charge you less rent. Now suppose you fixed a board on the steps and later it broke, causing you to fall and break your leg. Even though the landlord owns the property and has insurance against liability, the landlord (or the landlord's insurance company) will probably not be liable because you had a duty to maintain the premises and you are the one who improperly fixed the step which broke. On the other hand, if the landlord supplied you with defective materials to fix the step, the landlord, the supplier, and the manufacturer may all be liable for your injury and your improper maintenance would be considered merely contributory negligence.)

If you signed a contract or received any documents or papers from the other party relating to the transaction, you should read them very carefully before filing suit. Sometimes they will limit your legal rights or your right to bring suit. If a business made oral promises about a product but the contract said that the product was sold "as is" and that "oral representations cannot be relied upon," you may be out of luck. Or if your contract with your stock broker says that you agree to binding arbitration, you may have given up your right to sue in court.

In some cases, the papers used by the party may not have any legal effect. Parking lot machines often hand out "tickets" that say they are not liable for any loss or damage to your vehicle on the premises, but in some instances, California law says otherwise and this overrules the wording on the parking ticket. Receipts you receive for bringing clothing to a tailor for alterations, a car in for repairs, or a computer in for required maintenance may say that the shop is not liable for damages but in many instances, California law allows you to recover anyway.

If you have any doubts about your rights, you should either check with an attorney, do some research yourself, or both. Many types of claims are explained in this book, but if you are industrious, you may want to do some extra legal research to find other causes of action or grounds for your suit. You can do legal research at the law library found in most county courthouses or at the law library in some law schools. Law schools often restrict use of their law libraries to their own students and attorneys, so check first. Some college libraries have substantial law sections, especially if they offer paralegal or other law related degrees.

The internet contains excellent sources of information, many of them easily searchable. For example, the entire California Code is available and can be searched by code section, keyword or subject. The web site is: http://www.leginfo.ca.gov/index.html

The California court cases available on the internet at no charge is limited at this time, but will be expanded over the years. The web site is:

http://www.courtinfo.ca.gov

You can also find services on the internet that will do your research for you (for a fee, of course) and there are some databases available for a fee. There are several books on the market explaining how to do legal research. If you cannot find one locally, contact your local bookstore or Sphinx Publishing at (800) 226-5291 for a copy of *Legal Research Made Easy*, by Suzan Herskowitz.

CAN YOUR PROVE YOUR CASE?

Even if you have a good case, you will not win if you do not have enough proof to convince the judge or commissioner that you are right. If all you have is a verbal agreement, it will be your word against the other party and the judge will have to decide who is more believable. If you do not have any evidence and the other side has evidence that supports their position, it is unlikely that you will win.

Be sure to read the rules of evidence in chapter 7. Also, ask a friend (the one that always tell you the truth) what he or she believes are the best points of the other side's case. As a participant in the situation you will not be able to effectively judge the merits of the arguments on either side as objectively as your friends. He or she may be able to point out the weaknesses of your case or a legal rule or other reason that you could lose the case.

IS IT WORTH YOUR TIME AND EFFORT?

Even if you have a valid legal claim, not all claims are worth bringing to court. Sometimes it may cost you more to take off work than the claim is worth. If there is a chance you will be countersued, then you are risking more than just your time and effort.

Of course, in many cases the principle is more important than the money to the wronged person, and you may enjoy the process of getting justice from someone who took advantage of you. But be sure to consider what the case will involve before you start it.

On the other hand, there is always the possibility that it might not be worth the time and effort for the other side to fight your case. If the amount involved is small (in their perspective) and they will have to take off work or hire any attorney, they may just pay you without a trial. So merely filing the case may get results.

CAN YOU COLLECT IF YOU WIN?

If the person you want to sue has no money, it may be a waste of time to get a judgment. You can't garnish the wages of the self-employed, unemployed, and those receiving most types of government income (unemployment, social security benefits, etc. are exempt). The most difficult parties to collect from are small corporations with no assets or unemployed people who have no assets.

Equity in the amount of at least fifty thousand dollars in a primary residence is exempt from collection and higher amounts are exempt under certain circumstances. On the other hand, a company or person with a lot of real estate or other assets may be worth pursuing. Your judgment can be placed as a lien on all or some of their property and you will be paid when they sell it.

The old saying "you can't get blood out of a turnip" applies here. Consider carefully whether the judgment you spent time and court costs to obtain will end up being a worthless piece of paper. (Of course, you can optimistically hope that the defendant may some day win the lottery and be able to pay you, but you are better off hoping that you will win the lottery instead and no longer care about the defendant's finances.)

If you are not sure if the party is worth suing, you might want to first read chapter 8 in this book before filing your claim. It explains how to find out the extent of assets owned by a company or person.

WHAT SHOULD YOU DO BEFORE FILING YOUR SUIT?

California law requires that you "demand" payment from the other person before you file your claim in small claims court. And while there is no requirement that the demand be written, it makes sense not to rely on your memory as to the date you requested payment and what you asked for. Some judges interpret the requirement to mean that a written request was made, so you should do so, by certified mail, so you can prove that the other party got your letter. Even though the letter is often called a *demand letter*, it is much more effective to be polite and business-like in your letter. A sample demand letter is provided in appendix C.

Before filing your suit, either before or after you have written the required letter, you should attempt to work out a settlement with the other person. In some circumstances you can try to negotiate directly with the other person, or you can have another person act as the go-between if you don't want to do it yourself. You can ask a lawyer, a friend, a spouse, or someone both you and the other person know and respect. (This person can also be a witness to prove that you tried to settle the case.)

The next chapter explains how you can use mediation to resolve your dispute. (You don't have to like each other to use mediation.) Appendix H contains a list of county sponsored and private mediation services available in each county.

WHAT IS THE DEADLINE FOR FILING SUIT?

Whenever you are negotiating to settle a case, you should be careful not to miss the time limit for filing your case. This time limit is a deadline, and the laws that set the deadlines are called the *Statutes of Limitations*. If you have not done so already, you should immediately turn to appendix G which contains a list of the various time periods for filing your case. You should then calculate the very last day you can file your lawsuit and write it in a calendar or a place where you absolutely cannot miss it. You should also write reminders in your calendar for six months before the deadline and one month before the deadline. Remember the book and a television-movie about a California lawyer who was so caught up in negotiating a several million dollar settlement for her client that she forgot about the deadline? A few minutes after the court closed on the day of the deadline, the insurance company representative "changed his mind" and decided not to settle. Luckily, it was a case where the federal courts had jurisdiction and she was able to call a lawyer in Hawaii where the courts were still open and get the case filed in time.

Even though the story above is fictional, missing the deadline has happened to many people, including and mostly lawyers. If the limitations is near and the person you are negotiating with seems to be delaying, you may have to file your suit to avoid missing the deadline. Even though insurance companies are required to inform you of how long you have to sue, you may not have paid attention to the information if it was written in a letter which contained a lot of other information. Or you may be negotiating with someone who does not have insurance. Remember, once the deadline has passed, the claim is forever barred.

Caution! If you are planning to sue a government agency, you *must* file a governmental claim first and you need to be aware of the time limits for filing the various types of claims. A list of the time periods for governmental claims is provided after the Statutes of Limitation in appendix G, and a claim against a government entity is provided in appendix C.

Caution! You should not sue anyone unless you have a valid claim. If you file a suit and the judge decides there is no legal or factual merit to it, he or she may decide the judgment against you and award costs to the party.

USING MEDIATION TO RESOLVE YOUR CASE

3

SHOULD YOU TRY MEDIATION?

Alternative dispute resolution is the term used for all the methods of resolving a lawsuit without going to court. The methods used most often include advisory arbitration, conciliation, and mediation. *Mediation* is, by far, the most popular, and is now being used to resolve employment, family, probate, civil, and even misdemeanor and juvenile criminal cases. *Conciliation* is a process where a neutral third party assists disputants in finding a solution by speaking with each party separately. There is no face-to-face meeting between the parties involved in the dispute. Conciliators use their training and skills to assist and educate the parties and help them resolve their dispute. *Arbitration* is a process where each party presents his side of the case to an impartial decision-maker. The arbitrator evaluates the information and evidence and renders a decision.

Mediation differs from conciliation, arbitration and going to court because in mediation the parties are aided in reaching their own compromise of the issues, rather than having a third party make the decision for them. It works best for parties who are motivated to resolve their differences quickly.

At its best, the parties address each others' interests, rather than their positions, and attempt a win-win solution rather than a decision where one party wins and the other loses. Parties can have their attorneys participation at any stage of the mediation if they choose to include them. Mediation can take place at any time during the dispute including the day of trial, or even after the decision from the court.

There are many other advantages to mediation. It allows you and the other party the opportunity to try to work out a settlement rather than taking your chances on the ruling of a judge or commissioner who may not be familiar with the type of business or with the laws which apply to the situation. A mediation takes place in a private area rather than a crowded courtroom where anyone can watch you put on your case. The mediator's role is to guide you through the process and to facilitate the meeting. The mediator helps you and the other party set an agenda, focus on the issues, and then helps craft solutions to all or part of the dispute.

Another advantage of mediation is that you and the other party can determine when to schedule the mediation. This is an especially important consideration if venue is in a county that does not hold night sessions and you don't want to lose a day of work. Some people like the informality of mediation and not having to "dress up" for court. There are no forms to file when you mediate a case. The only paperwork necessary will be the agreement if you resolve the case. Many people feel that the most important advantage is that people who mediate agreements are much more likely to abide by its terms because they feel connected with the process of reaching the outcome.

When cases are mediated, the range of solutions is much greater and more creative than a judge would be allowed to fashion from the bench. For example, in a case where money is owed, the parties can decide to trade their services or merchandise instead of repayment in cash. They can make an agreement where goods or services are given to a person who is not part of the dispute. They can work out a payment schedule based on irregular incomes. They can apologize and renew their business or personal relationship. The parties are limited only by their imaginations, their willingness to cooperate, and their desire for a reasonable and fair result.

WHAT GOES ON IN A MEDIATION?

The process begins when one of the parties decides that he would like to mediate and contacts a mediator or agency that provides mediation services. The contact with the other side is usually made by the mediator who then explains the mediation process to the other party. If both sides agree, a mediation session is scheduled.

The parties meet with the mediator, usually in a neutral place but it can be anywhere where everyone feels comfortable. When everyone is in the room, the mediator commends the parties for choosing mediation and asks for their commitment to the process.

The mediator then makes an opening statement where the procedure is explained. The mediator makes sure that the individuals who attend have full authority to settle the case, whether or not they use it. The parties each make an opening statement after which the mediator may probe and ask questions. The parties then communicate directly with each other while the mediator guides the discussion. Every mediation is different, but most parties exchange relevant information, talk about their point of view and try to understand the other party's position.

At some point during the discussion, the mediator may suggest a *caucus*, which is a private meeting with each party. The mediator may use the caucus to review the strengths and weaknesses of the case and to try to channel the party in a more constructive direction. The mediator may also give feedback on the person's style of negotiation and suggest reasons why the other party may not be accepting their proposals. During caucus, each party has an opportunity to tell the mediator information that he or she doesn't necessarily want to disclose to the other party. The mediator will keep this information confidential if the party desires or offer to bring messages to the other side.

The parties will then go back into joint session, and the mediator will attempt to help the parties integrate their interests into a workable solution. If they reach an agreement on all or part of the issues the mediator helps them write an agreement. The agreement can be used as evidence of a contract in a later small claims action if it is breached, but everything that was said during the mediation is private and confidential. If the parties do not reach an agreement, they still have the right to file their claim in court.

Many counties, bar associations, non-profit, consumer, and private organizations have mediation services where the parties meet together with one or two trained neutrals who help you resolve your case. (A list of these services is included in appendix H.) The small claims advisor in your county usually has a list of local attorneys, psychologists, accountants and other professional mediators who charge a fee. But check first with the agencies because many of the professional mediators do volunteer mediation with non-profit agencies as a public service. Many of these organizations have very reasonable fees for mediation, sometimes just to cover the costs of the neutral meeting room.

FILING AND SERVING YOUR CASE 4

WHO CAN SUE AND BE SUED?

Before you file your lawsuit you must be sure that you are suing the proper legal entity and that your own legal status is designated properly. If this is not done you may lose your case or your judgment may be worthless.

MINORS
Minors are people under eighteen years of age who have not been emancipated under the law. They cannot sue or be sued except through their parent or legal guardian. If you are a minor who wants to sue someone, you must use the PETITION AND APPOINTMENT OF GUARDIAN AD LITEM (Form 3 in appendix B).

If you wish to sue a minor it makes sense to sue his or her parent or legal guardian. However, you should be aware that a parent is not liable for the acts of his or her child except for auto accidents where the child was authorized to drive and for acts that are "malicious and willful."

INCOMPETENT PEOPLE
Incompetent is a legal word meaning that due to some physical or mental condition, a person is unable to bring or defend a suit on their own behalf. If you wish to file a suit on behalf of an incompetent person you must use the PETITION AND APPOINTMENT OF GUARDIAN AD LITEM (Form 3) to have yourself or another person appointed.

If you are suing an incompetent person you should name their guardian ad litem if they have one, otherwise the court will need to appoint one. The incompetent would be named in the lawsuit as: Lorraine B. Little, by and through her Guardian ad Litem, Silvia T. Little.

SPOUSES   A husband or wife who sues or who is sued with his or her spouse, may appear and participate on behalf of the spouse if the claim is a joint claim. However, the spouse must give his or her permission and the court must agree that the interests of justice would be served. The lawsuit would name them as Florence Flighty and Filbert Flighty, or Filbert Flighty and Mrs. Filbert Flighty, or Florence Flighty and Mr. Flighty.

SOLE PROPRIETORS   The appearance in court must be made by the business owner unless the suit is only for collection of an unpaid bill. Under those circumstances the sole proprietor can send an employee who prepares or keeps the business records, subject to Evidence Code 1271, (See chapter 7) and is knowledgeable about the facts and circumstances of the unpaid bill.

If you are suing a sole proprietorship, check the fictitious name listings at the county clerk's office to find out the correct name of the person who owns the business. Sometimes businesses are owned by many more people than the one person who may have identified himself to you as the owner. Name both the owner and the company name in your lawsuit and name the owner individually. The format would be as follows: Ura Skunk, an individual and Ura Skunk d.b.a. (doing business as) Silly Smells.

PARTNERSHIPS AND OTHER UNINCORPORATED ASSOCIATIONS   A partnership and other unincorporated associations, even though made up of individuals, can sue in the name by which it is known, the name it has assumed or in the name of all the individuals. Any partner may make the appearance in court.

When bringing suit against a partnership or unincorporated association, the safest route is to name each individual and the partnership.

CORPORATIONS   The suit should be brought in the name of the corporation and the claim should be signed by an officer or director or a regular employee appointed by the corporation's board of directors. The key point is that this person must have been hired to perform other duties in addition to making appearances in small claims court.

When you are suing a corporation, you will probably need to check with the Secretary of State's office to obtain the names and addresses of the officers and of the "agent for service of process." In a suit against a corporation, the defendant should be named by its corporate name, or its corporate name and its subsidiary.

You can find out the exact name of a corporation and the agent for service of process by visiting an office of the Secretary of State or by sending a fee to their Sacramento office. The fee is currently $4. To find out if it has changed call (916) 653-7315. The address is:

> Secretary of State
> 1500 11th Street
> Sacramento, CA 95814
> Attn: The IRC Unit.

The branch offices are located in Fresno, Los Angeles, and San Diego.

A corporation with assets is a good target, but a "shell" corporation with no assets is not. It can be dissolved, making your claim worthless. An individual may have no assets or may file bankruptcy, but it is not as likely or as easy as dissolving a shell corporation. A new corporation can always be started, but an individual is stuck with his credit record for years.

In such a case, it is better if you can sue some of the individuals in the corporation. This can be done if the individuals signed documents without their corporate titles; or if the company name was used without the words "Inc.," "Corp.," or "Co." after it; or if the individuals committed some sort of fraud. It can also be done where a corporation has been undercapitalized and in a few other circumstances.

Ignoring a corporate entity and suing the individuals behind it is called *piercing the corporate veil* and much has been written about it in legal books and periodicals. If you think you will need to pierce a corporate veil to win your case, you should research the subject further in your nearest law library. To find out who the officers of a corporation are you can obtain a "Statement of Officers" from the Secretary of State for $5 from the address above.

ATTORNEYS

Attorneys can only appear as "real" parties, not as representatives of anyone else. If an attorney and someone else are injured in an automobile, the attorney can represent himself but not the other person who was in the car. When an attorney is a member of a partnership of lawyers, (many law firms are set up that way) the attorney can represent the partnership. If all of the officers and directors of a corporation are attorneys, any one of them may prosecute an action on behalf of the corporation.

ASSIGNEES

Assignees generally cannot appear in small claims court. The exceptions are trustees in bankruptcy, and holders of security agreements, retail installment contracts, or lien contracts.

OWNER OF RENTAL REAL PROPERTY

In a suit involving rental property, the appearance can be made by either the owner of the property or the property manager if the manager has other duties and was not hired for the specific purpose of appearing in small claims court. The claim must relate to the rental property.

When serving the landlord, it is permissible to serve the manager of the building if the manager will not provide the owners address and if the manager rented the apartment to you.

NON-RESIDENT OWNER OF REAL PROPERTY

A non-resident owner may defend the small claims case by submitting declarations, or by another person who does not receive compensation for making the appearance, or both. This provision is only for the defense of the action and does not include a counter-claim.

DEPARTMENT OF CORRECTIONS AND YOUTH AUTHORITY

If either the Department of Corrections or the Youth Authority is a plaintiff, they can appear by a regular employee but when named as a defendant, they are permitted to appear by declaration to challenge the pleading defects.

MEMBERS OF THE ARMED SERVICES AND INCARCERATED INDIVIDUALS

If a member of the Armed Services is stationed outside the state of California on an assignment that is scheduled to last more than six months, the member may file the claim by mail for a claim that arose before the out of state assignment was made. The member can choose whether to submit declarations testifying to the facts under penalty of perjury or have someone who is not a lawyer, not compensated, and who has appeared in small claims court on behalf of others less than four times during the past twelve months, appear instead. A person who is incarcerated in a county jail, a Department of Corrections facility or a Youth Authority facility is allowed the same choices as someone in the armed services.

GOVERNMENT ENTITIES

Except for the federal government, you can sue any government agency in small claims court. You can also sue an employee of the government, if the employee caused you injury while "in the course and scope" of employment. It is very easy to confuse one government entity for another and sue the wrong one. For example, even though a street may run through a city or town, it may be under the jurisdiction of the state. Some hospitals may appear to be private hospitals but they come under the umbrella of the government.

In order to sue a government entity, you are required to file a claim against the proper agency within six months of the *accrual date*, which is usually the date the incident occurred. The claim must be rejected to file your small claim action. If you do not get an acceptance or a rejection within forty-five days, the claim is deemed rejected by operation of law. A copy of the rejection form, if you received one should be attached to your small claims action when you file it. You only have six months from the date of rejection to file your lawsuit.

If you missed the claim filing deadline, don't give up. There are many exceptions for late claims and there are a few specific situations where a claim is not required at all. You will either need to do some research in the law library or consult with an attorney to find out how to file an application for a late claim.

The claim against the government entity must contain your name and address; the address where notices should be sent; the date, place, and circumstances giving rise to the claim; the name of any government employee responsible (if you know); a description of the injury; and the specific dollar amount of damages being claimed. Some government entities have their own claim form but most will accept any format that contains the required information. A claim against the state must be delivered to an office of the Board of Control and a claim against local agencies must be delivered or mailed to the clerk, secretary, or governing body. If you are unsure of the name or address of the government you are suing, the county clerk in each county should keep a roster of public agencies for you to review. Most government agencies will give you the name and address of the person and the place to send a claim over the phone.

OTHERS   The judge in a small claims action has been given the discretion by the legislature to allow another person to help someone who cannot effectively present or defend their case. This issue most often arises when a non-English speaking person is either the plaintiff or the defendant. The small claims court usually has a list of interpreters who can help non-English speaking plaintiffs. Some charge for their services, some do not. If there is no available interpreter on the day of the hearing, the court will usually postpone the hearing to allow the party to find one. If there is no available interpreter on the new date, the judge may use his or her discretion to either postpone the matter again or to allow a family member or friend to interpret.

WHERE TO FILE YOUR SUIT

You must file your small claims suit in the right county. The official legal term is *venue*. The general rule is that venue is the county where the defendant lives. Venue, however, has lots of rules which expand this definition and the plaintiff may choose among any of the counties where venue is proper, even if the location is inconvenient for the defendant. Some of the other places where venue would be proper are:

- ☞ where a business or branch office is located,

- ☞ where a corporation does business,

- ☞ where an injury occurred,

- ☞ where a buyer signed a contract (automobile or retail installment contract),

- ☞ where buyer resided when contract was signed (automobile or retail installment contract), or

- ☞ where buyer presently resides (retail installment contract only).

The defendant can write a letter to the court explaining the inconvenience and hope that the court will transfer the case. However, if moving the case is going to cause hardship for the plaintiff, there is much less likelihood of transferring it out of the county where it was filed.

If the defendant is a business, venue is proper in the county where the business or branch office is located. A case against a corporation is venued where the corporation has its principal place of business or where the contract was breached or the obligation or liability arose. A tort action such an automobile accident case is venued in the county where the injury occurred, and if a tort action is being brought against a corporation, the liability arose where the injury occurred.

If you are seeking recovery for a bad check, or suing your landlord for return of your security deposit, then you should file your claim in the county where the check was issued or where the rental property is located. A case based on contract can be filed in the county in which the contract was signed or where it was to be performed. A case based on a retail installment account, a sales contract or motor vehicle finance sale can be brought where the buyer lives, where the buyer lived when the contract was signed, where the buyer signed the contract or where the goods or vehicle are permanently kept.

An objection to the proposed venue can be made in a written letter to the court or by an appearance on the day of the hearing. If the defendant does not appear, the court will investigate the facts and make a determination as to whether venue is correct. If it is not, the case will be dismissed without prejudice. If venue is correct and the defendant is not present, the case will be continued for at least fifteen days. If all the parties are present and agree to proceed, the case will be heard.

WHAT ARE THE FEES?

The fee to file your claim is $20. If you have filed more than twelve cases during the previous twelve month period, the filing fee is $35 for subsequent filings. (Unlike the airlines, the court does not reward frequent usage.)

There is an additional fee of $6 to have the court clerk serve the defendant by certified mail, or you can pay $25 to the marshal or sheriff for personal or substituted service. Marshals usually require thirty days lead time. The marshal can also serve subpoenas. The court will waive the fees if you cannot afford to pay them. This is not a decision you get to make. Form 5 in appendix B contains the information sheet which states the conditions you have to meet for a waiver of fees.

There is also a fee of $10 to request a postponement of the court date, a $14 fee for a judgment creditor examination and a $14 fee to file a motion to vacate the judgment.

How Much Should You Sue For?

When filing a suit you should always ask for the highest amount allowed for the claim. For example, if someone hit your car and you got estimates of $100, $150, and $175 to fix it, you may be happy if that person paid you $100. If they offer to settle the case, you should seriously consider accepting it. But if you have to sue for damages, sue for $175, plus any other amounts you can reasonably add to the bill such as car rental, lost time at work, taxi fares, etc. You might not get the full amount, but asking for it will provide the judge with room for compromise.

How Do You Begin?

To begin your case, you must file a PLAINTIFF'S CLAIM AND ORDER TO DEFENDANT (Form 2 in appendix B). The claim form is the same whether your case is based on breach of contract or negligence. In only one circumstance is there an "attachment" and that is for a dispute between you and an attorney over fees after a non-binding arbitration has taken place.

You are not required to go into a lot of detail on the claim form. However, you will need to know all of the elements required for each type of case when you prepare it and when you present your case during trial. The next chapter explains the various types of lawsuits and the necessary elements.

Forms

We have included the approved "Judicial Council" forms in this book in appendix B to save you a trip to the courthouse. However, some counties have devise their own forms for some situations. Check with your court clerk as to whether you can use the Judicial Council form for the procedure you are filing. You can also download forms from the internet. See appendix B for more information.

There are forms for most actions you may wish to take in your case, such as listing additional plaintiffs or defendants, requesting a postponement, dismissing your case. Check the list in appendix B for the form you need.

STATUTES

The statutes governing small claims court are contained in appendix A of this book.

SERVING THE PAPERS ON THE DEFENDANT

CERTIFIED
MAIL

One requirement in successfully suing someone in any court is that they be properly served with the papers. The purpose for this rule is to be sure the defendant knows about the suit and has the right to respond to it. As explained below the papers may be served by certified mail, but if the defendant refuses to sign for them you will have to use personal or substitute service. For this you will need the home or business address of the defendant. If you do not know the defendant's physical address, read the section beginning on page 38.

Service of a lawsuit is less formal in small claims court than for municipal and superior court actions. Service of the claim may be made by the clerk of the court mailing the claim to the defendant by restricted certified mail, which means that only the defendant can sign for it. Service is complete when the defendant signs the return receipt, which must be at least ten days before the hearing if the defendant lives in the same county and fifteen days before the hearing if the defendant lives in a county different from the one where the action is filed. This kind of service is the cheapest and the easiest but least reliable because the defendant can refuse delivery and write "return to sender." If someone else signs by mistake, the service is not valid. The service by certified mail can only be done by the court clerk and you have to rely on the court and the post office directing the return receipt to the right file.

PERSONAL
SERVICE

Another way to serve is *personal service*. This is accomplished when the defendant identifies himself to the server (unless the defendant is known to the server) and handed the lawsuit. If the defendant refuses to accept the lawsuit, it can be dropped at his or her feet. This service may be done by any individual over eighteen who is not a party to the lawsuit, a registered process server, the sheriff, or the marshal. Commercial process servers are listed in the phone book. It is best not to have witnesses to the lawsuit do the service. Law firms almost always use process servers and you can ask any legal secretary to recommend one to you.

SUBSTITUTE
SERVICE

A defendant can also be served by *substituted service*. This means that the claim can be left at the defendant's office with the person in charge or at the place of residence with a person who is an adult. After the claim is substitute served, it must be mailed within ten days to the defendant at the address where the claim was served. In addition, the mailing must be at least twenty days before the hearing, or twenty-five days before the hearing if the defendant lives out of the county. Substituted service can be done by anyone over eighteen.

OUT-OF-STATE
DEFENDANTS

If the defendant does not live in California, he or she must be served within the state's boundaries except under two specific circumstances. There is a special method of service for the non-resident owner of real property who does not have an agent for service of process in California. The owner can be served by any of the methods described above. The other exception is an out-of-state owner or driver of an automobile involved in an auto accident in California. The claim is served on the Director of the California Department of Motor Vehicles.

PROOF OF
SERVICE

You should make sure that the proper *proof of service* has been filed in the court file prior to your hearing. Usually, this is a paper signed by the sheriff or process server stating that the papers were properly delivered to the defendant. Most process servers will file the proof of service done by their agency, but if a friend or family member served the defendant, you will have to file the proof of service yourself. If the court served the defendant by certified mail, make sure the receipt is in the court file.

WHAT IF YOU CAN'T FIND THE DEFENDANT?

It is not unusual to discover that the individuals and businesses you want to sue are not easy to locate. They may either have unlisted phone numbers, post office boxes, fictitious names, or they have gone out of business. You can always hire a private investigator to do a search for you. A thorough search will reveal property, bank accounts, tax liens and prior lawsuits against the company or individual. This information can be very helpful in determining whether your lawsuit is worth pursuing and how to go about collecting on your judgment (more about this later.)

If you want to start or do the search yourself, there are several things you can do. If you are familiar with the last known address, you can mail a letter to the old address requesting an "address correction only" from the post office. Sometimes the post office does not have the old address on file, either because a forwarding address was not given to the post office or the forwarding order expired. If the only address you have for a business is a post office box, you are permitted to obtain the name and address of the holder of the box if you can show that the box is used for business purposes. Libraries also contain "reverse directories" which provide the address that goes with the phone number. The tax assessor has records linking property addresses to their owners, as well as death, birth and marriage records, all available to the public to peruse.

There is a commonly held belief in California that personal information can no longer be obtained from the Department of Motor Vehicles. While it is true that the DMV has made it more difficult to obtain information, it is certainly not impossible. The DMV does not consider a post office box to be confidential information and will make that information available after you fill out a form. If you want the street address you will have to provide justification (such as the need to serve the lawsuit) and some information you already have about the defendant. The key is following the DMV's instructions to the letter because the applications for information are scrutinized very carefully.

The internet is very helpful in locating both individuals and businesses. There is an excellent selection of directories providing all kinds of information. One links area codes and prefixes with locations. Another links phone numbers with business and residence addresses. One good site is:

http://www.switchboard.com

The social security death index will provide information as to where a person was born or died. You can find information revealing the financial status of most major and some not so major companies. There are also services on the web which will perform fairly sophisticated searches for less than $20. If you are not computer-savvy, you can probably find one or two "web junkies" among your family and friends who can help you in your quest for information.

Types of Cases 5

This chapter contains a brief explanation of the most common types of cases that can be brought in small claims court. If your case falls into more than one category, list all of them on your claim. For example, if you are suing an auto repair facility for negligent repair of your auto, you may also have a case for breach of contract, and breach of warranty.

If your claim does not fall into any of these categories it does not mean that you do not have a case. There are many legal theories and more are evolving every year. If you feel you have a case you should either do some legal research yourself or consult with an attorney as explained in chapter 2.

Even if you can prove all the elements of a particular claim, you should try to anticipate any defenses the defendant will have. Before filing your case, be sure to read chapter 6 to find out if any of the defenses mentioned apply to your case and could negate your claim.

For example, if you are in business using a fictitious name and have not filed a fictitious name statement, make sure you do so before you file suit. Another common defense is that the suit is beyond the period allowed by the statute of limitations. Before you file, be sure to check the list in appendix G.

Bad Checks and "Stop Payment" Checks

A person who writes a check for which there is either no account or not enough money in the account to pay it, is liable in civil court for the face value of the check and penalties of up to three times the face value of the check with a minimum of $100 and a maximum of $1500 (CC 1719). Likewise, if someone has stopped payment on a check written to your business or to you personally, you may also be able to take advantage of the penalty provisions of this statute. You must send a demand letter to the maker of the check by certified mail, in which you tell him or her that you plan to seek these extra damages. Be sure to save the receipt for certified mail because you will need to prove to the court that you sent this letter.

If your case is based on a bad check, the notice from the bank containing the information about the check coupled with a receipt showing the services you provided or the merchandise purchased should be sufficient to prove that the defendant owed the money to you. If your case is based on a "stop payment," you will have to prove that the stop payment order was not based on a good faith dispute with you. This may be difficult to prove if the person who stopped payment called you immediately after he or she stopped payment to explain the reason for doing so, and either returned the merchandise or wrote you a letter stating the facts of the dispute (the car engine burned up on the way home from the repair shop).

You will also need to show that you made a reasonable attempt to resolve the issues (mediating the dispute is considered a reasonable attempt) and wait thirty days from the date you mailed the notice before you file your case.

BREACH OF CONTRACT

Breach of contract is an action to recover money damages for failure of a party to abide by the terms of an oral or written contract. To win a suit for breach of contract your must prove that there was an agreement, that the defendant either did not perform or performed improperly. You must also prove that you either performed or were ready to perform your part of the agreement.

If the breach was failure to pay a sum of money or to deliver some item, the proof and the evidence will be easy. But if the breach involved the quality of an item or service, the proof required will be more complicated. Some examples:

Mike agreed to pay John $2,000 to purchase his 1957 Chevy "if it runs." The car had been sitting in John's garage for years and wouldn't start. John got it started the next week, Mike drove it around the block. He then paid John $1,500 cash and $500 by check and drove home. On the way home the car broke down and the service station that towed it said the engine was beyond repair and would have to be replaced at a cost of $1,000. Mike stopped payment on the check and sued John for the $1,000 it would cost for a new engine. John countersued Mike for the $500 for the stopped payment on the check.

To Mike it is a simple case. He was supposed to get a car that runs for $2,000. To John it is also a simple case. The car did run and he was supposed to get $2,000. To a judge looking at the case, it is much more complicated. Some of the questions the judge will have are: What exactly was said between the parties? Did John make any representations about the car? Did John tell Mike that the car hadn't been driven in years? Is either party an expert on cars? What exactly was wrong with the engine? Did Mike get other estimates on the engine?

Actually, Mike and John should probably go to mediation to come to a settlement with which they are both happy. But if they insist on fighting it out in court, they should do their homework and have evidence that will answer all the questions the judge will have. This may mean written estimates and witnesses who heard their negotiations or saw the car before and after it broke down.

CONTRACT RESCISSION

A contract can be canceled if a party to the contract was induced to enter into the contract through fraud or misrepresentation, or if the bargain fails through no fault of the party.

For example, a contract to cut down a tree can be rescinded if a storm uproots the tree before the contract could be performed. A contract can also be rescinded if the contract was unlawful, unconscionable, or against public policy.

The point of rescission is to restore the parties to the position they were in prior to entering into the contract. Therefore, a party requesting rescission must return everything of value he received under the contract if it is possible to do so. There is also a requirement of giving notice to the other party. If a small claims case for rescission is filed, it is deemed to be both notice and an offer to restore the benefits.

Rescission can be used as the basis of a claim for damages or as a defense or counterclaim. It is important to note that parties who have entered contracts through misrepresentation or fraud may be entitled to punitive damages which are not available in small claims court. If rescission is based on a consumer contract, damages in the form of penalties may be available to the claimant.

Warranty

A claim for a breach of warranty is one of the most useful. There are two types of warranties, *express* and *implied*, and there are three kinds of implied warranties.

EXPRESS
WARRANTY

An action for breach of express warranty exists when a product or service does not live up to oral or written statements describing how well the product will perform. To win such a case, a person must prove that the 1) the product had a warranty, 2) the product did not perform as represented, 3) that the person relied on the warranty to purchase the product, and 4) that damages were suffered as a result.

IMPLIED
WARRANTY

The theory of implied warranty is used when a product does not live up to its basic purpose. Most new products, and some used ones, come with implied warranties, but the warranties rarely cover everything that can go wrong. The three types of implied warranties are as follows:

Warranty of Title. If you were sold an item that the seller didn't own and that you had to return to the rightful owner (such as stolen property), you could sue the seller for breach of the implied warranty that he had title to the property he sold you. To do so, you must prove that: 1) you paid for the item, and 2) you did not obtain title to it.

Warranty of Merchantability. When goods are sold by a dealer in such merchandise, unless they are sold "as is," there is an implied warranty that they are fit for the purpose for which they are made. If a washing machine does not wash, it is not merchantable. If bread is moldy, it is not merchantable. To win a claim for breach of the warranty of merchantability, you must prove that the goods were not merchantable when received. If, for example, a car broke down two weeks after it was purchased, you could not collect for breach of such a warranty unless you could prove that at the time of the sale the car was in such a condition as to make it unmerchantable. If a part was ready to break, you would probably win. If it broke because you hit a bad bump in the road, you would probably lose.

Warranty of Fitness for a Particular Purpose. When a seller represents himself as being knowledgeable about a product and sells it to a person for a known particular purpose, there is an implied warranty of fitness for that purpose. For example, if a body building gym sells a piece of pipe for use as a weight lifting bar and the bar bends when weights are attached, there would be a breach of a warranty even if it was a perfectly good pipe for other purposes. To win a suit for an implied warranty, you need to prove that the seller was knowledgeable about the product and that you relied on this knowledge when you purchased the item.

LEMON LAW CASES

California's "lemon law" entitles the buyer of a defective vehicle that is still under the original warranty to the presumption that they are entitled to replacement or refund. The presumption is based on the manufacturer making at least four attempts to fix the problem or the fact that the vehicle has been out of service for thirty days. There are of course, many hoops to go through before you find out that the manufacturer is not going to give you a replacement vehicle, including written notice to the manufacturer and submission of the dispute to the manufacturer's arbitration program.

If you have a new car, the value of your vehicle will be well in excess of the small claims limit, and you will probably want to file your case in municipal or superior court. But this is not true of every potential lemon law case, especially where the law applies to used vehicles. If the value of your vehicle comes within the small claims limit, or you are willing to forgo the amount of your claim in excess of the limit, you can bring the case in small claims court, whether or not you go through the lemon law procedure. However, failure to go through the arbitration procedure with a manufacturer who uses a certified arbitration program will prevent you from taking advantage of the "presumption." It is very important to carefully read the statute and the rules governing the arbitration program before filing your case.

If you have a car that is out of warranty, and is defective, you can sue the car manufacturer for breach of the warranty of merchantability if you have been trying to get them to fix the problem since the time the vehicle was still under warranty. First write a demand letter asking the manufacturer to stand by their warranty and give them a specific amount of time to honor it. Then file your case. You will need to be very careful in naming the car manufacturer by their legal name. Choose the court which is most convenient for you since venue is everywhere they do business. You should also check with the NHTSA and request the federal government's file on your vehicle to see if there are enough reports about the defect to have put the manufacturer on notice of the problem under 15 USC 1402. If you can prove that a problem with the car was concealed from you there is a possibility you can get the car contract rescinded. If so, you will want to file your case in municipal or superior court so you can get punitive damages.

If you bought your vehicle "as is," you should analyze the entire situation. Was the "as is" sign conspicuous? Were you being rushed? Did the salesperson tell you that the "as is" sign didn't matter; that they would fix or replace the vehicle anyway? Is your case against the manufacturer or seller? ("As is" only protects the seller.) Was the sign confusing? Did they already void the "as is" by performing some repairs? Was there a failure to disclose defects, thereby constituting a deceptive sales practice?

Consumer Contracts

In response to consumer complaints, the state of California has amassed an enormous number of statutes governing consumer contracts. Appendix E contains a list of the California and Federal consumer laws most often encountered in small claims actions. There is also a list of the cancellation periods, known as "cooling off" periods. The consumer laws contain these cancellation periods because the legislature was aware that many people have difficulty saying "no" to high pressure salespeople. For example, home repair contracts made after a disaster such as an earthquake can be canceled for up to seven days after the contract is signed, but only for up to three days under normal conditions. If a contractor failed to permit you to cancel the contract during the cooling off period, and assuming you have proof that you attempted to cancel, you will substantially increase your chances of recovering your money in small claims court. Even if you don't have written proof, be sure to include the information on your claim and let the judge or commissioner know during your presentation that you attempted to cancel the contract. There's always the chance that the contractor will not deny his refusal to allow you to cancel.

All of the statutes are available in law libraries, on the internet, and through the Department of Consumer Affairs, a state agency which oversees compliance with these statutes. If you think your small claims suit may be based on a consumer protection statute on the list, be sure to research the statute thoroughly prior to filing a lawsuit because many of them contain special procedures. You should also consider the fact that most of the violations of the consumer statutes provide for attorney's fees, thereby making it reasonable to obtain legal representation and file your case in a court where the limits are higher.

Below are several types of consumer contracts which are covered by statutes.

HOME
IMPROVEMENT
CONTRACTS

Contracts made under the Home Improvement Act and The Swimming Pool Act are overseen by the Contractors State License Board, an arm of the Department of Consumer Affairs. The Board licenses contractors to provide services to improve real property, including remodeling, room additions, repairs of mobile homes, electrical work, and many other improvements only after the contractor meets certain requirements such as posting a bond for $7,500. The bond is provided by companies called "bonding" companies. (The name of a contractor's bonding company can be obtained by calling the Board at 800-321-2752.) You may have a better chance of collecting damages from a bonding company than a fly-by-night contractor so be sure to name and serve the bonding company in your lawsuit. The one catch is that the bonding company can only be sued for up to $2,500.

To be successful in a suit against a home contractor, the work must be defective. You cannot sue the contractor merely because the contractor was not licensed.

If you win your lawsuit against the contractor, be sure to notify the Board because it will not renew a contractor's license if there is an unpaid judgment on the contractor's record. Also, if you are being sued by a contractor, be sure to find out if the contractor was licensed at the time the work was done because under most situations, the contractor cannot sue on home improvement contracts unless the requirements of licensing were substantially met.

UNLAWFUL COLLECTION OF PERSONAL INFORMATION

When a consumer pays with a credit card or check, the law restricts the amount and type of information a merchant can collect. Merchants are prohibited from requesting or requiring a consumer to write any personal information, including address or phone number on any document associated with a credit card transaction, nor can they ask for personal information and write it down anywhere. The merchants can require that you produce a picture I.D. but they cannot record any information from the I.D.

There are, of course, several exceptions to these restrictions. For example, if you use a credit card to obtain a cash advance, the law does not apply. The law also does not apply when you put down a deposit using a credit card, when the information is needed for shipping purposes, or if some federal law or regulation requires obtaining the information. One other exception is the situation where a credit card is issued by a gasoline station. Merchants are sometimes required by contract to collect the personal information.

You can, of course refuse to show merchants your I.D. If they refuse to make the transaction, you can complain to the credit card issuer since the refusal is not permitted under the rules of most of the major credit card companies.

Merchants who accept a check for retail goods or services cannot require a consumer to provide a credit card or record a credit card number. If the check is used for a deposit, a cash advance or to pay a credit card bill, the merchant can require that you produce the credit card number.

If the merchant violates these rules, he or she can be sued in small claims court for the unlawful collection of personal information. Because it is very difficult to place a value on personal information, you may want to consider suing for the highest amount possible. (If this is your first or second small claims action in one year, the amount is $5,000; otherwise you are limited to suing for $2500.) The amount you recover may depend on whether the judge feels that the request was a mere slip-up of a new employee or a deliberate policy set by the store. If the merchant has a practice of violating the credit card laws, there may even be a basis for a "class action." Some judges feel that privacy rights are very important while others feel that the gathering of this information is not a substantial intrusion in the modern world.

TELEMARKETING CALLS

Who hasn't run out of the shower to get the phone, only to find out that it was an unsolicited phone call? You can use the small claims court to stop them.

Next time they call, ask to be put on the do-not-call list. The telemarketer is permitted one mistake during the next year. After that, you can sue for $500 for each unwanted call. The law also applies to unsolicited faxes, automated calls, and calls received before 8 a.m. or after 9 p.m. It does not apply to non-profit agencies, political organizations, polling companies, or businesses with which you have an established relationship.

CASES AGAINST CREDIT REPAIR AGENCIES

The stated purpose of Credit Services Organizations (CSOs) is not to provide credit, but to obtain loans and extensions of credit for consumers who have credit problems. They also offer to help consumers repair or correct their credit history. While there are legitimate credit repair organizations, some of them operate unscrupulously, selling services that consumers can obtain themselves for no charge, or selling incorrect and inaccurate advice.

The law now requires these organizations to register with the state, obtain a bond, provide notices to the consumer telling them what they can and can't do, and how and when they can charge for their services. A full listing of the requirements can be found in California Civil Code Section 1789.

A suit can be brought in small claims court for any damages caused as a result of a violation of the statute. Before filing in small claims court, you should be aware that it is possible to obtain both punitive damages and attorney fees under the statute, perhaps justifying a case in municipal or superior court.

PROMOTIONAL GIVEAWAYS

Have you ever wondered whether people actually get a free television or diamond bracelet just for attending a sales presentation? The answer is that failure to disclose the odds of receiving the incentive, as well as other specific information about the promotion is not only a misdemeanor under Business & Professions Code 17534, but private parties can sue for treble (triple) damages and attorney's fees if the promised gift is not received.

PRODUCTS LIABILITY CASES

A products liability case exists when a person is injured or suffers financial loss as the result of a defective product. This kind of case may be brought against the manufacturer, assembler, component supplier, advertising agency, distributor, retail establishment, repairer, and anyone else in the chain of commerce. There are several theories under which you can bring your lawsuit. The easiest one to prove is strict liability, which makes the defendant liable even if there is no negligence or wrongdoing. To win a case under strict liability, it is only necessary to show that a particular product, when used as intended, caused the injury. A products liability case may also be brought under the theory of warranty discussed on page 45.

You can also bring a products liability case based on negligence.

One example of a negligence situation is when defective food is served in a restaurant due to the failure of the establishment to take proper precautions to refrigerate the food.

If you don't know whether the defect in your product is a manufacturing defect or whether it occurred later, it may be reasonable to name and serve all of the parties in the "stream of commerce" and let them fight it out among themselves. In some cases, each defendant will make a better case against another defendant than you could because of a greater familiarity with the product. In cases where it is obvious where the defect arose, you are likely to raise the ire of the judge or commissioner if you parade ten defendants into court. But don't let the inexpensive price of an item scare you off if the damages it caused are substantial. A faulty washing machine hose can result in an expensive flood.

Before bringing suit, you should find out if any of the California consumer statutes cover the product and whether there are any special requirements you need to follow. At the very least, you should give notice to all the defendants before you sue them, giving them a sufficient opportunity to resolve the problem without going to court.

Auto Accidents and Other Negligence Cases

You can bring an action to recover money for damages sustained in an automobile collision as a result of negligence of either individuals, government entities, companies, and the owner of the vehicle (including rental car agencies). It is especially important to remember to sue both the owner and the driver.

In California, a suit for personal injury must be filed within a year of the date of the accident with very few exceptions to extend the filing period. (Children have until their nineteenth birthday to file a lawsuit for personal injuries, even if the injury occurred when the child was only five years old.) If the negligent person or entity is the government, you only have six months to file a claim against the government.

When you compute your damages, be sure to include your actual medical expenses, even if they were paid by your medical insurance company. If you belong to an HMO, finding out the value of your medical treatment is a little more complicated, but there are books which list approved billing rates for all medical procedures. Check with the bookstore or library of a medical or nursing school near your home.

You can also sue for out-of-pocket expenses, lost wages, including the value of any sick or vacation days used up, time taken off for doctor's appointments, the cost of repairing or replacing your vehicle or other damaged items, the cost of a rental vehicle, mileage for medical care and a reasonable amount for pain and suffering. These damages can quickly add up, so make sure your case is small enough to file in small claims court. A general rule of thumb is that to be cost-effective enough to hire an attorney, the case needs to be worth more than $7,000; otherwise, you would gain nothing since the the lawyer's fees would be approximately $1500-$2,000.

The value of your case is rarely the figure first offered to you by the claims adjustor. It is the claims adjustor's job to pay you as little as they can. Generous claims adjustors do not keep their jobs very long. Most attorneys will give you a free consultation on a personal injury case since they do not charge fees until the case is concluded. Gather a few opinions on the value of your case. And if any attorney tells you that he can get you a lot more money than you can get for yourself, try offering one third of your settlement for every dollar above the $5,000 you can get for yourself in small claims court. If the attorney is still interested, your case is probably worth more than $7,000.

Class Actions

Even though there is no official class action designation in small claims court, it can sometimes be the best place for a neighborhood group to force bad neighbors to stop illegal drug activity on their property or to stop polluters under the legal theories of negligence and nuisance.

The procedure starts with the organization of a core group by residents of the neighborhood. The core group will be able to prepare a stronger case if they are joined by and obtain the cooperation of the police department, local elected representatives, and other city agencies and non-profit organizations. Every member needs to monitor the situation carefully and keep detailed records.

Before filing suit, the owners of the property need to be identified and a certified letter should be sent to all of them from the group informing them that the neighborhood group is planning to sue on a certain date unless the nuisance is eliminated. Everyone then files a separate claim, (using the same wording) including children who sue by their guardians ad litem. Each claimant should ask for the maximum amount of money in damages and all costs incurred in filing the suit.

Court clerks who are notified in advance of unusual circumstances that are planned for the courtroom are far more likely to want to be cooperative in making the procedure go smoothly. These kinds of cases require coordination to make sure that all of them are heard on the same date, that a judge or commissioner is available to hear the cases on the chosen date, that the police officers and police records, health department data and other evidence have been properly subpoenaed, that the proofs of service are filed in advance and that every claimant has a complete file of evidence and questions to ask the defendant when his or her case is called. Each plaintiff will need to describe the extent they have been deprived of enjoyment of their property and their symptoms of emotional and mental distress.

Since the whole point of the small claims actions is to get rid of the nuisance, several small money judgments which add up to a substantial sum may catch each defendant's attention, since the same tactics can be used several times if the nuisance continues.

LANDLORD PROBLEMS

DEPOSITS

Whether it is called last month's rent, pet deposit, security deposit, new tenant fee, or cleaning fee, if it is for the purpose of protecting the landlord from damage or default, it is fully refundable if the tenant fulfills his or her obligations under the rental agreement.

As a tenant, you can sue in small claims court if the landlord refuses to return the deposit (or permit access to meet the conditions for return of the money), or if the amount collected is in excess of two month's rent on an unfurnished rental and three months rent on a furnished rental. You can also sue if the landlord uses more than a reasonable amount of the deposit for any purpose other than unpaid rent, cleaning, and replacement or repair of the apartment caused by the tenant or his guests. The landlord may not use the deposit for normal "wear and tear," and this issue is where there are the greatest number of disputes. Good evidence of normal "wear and tear" includes rental agreements that contain a description of the premises, photos taken just before you move in to compare with photos taken just before you move out, and a letter written to the landlord describing the premises as soon as you become aware of them after moving in.

The landlord is required to either return the deposit within three weeks after you move out or to send you an accounting of how the deposit was spent. After first writing a letter to the landlord requesting the return of your deposit (see appendix C for an example), return receipt requested of course, you can sue for the return of the deposit and up to $600 in penalties if the refusal to return the deposit was in bad faith. In those counties where the landlord must pay interest on the deposit, you can sue for the accumulated interest as well.

RETURN OF
PROPERTY

If you left something on the premises by mistake, or under some other reasonable circumstances, (your piano mover didn't show up on moving day) the landlord is required to return it as long as you follow specific steps set forth in the law. If the landlord refuses to return the property within a reasonable time after you have followed those steps, the landlord will be liable for damages for the value of your property and up to $250 in penalties.

The steps you must take include writing a letter, paying the landlord's reasonable costs of removal and storage, and removing the item from the landlord's premises within three days. After the landlord receives your letter, he or she must write a return letter within five days individually listing all the items and the cost of removal and storage for each.

UNINHABITABLE
RENTAL UNIT

A tenant can sue a landlord in small claims court if a landlord does not make needed repairs to a rental unit in a timely fashion. In order to win such a lawsuit, the tenant must prove that the unit is uninhabitable, that a housing inspector notified the landlord in writing to repair the condition, and that the condition lasted at least sixty days after receiving written notice from the housing inspector. If the landlord is liable, a tenant can collect up to $1000 in special damages incurred as a result of the condition. For example, if you had a leaky roof during a rainstorm, you can collect the expense of staying in a hotel as special damages.

In order to determine if the unit is legally unliveable or uninhabitable, the landlord must comply with housing and building codes in addition to maintaining the integrity of the structure, plumbing, utilities, ventilation, cleanliness etc. On the other hand, the tenant has the responsibility to keep from damaging the unit, common areas, equipment, or fixtures. Basically, if the tenant caused the conditions that made the unit uninhabitable, the tenant will not be successful in a suit against the landlord.

TENANT PROBLEMS

Eviction actions are not handled in small claims court, but a landlord may have reason to sue a tenant in small claims court after a tenancy has ended. This section discusses such claims briefly. For more information see the book *Landlords' Rights & Duties in California* by John J. Talamo and Mark Warda, available from your local bookstore or through the publisher by calling (800) 226-5291.

DAMAGE TO RENTAL UNITS If a tenant has done damage to the unit greater than the damage deposit, the landlord may want to take the tenant to court. Of course, he must take into consideration all the factors discussed in chapter 1, such as whether it is worth the time and whether a judgment against the tenant would be collectable.

To win such a case you must have good evidence that the damage was done to the unit during the tenant's occupation. This would require testimony or photos of the unit before and after the tenant rented the unit. Normal "wear and tear" would not usually be chargeable against a tenant. If a unit had not been painted in five years, the cost of painting could not be charged to a tenant who only rented it for the fifth year unless unusual damage was done to the walls.

UNPAID RENT If a tenant leaves a unit owing back rent, a landlord can sue the tenant in small claims court. This would usually be a simple case to prove unless there was some sort of complicated agreement between the parties for payment of rent in other than cash. For example, if the tenant was to do some work to the unit in lieu of rent, then the exact terms of the agreement as well as photos and an expert opinion of the quality of the work would be helpful to the judge.

ATTORNEY-CLIENT PROBLEMS

If you lost money or property because of negligence or other wrongdoing on the part of your attorney, you can sue the lawyer in small claims court to recover the money or the value of the property. If you have a dispute with an attorney concerning fees, you can request a trial de novo in small claims court after first going through a non-binding arbitration. See the ATTORNEY-CLIENT FEE DISPUTE (Attachment to Plaintiff's Claim), Form 37 in appendix B for this purpose, and to vacate, correct, or confirm either a binding or non-binding arbitration award. Confirmation is required before collection procedures are initiated. You will have thirty days to file after the date the arbitration award was mailed.

DEFENDING YOURSELF 6

DO NOT IGNORE THE SUMMONS!

Typically, you will first become aware that you are being sued when you receive a copy of the summons and complaint. Be sure that you read all of the documents you receive carefully. They will tell you why you are being sued, and when and where you must respond.

Some people consider themselves "judgment proof" and make the big mistake of ignoring a small claims case. If the party does not show up on the day of trial, the judge does not have to decide who to believe and the judgment could end up being much more than the case was worth. Defendants who plan to file for bankruptcy, and as a result, ignore a small claims case, may be very surprised to find out that not every judgment will be wiped out. And even though judgments are only good for ten years, they can easily be renewed for another ten years. What a surprise it will be for the "no-show" to find a lien on their house when it is finally sold fifteen years in the future!

Many defendants merely show up in court and give their side of the story without any preparation. This is certainly better than not showing up at all. But the problem with this type of defense is that it increases the likelihood of having insufficient proof to substantiate the defendant's position. These defendants appear unorganized, confused about the law and rules that apply to their case, and mixed up about the chronology of events that make up their defense. Anyone who plans to offer this kind of defense will benefit from spending a few hours sitting in small claims court and watching some cases. It will be easy to pick out the parties who are prepared and those who are not. I strongly urge any defendant who has opened this book to this chapter first, hoping to avoid reading the information that relates to plaintiffs to go back to the beginning and read the entire book. All the information is helpful to defendants too.

If you have a counterclaim against the plaintiff, you are a plaintiff on your case as well as a defendant. Keep in mind the fact that you have both roles. You will have to prepare the counterclaim in the same way a plaintiff prepares the claim. You will need to know the rules of evidence, and the ins and outs of preparing and presenting your case.

WHAT SHOULD YOU DO FIRST?

Before you spend a lot of time and money on the defense of the lawsuit, you need to know whether the case is worth defending. If you know the claim is true, you should contact the other party and try to settle the matter. You should not waste the court's time and incur additional expenses if you know you owe the money you are being sued for. If you don't have the money, you could offer to sign a promissory note to make regular payments or you could sign a stipulation in the court case to make payments.

This is often a personal decision. For example, if you are unemployed, and have lots of free time on your hands, you may be more inclined to delve into the lawsuit than someone who is employed. Some people feel that the amount of money that is at stake is the main issue. They will need to make a calculation of the amount of damages in dispute and decide if the money is worth their time. Or if they have no money to pay and they know they owe it, they may be able to work out a payment plan with the plaintiff. One way of handling the situation is to write a letter to the plaintiff and make an offer to settle the case. You may get a counter-offer, or your offer will be rejected or accepted.

Another possibility is to contact a mediation service and tell them you want to mediate your dispute. They will contact the plaintiff for you. Some people feel that in certain situations, it is not the money, but the principle that they want to defend. This type of case lends itself to the type of mediation where the interests and positions of the party are explored in reaching resolution.

There are several defenses based on improper procedures by the plaintiff and you will need to determine which ones apply and whether they were followed in your case. For example, were you named and served correctly? Is the plaintiff named correctly? Was the case set in a court that has venue? Has the plaintiff fulfilled all the prerequisites to filing a small claims suit? Is the contractor licensed? Did the plaintiff write the required demand letter? Any one of the above can be fatal to the plaintiff's case (or counterclaim). These defenses are discussed later in this chapter.

Decide if you have defenses based on principles of law. For example, if the plaintiff fell in the parking lot in front of your store, are you responsible for the plaintiff's injuries? Who owns the parking lot? Are you responsible for the upkeep? You may have to do some investigation into the facts of the situation.

Should you contact an attorney? There are several reasons you may want to seek legal advice. Perhaps the principles of law are complicated. If there is more than one plaintiff asking for the $5,000 limit, you may have a situation where legal advice is essential. Or you may have a potential case against the plaintiff where you are unsure whether it should be heard in small claims court. Maybe you just need reassurance that you can handle the defense yourself, or that you are on the right track.

One other important factor that is often overlooked is the possibility that your homeowner's, auto, or business insurance policy covers you on the plaintiff's claim. Send a copy of the plaintiff's claim to your agent and your insurance company (certified mail) and ask them to provide a defense and pay the claim if necessary. Sometimes, if the insurance company is unsure about whether the policy covers you, they will pay anyway to avoid future litigation over the issue. In many situations, they will do the investigation of the facts and save you a lot of time even if it ends up that you are on your own.

WHAT ARE YOUR DEFENSES?

Before you decide to settle the case you should review your defenses in the matter and see if the claim is legally enforceable. There are many possible defenses to a claim that you (and the plaintiff) may not know about.

IMPROPER
SERVICE OF
PROCESS

Read all of the following possible defenses and see if any of them apply to your case. If you think any might, be sure to mention them to the judge if your case does go to court. Some of the defenses may just delay the case, and if you are in a hurry to get it over with, you might not want to use them even if they do apply. Many of them are defenses that could win the case for you.

If the claim is not served on you or your company properly then the court does not have jurisdiction and the judgment is void. However, if you appear in court and do not object to the service then you waive the right to contest it.

Or you can appear only for the purpose of contesting the service. If you ignore it, you may have more aggravation later in having a judgment set aside or in trying to stop seizure of your property. If you appear to contest the service, you may be able to have the service set aside so that the plaintiff has to start over. But then, you may just aggravate the judge who will eventually hear your case.

VENUE Are you being sued in the right court? See page 33, WHERE TO FILE YOUR SUIT, to find out if you are being sued in the right court. If not, you might be able to have the case moved (or you might prefer not to). This may just delay the case, but perhaps the plaintiff will drop the case if he has to travel to another county. You can write a letter to the court explaining why venue is improper and hope that the judge agrees with you. Another possibility is to show up and bring it up at that time. If you choose to write a letter, make sure you receive notice from the court indicating whether the case has been continued or dismissed.

CORPORATE REGISTRATION If the plaintiff is a corporation, it must be current in its registration to maintain a suit. You can call the Secretary of State in Sacramento at (916) 653-7315 to check on a corporation's status. If it is not current, you can order a certificate of proof of non-active status (current fee $5) from the following address:

> Secretary of State
> 1500 11th Street
> Sacramento, CA 95814

This may only delay the suit, but if the corporation is a few years behind in filing, it may be too much trouble and expense to file and then start up the suit again. The fees are hundreds of dollars to reinstate a corporation.

FICTITIOUS NAMES If the plaintiff is using a fictitious name that is not registered, then he may not bring a suit. This will usually just delay the case a couple of months while the plaintiff is publishing the ad and filing the registration. But again, the plaintiff may feel it is too much trouble and not go through with the case.

Under sections 17900-17930 of the Business & Professional Code, every business doing business under a name which is not its legal name must file a Fictitious Business Name Statement in the counties where the business operates. The registration expires after five years or forty days after a change in ownership. Check with the clerk to see if the plaintiff has properly registered. If not, bring it up to the judge.

LACK OF
CONSIDERATION

Promises to make gifts are not enforceable. Therefore, if you signed a promise to pay someone and never received anything in return, the promise would be unenforceable. This can be used in many kinds of cases. Some examples:

☛ If you promised to give your neighbors your old car when you got a new one, they could not win a suit for the car if you changed your mind, since they didn't do anything for the car. However, if you told them you would give them your old car if they mowed your lawn every week, and they did mow your lawn, then they could sue you and win.

☛ If you agreed to pay $1000 for a diamond ring and signed a promissory note to the seller, then discovered the stone to be glass, you could probably avoid paying the note because you got nothing for it. (You could probably also use the fraud or the mutual mistake defenses.) However, if you borrowed the money from a third party such as a bank, you could probably not avoid repaying the bank for the loan because the bank is not responsible for the condition of the item you bought.

Also, if you bought something and signed a promissory note and then the dealer sold the note to a bank or other lender, you could probably not avoid paying the note, since the bank would be considered an innocent buyer of the note and the law encourages the easy sale of "commercial paper." Many businesses that sell questionable products quickly sell the loan papers so that the buyers cannot stop payment.

STATUTE OF
FRAUDS

Certain agreements are not enforceable if they are not in writing (California Civil Code §1621). Even if the facts are true and money is owed, the Statute of Frauds provides that these agreements just won't be enforced by the court if they are not written. The writing need not be a formal contract. Cancelled checks and short memoranda signed by the promisor have, in some cases, been held to be sufficient. The following are circumstances when the agreement must be in writing:

☛ sales of any interest in real estate;

- most leases of real estate for more than one year;

- promises to pay the debts of another person;

- agreements that take longer than one year from the making of the agreement to perform;

- agreements that cannot be performed within the lifetime of the promisor; and

- authorization for an agent to buy or sell real estate.

SPANISH LANGUAGE There are some circumstances where businesses are required to provide a Spanish version of the contract at the time the contract is signed. These include leases for residential units for a period of more than a month, unsecured loans, and certain legal contracts. Furthermore, if a defendant can show that the material terms of the Spanish contract were different than the English language on that was signed, the judge may very well rescind the contract.

MINORS An agreement entered into by a minor, unless emancipated, is generally not enforceable in court. The exceptions to this are if the minor continues to fulfill the agreement after reaching majority or if the agreement was for a "necessity." Thus, if a minor signed an agreement to buy a car, it would probably not be enforceable, but if he signed a check to pay for food it probably would be. (California Civil Code 1556 and 1557.)

PAYMENT Obviously, if you have already paid the money claimed to be owed, this would be a defense to the claim. Perhaps the money was credited to a wrong account or not credited at all. To prevail with this defense you should have some evidence that you have made payment, such as a cancelled check or a receipt.

ACCORD AND SATISFACTION If a debt is in dispute and the parties agree to a settlement, such as acceptance of fifty percent of the debt, this should finally settle the matter. If one party later claims the whole amount in a suit, the settlement agreement would be a defense. This agreement of *accord and satisfaction* should of course be in writing, but even if it is not, it may be enforceable.

STATUTE OF LIMITATIONS

The laws of every state give time limits on how long claims can be brought. After a certain time, claims will not be allowed by the court, no matter how valid they are. Thus, if a person waits too long to file a suit, his or her claim may not be enforceable. The time limits for the different types of claims are set out in appendix G.

FRAUD OR MISREPRESENTATION

If you were defrauded in a transaction, or if important facts were misrepresented to you, you may have a valid defense. For example, if you bought a car and later found out the odometer was set back, you can use that as a defense if you are sued for the price of the car. Usually though, such claims should be used for a counterclaim. (See chapter 6.)

MISTAKE OR ERROR

If both parties were mistaken about an agreement they entered into, it can usually be voided. For example, if both parties believed a gem to be a diamond, but it turned out to be a fake, then a sale of it could be rescinded. If only the seller knew it was a fake, this defense would not work, but the fraud defense might.

BREACH OF CONTRACT

If the plaintiff did not fulfill his side of an agreement, he may not be able to sue you to collect on it. Thus, if improper goods or services were provided, the seller should not be able to collect. For example if you hired someone to paint your house and they did a sloppy job, or if you contracted for a catering service for a wedding and they showed up four hours late, they would have breached the contract. In the painting example, you can also argue that they breached an implied warranty to do the job in a workmanlike manner (see below). Explain to the judge that the plaintiff failed to fulfill his side of the agreement.

IMPLIED WARRANTIES

Even if a provider of goods and services does not provide a written warranty, the law implies three types of warranties in most business transactions, these are that the seller of goods actually owns them and can legally sell them, that the the goods or services are merchantable, that is that they perform the function they are supposed to, and thirdly, if the seller is knowledgeable about them and sells them for a particular purpose that they will fulfill that purpose. For more details on warranties see page 45.

USURY   *Usury* is defined as charging excessive interest. Usury laws are complicated, consisting of a combination of federal and California law. In general, the law permits parties to contract for interest on the unpaid balance on a *personal loan* at a rate not exceeding ten percent per year. Furthermore, there are many exceptions to the general rules. For example, a loan to be used primarily for home improvement or home purchase is not regarded as a personal loan and therefore, the allowable rate is five percent over the amount charged by the Federal Reserve Bank of San Francisco. The penalties for violating usury laws are severe, and people who believe that they have been charged excessive interest rates should research the laws or check with an attorney.

ARBITRATION   To avoid litigation, many parties are putting *arbitration* clauses in their contracts. These clauses provide that the parties agree that in the event of a dispute under the contract they agree not to file suit but to go to an arbitrator. There are several different versions of these clauses. Some of them require non-binding arbitration before suit is filed. Others say that the arbitrators decision will be final. If the contract being sued on has such a clause, the judge may be required to dismiss the case if the clause has not been followed. Of course if a party is suing about a matter which is not covered under the contract, or the arbitration clause, then the clause would not apply.

DURESS   If an agreement is made under *duress*, then it may not be enforceable. For example, if someone confronts you with a gun and says "sign a $1,000 check to me or I will shoot you," you could stop payment on the check since your agreement would have been given under duress.

Duress has to be serious, however. If a mechanic says he will not return your car unless you pay for it and you pay because you need the car even though you feel the work was done wrong, this might not be considered to be duress, because you have other options. For example, you could have sued to get your car back. But small claims court judges are flexible and it might work in where you can convince the judge of the necessity of having the vehicle.

ILLEGALITY	Agreements that are illegal cannot be enforced in court. If you write a check to pay for illegal drugs, prostitution, or illegal gambling, the court will not help the person you paid collect the check.
LICENSE	In certain situations people can give up their right to sue by granting a written or an implied license to the other person. For example, if two people agree to a boxing match, one of them cannot later sue the other for battery if he is hurt. By agreeing to participate in a fight he impliedly gave the other person a license to hit him. If the fight were under the auspices of a club or organization, the parties were probably required to sign an agreement that contained a license as well as a waiver of the right to sue.
WAIVER	A *waiver* is a contract where people give up their right to sue. Restaurants, bars, social clubs, and other groups that hold any types of contests usually require all participants to sign *waivers* of their right to sue. The participants are usually too excited about entering the contest to read what they are signing, but if they try to go to court they learn that they have waived their right to sue.
	School districts, sports organizations, and even police departments who use minors as informants may require that a waiver be signed. Interpretation of a waiver can involve several complicated legal issues which may require research of the case law on the validity of the waiver.
RELEASE	Similar to a waiver is a *release*. For example, suppose a landlord and a tenant get into a lawsuit, each making claims against the other. They don't want to take a chance in court, so they agree to settle. They both sign releases of the other and dismiss the case. If six months later the tenant finds a cash receipt proving that he paid more rent than he realized, he probably wouldn't be able to sue because he already signed a release. Releases may also require analysis to ascertain whether the "injury" was contemplated by the parties when the release was signed.
SALES OF GOODS	Sales of goods are governed by a set of laws called the Uniform Commercial Code. If you are being sued over a transaction involving a sale of goods, there might be some rule which covers your case. For

example, if you sold defective goods and the buyer did not give you proper notice that they were defective, then he may not be able to win a suit against you.

BANKRUPTCY

If a person files *liquidation bankruptcy*, most of the debts listed can be wiped out and completely discharged forever. If a person files a bankruptcy petition while a case is pending, all actions against the person and his property must stop. If you are the plaintiff, and a defendant tells you that he has filed bankruptcy, you should call the local federal bankruptcy court to confirm that it has been filed. If you take any action after you have been informed of a bankruptcy, then you may be held in contempt of federal court. If you are told that an attorney is handling the bankruptcy, all future contact must be through the attorney.

In a *reorganization bankruptcy*, the debts will not be wiped out, but the court will approve a schedule for payment of them. Still, a creditor may not take any actions against the debtor while he or she is in bankruptcy.

SETTLING THE CASE

Whether or not you have any defenses to the case, it is usually better to negotiate a settlement than to take a chance with a judge's decision. No matter how sure you are of your case, you can easily lose if your witness doesn't show up, the other side is more believable, or if any number of things go wrong.

It is often better to take only a partial victory than to risk complete defeat. If the plaintiff understands that he may never be able to collect his judgment, he might accept 50¢ or even 25¢ on the dollar for a cash settlement.

Even if you know you owe the full amount, you should try to avoid a judgment being issued against you. This will be damaging to your credit rating. The best arrangement for both sides is to enter into a Stipulation to Stay Entry of Judgment. This is an agreement by which the parties agree that if the defendant makes payments according to a certain schedule, no judgment will be entered. If you can come to such an agreement, check with the judge or court clerk to see if your agreement can be entered in the court file and approved by the court. It is important for the defendant to keep payment by the schedule or else the judgment will be quickly filed. If the payments are made, no judgment will ever be filed.

Some counties have dispute settlement programs where parties can talk to a mediator and avoid the trouble of court. But such mediation is not binding, and a person who does not get his way may go to court anyway.

COUNTERCLAIMS

The best defense is a good offense, so the best way to defend yourself is to find a reason to counterclaim against the plaintiff. If the only claim pending is the plaintiff's claim against you, the plaintiff will be eager to try the case because the worst that can happen is that he won't win. However, if you file a suit against the plaintiff, there is a risk of losing that was not present before. There is also a better chance of having the case against you dropped or of settling the case when neither party wants to chance losing.

In most states, if you have claims based upon the transaction the plaintiff is suing over, then you must bring up these claims in a countersuit in the same case. This is called a *compulsory counterclaim*. However, in California, the Code of Civil Procedure, §426.60 provides that this rule does not apply so that related claims can be the subject of a new lawsuit.

However, because it is cheaper and less time-consuming to handle your claims in the same suit the plaintiff has brought, you should do so. Only if you weren't aware of a claim until after the suit was over, or if your claim is higher than the $5,000 limit of small claims court, would you want to file a new case.

If the value of the claim you have against the plaintiff is more than $5,000, the defendant can either waive his or her right to the amount in excess of $5,000 or file a motion to transfer the case to either municipal court (if less than $25,000) or superior court, (if more than $25,000).

After you are served with the PLAINTIFF'S CLAIM AND ORDER TO DEFENDANT (Form 2), your claim must be filed on the plaintiff at least five days before the hearing, or one day before the hearing only if you were served with the plaintiff's claim less than ten days before the hearing. The time periods are very important. If you are late with your service, the judge probably will not hear your counterclaim.

CROSS-CLAIMS AND THIRD PARTY CLAIMS

If you discover or know that a third party is responsible for the plaintiff's damages, and that person is not named as a defendant in the plaintiff's case, you may need to file a separate action against that person. If the claim against the third person will be in small claims court, try to get both set for the same date and put a note on the claim form that it is related to Case Number *(insert #)* which is set for *(insert date)*. You will probably need to follow the procedure for a continuance, but it doesn't hurt to save the court some time and work in locating the plaintiff's case.

REQUESTING A CONTINUANCE

If you are the defendant, or the plaintiff on a counterclaim filed by the defendant, the failure to show up in court is likely to end up as a default judgment against you and there is no guarantee that the judge will vacate the default judgment later. Furthermore, you will have lost your right to appeal the merits of the case to superior court.

On the other hand, you can request a postponement of the small claims action if the date falls during a planned vacation, an important occasion, a busy time at work, you have a preference for an evening or Saturday hearing, or any other legitimate reason. You can obtain a continuance of fifteen days or more by making a request to the small claims clerk at least ten days before the hearing and paying a $10 fee. You can accomplish this in person or in a letter, but make sure you send a copy of the letter requesting the continuance to all the other parties to the action. As a final resort, you can show up in court and ask the court to set a new date. Most courts will do so if the request is reasonable. For example, if you were not served or served improperly, it is reasonable to obtain a continuance.

METHODS OF PAYMENT

If you prefer to make payment to the court and have the court pay the plaintiff, you can file a REQUEST TO PAY JUDGMENT TO COURT (Form 25) with the entire amount of the judgment. This service is not free and fees vary for the service. Another option is to pay the judgment in installments. This is accomplished by filing a REQUEST TO PAY JUDGMENT TO COURT (Form 25). This procedure is not automatic. A hearing must occur where the court reviews the income of the debtor to determine how much should be paid each month.

SHOULD I APPEAL?

If you decide to appeal, the Notice of Appeal (Form 20 in appendix B) must be filed within thirty days of the date of the small claims decision or if the clerk mails the NOTICE OF ENTRY OF JUDGMENT (Form 18), within thirty days of the mailing as indicated on the form. (See chapter 10.)

If you won on your counterclaim, write a letter to the plaintiff asking for payment before you start collection procedures. Follow the procedures for collection that are discussed in chapter 9. After the judgment if paid, you will be required to file an ACKNOWLEDGMENT OF SATISFACTION OF JUDGMENT (Form 36) with the small claims court.

RULES OF EVIDENCE 7

The purpose of evidence is to help convince the judge that your claims are true. In small claims court the rules of evidence are much more relaxed and informal than in courts where attorneys present the cases. You won't find a lot of objections being made because it is assumed that the judge knows which evidence is most reliable and admissible without help from the parties. Nevertheless, if you know of some major problem with the other side's evidence that would not be obvious to the judge, you should speak up. For example, if the other side brings photos showing damage to their vehicle that you know was already on the vehicle before your accident, you will need to tell the judge because there is no way the judge would have this knowledge.

When your case is in municipal or superior court, there are rules of discovery which allow one side to ask the other side questions about the case and get answers under penalty of perjury. Discovery also allows the party to obtain important documents from the other side that they either know the other side has, or thinks the other side may have. None of these pre-trial discovery procedures are permitted in small claims court. The only hope a party in a small claims case has to obtain documents from the other party to prove his case is to require him to bring the relevant documents to the hearing by issuing a SUBPOENA DUCES TECUM (Form 14).

The good news is that the *hearsay* rules do not apply in small claims court either. These are rules that require witnesses to have first-hand knowledge of matters about which they are testifying. If the information is second-hand, most other courts will not allow it into evidence, unless it falls into specific exceptions. Hearsay is a very complicated concept, as evidenced by the number of overruled objections that you see in televised trials. Hearsay rules do not apply to small claims appeals either so you can prepare your case without worrying about whether you will be able to use the same evidence if the defendant loses and appeals the case.

THE FOUR TYPES OF EVIDENCE

Whether you are trying a case in superior court, municipal court, or small claims court, there are four basic types of evidence: real, demonstrative, documentary, and testimonial.

REAL EVIDENCE Real evidence is usually a thing that was involved in some event such as a crumbled fender, the written contract, the bad check or the ruined coat. This type of evidence has several advantages. It gives the judge the opportunity to actually see what happened. It is also much more reliable evidence than just telling the judge what happened. If you can bring this type of evidence with you to court, do so. Obviously, you won't want to disturb the courtroom by wheeling a huge trash bin into the court, but you could have it in a truck in the parking lot in case you can interest the judge enough to go outside and view it. Bring photos just in case the judge doesn't want to take the time to leave the bench.

The problem with real evidence is that you also have to convince the judge that it hasn't been changed since the day of the incident. For example, if you continue wearing the jacket you claimed was damaged by the dry cleaner, it will be difficult to prove that it is in the same condition. Whenever you have real evidence, try to preserve it in a separate place.

If someone else has the evidence you need to prove your case, make sure you remember to serve a subpoena to bring the item to court.

DEMONSTRATIVE
EVIDENCE

Maps, diagrams, charts (such as time lines), scale models, photos, computer animations, site plans, and videos are all demonstrative in nature. Several studies have shown that people are more likely to remember oral testimony when they have been shown a visual at the same time. If your case could be more easily explained, bring items to court that illustrate what happened. Sometimes, the use of demonstrative evidence can be very compelling because it is in a format which is easy to understand, especially when you are trying to explain something that is difficult to put into words. For example, if you are trying to show the judge where vehicles were in relationship to each other after a collision, a drawing would help the judge understand. The problem with this type of evidence is that you sometimes need a witness who can testify that the demonstrative evidence is accurate.

DOCUMENTARY
EVIDENCE

The category of documentary evidence is very broad. It includes medical and inventory records, contracts, invoices, statements, public records, newspapers, magazines, and computer print-outs.

Documentary evidence runs into the same problems every time. For each piece of documentary evidence that you have, you should ask yourself the following two questions:

1. *Is there a parol evidence problem?*

Parol evidence is another term for oral evidence. This rule holds that oral evidence may not be used to contradict a written agreement. An exception to this rule is that when a written agreement is ambiguous, then parol evidence may be used to explain what the parties intended.

For example, if a lease says that the rent is $500 per month, you cannot expect to win if you tell the judge that the landlord agreed to accept $50. However, if you start taking care of the lawn and the landlord accepts $450 for the next six months while you take care of the lawn, then oral evidence could be used to explain what the parties intended.

2. *Is there a best evidence problem?*

Best evidence is pretty straightforward. If there is some other evidence that is better than the document you have, you will need to explain why you don't have the better evidence. For example, if you bring a newspaper to prove what the weather was on the day of the incident, a forecast is not as good as a newspaper story describing what the weather was on that day. A newspaper story is not as good as official records of the weather. Whenever you think that the documentary evidence is going to be an issue in your case, bring the original of the document, subpoena the originals, or get certified copies from public agencies.

TESTIMONIAL EVIDENCE

One of the best kinds of evidence you can have is a disinterested witness. Parties and members of their families can be witnesses, but it is much better to have a witness who does not appear to be biased.

It is also very important to find out what the witness will say before bringing them to court. If there is more than one witness to an event, only bring the best witness.

To make sure a witness will appear in court with or without documents, you can subpoena him or her. Even if you are sure the witness will show up, it is sometimes better to use the subpoena process because the witness's employer is more likely to cooperate with an employee who presents a subpoena as the reason why they will be late or absent from work. A subpoena tells the witness where to go, when to be there and what to bring. A subpoena lets the court clerk know the number of the case and where the witness should report, when the case is being heard in another courtroom.

If you want to subpoena someone, you will need to obtain a subpoena from the small claims clerk and fill it out (or use Form 15 in this book). If you want to subpoena records but you do not know the name of the person who is in charge of the records, write "custodian of records" on the subpoena where you fill in the name and address. You will also have to fill out a declaration stating which documents you need and why you need them. A copy of the subpoena must then be delivered to the witness. Unlike service of the lawsuit, you can do this yourself. Actually, anyone over eighteen can serve the subpoena, including the marshal or sheriff. The original is returned to the court with a PROOF OF SERVICE (Form 8) before the trial.

If the witness you subpoena is one of your friends, they may not want payment, but you must pay a witness who asks for payment at the time they receive the subpoena, so have the money ready ($35 and 20¢ a mile). If you win, you will be able to collect the cost of subpoenaing the witnesses if the judge feels that the testimony of the subpoenaed person or records was reasonable.

A word of caution. If you know that a witness will be at the trial to testify for the other side, you don't have to subpoena him or her. However, if the witness doesn't show up, you are out of luck if you need that witness's testimony to prove your part of the case.

TESTIMONY BY DECLARATION

Suppose your only witness can't come to the hearing. There is a procedure you can utilize where the witness writes a statement containing what he or she knows, declaring under penalty of perjury that everything in the statement is true and correct. If you plan to proceed in this manner, make sure the declaration is in the correct format because the judge will not give any credibility to a letter that is not dated or signed. There's even a possibility that the judge will not accept the written statement at all. Plus, a live witness who shows up at the hearing is more memorable.

TESTIMONY BY TELEPHONE

It is best to check with the court clerk to see if you will be allowed to present telephone testimony by someone who cannot come to court. Some judges allow it and some do not.

Expert Witnesses

In some cases, the testimony of an expert witness is the most convincing evidence for your case. For example, when trying to prove some repair work was done incorrectly, it is best to have a skilled technician or mechanic testify that he or she examined the work and it was done wrong. Your own testimony or the testimony of your accountant brother-in-law is not as compelling.

There are many ways to find an expert. Sometimes, a competitor of the defendant will know people who are expert in the field. The literature on a certain subject may contain the names of people who are knowledgeable in that area. The *Jury Verdict Reporter* publishes a semi-annual index of all experts who have testified during the past six months. This index is available in many law libraries.

You will probably have to pay an expert a substantial sum of money to examine the work and to come to court on your behalf. You can submit a written declaration prepared by the expert, but it will not be as effective as having the expert in court.

Oral Agreements

It is not necessary that an agreement be in writing to win in court. In most cases an oral agreement is fully enforceable. The only problem is convincing the judge that there actually was such an agreement.

Usually in a case involving an oral agreement, either one person will deny that there was an agreement or the parties will disagree over the terms of the agreement. It will be up to the judge to decide which side is telling the truth. Sometimes the judge will find inconsistencies in one side's story, and other times the judge will just have to use his or her gut feeling to decide who is telling the truth.

Occasionally there will be some evidence to support an oral agreement. For example, if you loaned a friend some money and she paid you $100 a month by check, you could bring your check register showing a $100 deposit from her every month. Or, you could subpoena her bank records to show that she wrote you a check each month. If she denies that there was ever a loan, she will have to come up with a good story about the checks to convince the judge that she is not lying.

JUDICIAL NOTICE

There are some things that are so generally known that you do not have to bring proof to court. These include the laws of the state and federal government, the fact that the world is round, and gestation takes nine months. Under judicial notice, you do not have to prove the fact, so evidence is not needed. For example, you do not have to bring an original or photocopy of the Constitution with you to court to prove its existence. In general, the procedure is to ask the judge to take judicial notice of a certain fact, and the judge will either agree to do so or decline. Whenever a fact can be reasonably disputed, it is unlikely that the judge will agree to judicial notice.

PROOF

The burden of proof in a civil case is called the *preponderance of evidence*. Many people, including several lawyers, mistakenly believe that preponderance refers to the amount of evidence when it really means that the party who has the more *convincing* evidence will win. Sometimes, the most convincing evidence consists of only one sheet of paper.

PREPARING AND PRESENTING YOUR CASE 8

HOW DO YOU PREPARE FOR TRIAL?

The most important thing to remember when preparing your case is to make it organized, clear, and complete. There are many different ways to go about this. Making a list of all the facts you need to prove and which witnesses or documents you will need to prove them can help you break your case into manageable activities. In some cases, reviewing each element of the law that must be proven will be most beneficial. Sometimes a chronological history of events provides the most organized evidence.

After you are familiar with what you have to prove and know which documents you will need, gather the evidence and make copies for the other parties. Make an extra copy for you to refer to while the judge looks at the originals.

Be sure you know in which courtroom your trial will be held. In counties which have more than one courthouse be sure you know which courthouse to go to. (Even lawyers have been known to show up at the wrong courtroom.)

It's a good idea to get in touch with all your witnesses to remind them of the court date and to let them know whether to expect a subpoena. Don't forget to thank them for helping you out!

Do You Need Advice?

As explained in chapter 1 there should be a small claims advisor available by telephone or in person in all counties in California. See appendix F.

Subpoena Process

Follow the procedures for subpoenaing witnesses and documents. In addition to the subpoena, it is a kindness to prepare written instructions to give to your witnesses telling them how to get to the court, what time they need to be there and what to do when they get there. Offer to pay for a babysitter if for no other reason than to prevent them from bringing children to court. (It's also kind to write down the location of the rest rooms, the cafeteria, and the price and location of the parking lot.)

Disqualifying a Judge

It doesn't happen often, but in some cases you may not want a particular judge, commissioner, or attorney (acting as a pro tem) on your case. For example, if you had a similar case before the judge previously and he or she severely criticized you, you may wish to use the disqualification procedures.

To do so, you must explain to the judge before you present your case that you have an honest belief that he or she is prejudiced against your case and you wish to have another judge preside over your case as allowed by Code of Civil Procedure §170.6. On the other hand, you are not required to sign a stipulation allowing a commissioner or attorney to hear your case if you prefer a judge. Be forewarned, requesting is frowned upon and will increase the time you spend in court while waiting for a very unhappy judge to hear your case.

PRESENTING YOUR CASE

As you get closer to the hearing date, you may find it helpful to write a concise statement of the case, one or two pages at most. You can use the statement as your opening statement to explain the case to the judge. It will also help you keep your thoughts organized.

A week or two before the hearing, present your case to a family member or friend who is unfamiliar with the facts and ask them to critique your presentation and let you know if there are any holes in your argument that you need to fill. A few days before the hearing, review and re-organize your evidence and arguments in the order you plan to present them. Make sure you don't eat or drink anything that you know will cause you to feel ill the night before the hearing.

If you have not settled the case and if the defendant has not defaulted (failed to show up), then a trial (also called a *hearing*) will be held. The purpose of the trial is for the judge to hear both sides of the case and decide who should win and the amount of damages. Even if the defendant does not show up, you will have to present your case.

The hearing is your only chance to present your case to the small claims court. You cannot tell the judge that you are not ready (unless it is a real emergency) or you forgot to bring some of the evidence to court.

If you normally eat breakfast, don't skip it on the day of trial. If the courthouse does not have a cafeteria, bring snacks. Although you can't eat inside the courthouse except in specifically designated areas, it may be a long day and a granola bar or a piece of fruit may be lifesaving treat.

Make sure you arrive at the courtroom on time. Sometimes the clerks give important instructions as soon as the court session begins. If you arrive late, you will miss the instructions.

Before your case is heard, you will have to sit patiently in the courtroom and wait your turn. It is a bad idea to bring children with you to court. Children get restless from sitting quietly for a long time. If they cry or behave badly, you will have to leave the courtroom. Gum chewing, eating, drinking, talking, and walkman radios are also prohibited. In some courtrooms, you are not allowed to read newspapers, magazines, or books while court is in session.

If you think you will need assistance, call ahead. The court has earphones to turn up the volume on the proceedings. If they know you will be in a wheelchair, they can make provisions for allowing your chair to be on the counsel side of the swinging door that separates the audience.

The procedure for presenting your case may include any or all of the following:

1. opening remarks by the judge;

2. plaintiff's opening statement;

3. defendant's opening statement;

4. plaintiff's evidence;

5. defendant's evidence on plaintiff's claim;

6. defendant's evidence on counter-claim;

7. plaintiff's evidence on claim of defendant;

8. plaintiff's closing argument;

9. defendant's closing argument;

10. rebuttals; and

11. judge's decision.

When it is your turn to present your case, come up to the "counsel table" appearing confident, competent, and truthful. State your name and wait for the judge to tell you to proceed. Speak clearly, reviewing your written statement to make sure you don't forget any major issues. If the judge asks questions and you don't know the answer, don't make up an answer (it's called *perjury*). Don't exaggerate or make claims for which you have no evidence. If the judge asks to see documents, hand them to the bailiff or the court clerk. Do not approach the bench unless the judge clearly asks you (this is unlikely).

Don't interrupt when it's the other side's turn to speak. Be mentally prepared to be patient and courteous throughout the entire procedure no matter what is said by the other party. Take notes instead. You will have an opportunity to dispute the evidence presented by the other side when it is your turn.

Judgment

After the case has been presented the judge will probably not give you the decision even if he or she has already decided the outcome. The judge is more likely take your case *under submission* to avoid dealing with an unhappy loser. You probably won't receive the decision for a few weeks. It will come in an envelope from the court clerk on a form called Entry of Judgment. The decision will not be final until the appeal period is over thirty days from the mailing of the judgment.

Caution! A small claims judgment will probably make its way on to the credit report of the losing party.

In order to avoid the consequences of having a major blip on your credit record, you can ask the judge to issue a *conditional judgment* with a follow-up hearing to fulfill the judge's requirements. Some courts do not issue conditional judgments. Check with the small claims advisor in the county where the case is venued before the hearing.

If the judge renders a judgment against two or more parties, he or she is required to clearly state the basis for liability and the amount of damages for each.

Costs
The prevailing party is entitled not only to the costs incurred in bringing the suit, but also to costs incurred in collecting the judgment and accrued interest. These costs include the filing fee, the costs of service and sometimes the costs of subpoenaing witness or documents. You have up to five days after the hearing to ask for your costs by using a special form called MEMORANDUM OF COSTS (Form 21).

VACATING A DEFAULT JUDGMENT

If you are a defendant and do not show up, your case may still be heard without you if the judge determines that service was proper after examining the proof of service filed by the plaintiff. The fact that you are not present does not absolve the plaintiff of the requirement of "proving up" the case (often called a *default prove-up*). The defendant has thirty days after receiving the NOTICE OF ENTRY OF JUDGMENT (Form 18) to file a REQUEST TO CORRECT OR VACATE JUDGMENT (Form 22), and complete a declaration stating the reasons why he or she did not show up. A hearing will be scheduled where the judge determines whether there was good cause for the absence. If the motion is granted, some judges will go ahead and re-hear the merits of the case immediately upon granting the motion to vacate. Other judges schedule a new date in the future. If you have not previously asked the court clerk or the small claims advisor whether this judge holds the re-hearing on the same day as the motion to vacate, be prepared to go forward with your case.

COLLECTING YOUR JUDGMENT 9

If the judgment is in your favor, the euphoria you feel upon winning may quickly fade if you wait until after the hearing to find out if the defendant has any property to satisfy the judgment. Winning the case doesn't necessarily mean that you will collect, at least right away. Sometimes a person or company is called *judgment proof*, meaning that the judgment obtained against the person or company is worthless because they have no money to pay it. It is important to note that judgments can be renewed every ten years and there is always the chance that the defendant will win the lottery or want to sell a piece of property upon which a lien is attached, making it possible for you to collect the money that is owed. If the defendant filed a Chapter 7 or 11 in bankruptcy court, you may still be able to collect the judgment.

ASK FOR YOUR MONEY

If you won the case, write a letter to the defendant asking for payment before you start a collection procedures. You can't start collection procedures until the appeal period is over anyway. Sometimes, the defendant (now known as the *judgment debtor*) will pay the judgment to keep his or her employer from finding out about it through garnishment procedures. You may receive payment because the judgment debtor does not want to lose another day from work to appear for a judgment debtor exam. At the end of the thirty day appeal period, the debtor will be required to submit a JUDGMENT DEBTOR'S STATEMENT OF ASSETS (Form 27), if the judgment isn't paid. That is another incentive for the debtor to pay up the judgment.

On the other hand, if you think the judgment debtor is likely to remove all his money from the only bank account you know about, or is likely to quit his job to avoid garnishment of wages, you may want to lay low until the appeal period is over so that you can attach the property before the judgment debtor can dispose of it. The steps you take prior to collection require careful analysis of all your options.

If you don't want to get involved in the collection process, you can hire a collection agency to obtain the funds for you. Most work on a percentage basis. You can hire an attorney who specializes in collection matters, but negotiate a fee in advance to avoid surprise later.

COLLECTION METHODS

JUDGMENT DEBTOR EXAMINATION

A judgment debtor examination is a procedure where the debtor is required to return to court and answer, under penalty of perjury, the creditor's questions about the location of assets. You can also subpoena the debtors financial records by obtaining a subpoena duces tecum from the court clerk. Appendix D contains a list of suggested questions for a judgment debtor examination. Before beginning the exam, ask the judgment debtor if you can tape record the exam. If you get permission, record the permission and the testimony. Having a recording will make it easier to listen and not be as concerned with getting the information down on paper.

RETAIL BUSINESSES

The sheriff can enter the retail establishment of a debtor and take enough money to satisfy the judgment from the cash register through a procedure is called a *till tap*. You will need to obtain a WRIT OF EXECUTION (Form 29) first.

Another similar procedure is where the sheriff goes to the place of business and sits by the cash register all day waiting for the money to come in. This procedure, called a *keeper levy*, is popular with collections against doctors or lawyers where customers trickle in all day. The keeper keeps the checks.

ABSTRACT OF JUDGMENT

An ABSTRACT OF JUDGMENT (Form 17) is a document which is recorded in the county where the debtor owns property. The effect of the abstract is that it places a lien on any property, or buildings on the property, that the debtor may own in the county. There is no requirement to ascertain in advance whether property is owned in the county or not. In fact, the lien operates on any purchase of property in the county by the debtor as well as any sale of property by the debtor.

If you know the debtor owns property but you don't know where, record an ABSTRACT OF JUDGMENT (Form 17) in several counties. You may get lucky.

WRIT OF EXECUTION— REAL PROPERTY

If the creditor does not want to wait until the property is sold, a WRIT OF EXECUTION (Form 29) can be obtained and filed with the county recorder. This authorizes the sale of the property to the highest bidder at a public sale. All of the money in excess of the judgment and interest are given to the debtor. These sales do not usually fetch market value on the property, so the debtor usually ends up losing a large part of his equity in the property.

WRIT OF EXECUTION— PERSONAL PROPERTY

The court can issue a WRIT OF EXECUTION (Form 29) against an individual judgment debtor, which is an authorization for the collection of property. The judgment creditor gives the WRIT OF EXECUTION to the marshall or sheriff with written instructions describing the property. The marshall is authorized to remove the property and put it in safekeeping. It can later be sold at a public sale. If the property to be seized is in a bank or brokerage account, the marshall directs the third party to turn over the property. If someone owes you money, that person is directed to pay the money to the marshall.

The debtor has ten days after the property is seized to file a CLAIM OF EXEMPTION (Form 31 for wages, Form 30 for other property) with the court. This claim states that the property is exempt from execution or necessary for the support of the debtor or the debtor and his family. The creditor then has ten days to request a court hearing to dispute the exemption. If the creditor does not request a hearing or the judge decides that the property is exempt or necessary for support, it will be returned.

Caution: There are two schedules of exempt property. The first one referred to is preferred by homeowners because it allows for a larger amount of equity in the home to be exempt. If you do not own your own home, you may want to choose the second set of exemptions because the personal property amounts are higher in many cases. Please note that neither list is complete and that an official list of exemptions can be found in Form 19, EXEMPTIONS FROM THE ENFORCEMENT OF JUDGMENTS. If you have substantial property, you may want to see an attorney to ascertain whether your property can be converted into "exempt property" using either schedule.

SET 1

1. Personal residence—if a homestead exemption is filed, certain amounts of equity, from $50,000-$100,000 are preserved.

2. Household furnishing—however items of extraordinary value are not exempt.

3. Automobiles—$19,000 in value is exempt.

4. Wages—75% of disposable earnings are exempt.

5. Life Insurance—$4,000 in cash value is exempt.

6. Government benefits—unemployment, disability, worker's compensation, welfare, pension, and health benefits are exempt.

7. Tools of trade—$5,000 is exempt if it is used by the debtor to earn his living; $10,000 if both spouses work in the same occupation.

8. Trust—if a debtor sets up a trust making himself the beneficiary, none of the assets of the trust are exempt, otherwise, when paid to the beneficiary.

SET 2

1. Personal residence—up to $15,000, or if no personal residence $15,000 of any property.

2. Household furnishings, clothes, books, animals—up to $400 per item.

3. Automobiles—$2,400 in value is exempt.

4. Alimony and child support.

5. Life insurance—$8,000 in unmatured cash value is exempt.

6. Government benefits—unemployment, social security, welfare, ERISA benefits are exempt.

7. Tools of the trade—$1,500.

8. Wrongful death recoveries needed for support and personal injury recoveries up to $15,000.

DRIVER'S LICENSE SUSPENSION

If you obtain a judgment for $500 or less in an auto accident case, you can file DMV form DL 30, (Form 28). The debtor's driver's license will be suspended. This is one of the best ways to get paid because a driver's license is more precious than property to many people.

VALIDITY

A judgment is good for ten years and can be renewed for ten more. In the meantime, they earn interest in the amount of ten percent each year.

AFTER THE JUDGMENT IS PAID

When the judgment is paid, the creditor is required to sign a form called ACKNOWLEDGMENT OF SATISFACTION OF JUDGMENT (Form 36). After it is signed, the debtor should file it with the court, just to make sure it gets filed. If an ABSTRACT OF JUDGMENT (Form 17) has been recorded in any county by the creditor, the debtor will not be able to buy or sell property in that county unless an ACKNOWLEDGMENT OF SATISFACTION OF JUDGMENT is also filed.

APPEALING YOUR CASE 10

If you are the defendant and you lose, or if you are a plaintiff who has been countersued by the defendant, and you lose on the countersuit, you are permitted to appeal. Insurance companies for the defendant can also appeal a judgment in excess of $2,500. The appeal will include a rehearing on all of the claims heard in small claims court, even if an appeal on that specific claim was not made. The purpose is to avoid the possibility that the superior court's decision will conflict with the small claims decision. Enforcement of the judgment is *stayed* while the appeal is pending. This means no other action can be taken on it.

You must file your NOTICE OF APPEAL (FORM 20) with the small claims clerk within thirty days of the date the judgment was mailed to you by the court clerk. A fee for filing is charged and varies from county to county. Since it usually takes a day or two for the judgment to reach you in the mail, you will not have a full thirty days. Watch your deadlines carefully. (Don't mail it. I know an attorney who mailed a NOTICE OF APPEAL of a superior court case where the verdict was over a $2,000,000. The mail was slow and he missed the deadline.)

The appeal will be heard by a superior court judge. You will have to start from scratch, presenting all of your evidence and witnesses again. This is called a *trial de novo*. The same rules and informality regarding evidence govern the hearing.

The amount of damages requested in the small claims suit will be the amount of damages requested in the appeal, even if the judgment against you was for less. For example, if the plaintiff won $250 after having requested $2,500, an appeal puts the defendant at risk of losing the entire $2,500 if the appeal is lost.

While some superior court judges treat small claims matters with the same importance of other matters that come before them, there are other judges who don't favor small claims appeals and make their distaste very obvious. They may rush the parties through their presentations, after they've made them wait in the courtroom for hours. They may use the opportunity to do other paperwork while they pretend to be giving the case their full attention. They may become impatient with the questioning and take it over themselves. Extraordinary requests will be denied. For these reasons, you may find it worthwhile to hire an attorney to represent you since most of them already have learned to deal with the idiosyncrasies of the judiciary. The sad truth is that many attorneys are not treated very well by judges either.

Another reason to consider hiring an attorney is that a judge can award the plaintiff an extra $1,000, plus lost wages if convinced that the appeal was not taken in good faith. This is in addition to the amount of the judgment, plus interest and costs that include attorney's fees in the amount of $150 if actually incurred, any lost earnings, transportation, and lodging expenses.

After the hearing, a new NOTICE OF ENTRY OF JUDGMENT (Form 18) will be mailed to the parties.

Appendix A
California Small
Claims Statutes

The following pages contain sections 116.110-116.950 of the California Code of Civil Procedure. These sections contain most of the laws that pertain to small claims cases.

CALIFORNIA CODES
CODE OF CIVIL PROCEDURE
SECTION 116.110-116.140

116.110. This chapter shall be known and may be cited as "The Small Claims Act."

116.120. The Legislature hereby finds and declares as follows:

(a) Individual minor civil disputes are of special importance to the parties and of significant social and economic consequence collectively.

(b) In order to resolve minor civil disputes expeditiously, inexpensively, and fairly, it is essential to provide a judicial forum accessible to all parties directly involved in resolving these disputes.

(c) The small claims divisions of municipal and justice courts have been established to provide a forum to resolve minor civil disputes, and for that reason constitute a fundamental element in the administration of justice and the protection of the rights and property of individuals.

(d) The small claims divisions of justice and municipal courts, the provisions of this chapter, and the rules of the Judicial Council regarding small claims actions shall operate to ensure that the convenience of parties and witnesses who are individuals shall prevail, to the extent possible, over the convenience of any other parties or witnesses.

116.130. In this chapter, unless the context indicates otherwise:

(a) "Plaintiff" means the party who has filed a small claims action; the term includes a defendant who has filed a claim against a plaintiff.

(b) "Defendant" means the party against whom the plaintiff has filed a small claims action; the term includes a plaintiff against whom a defendant has filed a claim.

(c) "Judgment creditor" means the party, whether plaintiff or defendant, in whose favor a money judgment has been rendered.

(d) "Judgment debtor" means the party, whether plaintiff or defendant, against whom a money judgment has been rendered.

(e) "Person" means an individual, corporation, partnership, limited liability company, firm, association, or other entity.

(f) "Individual" means a natural person.

(g) "Party" means a plaintiff or defendant.

(h) "Motion" means a party's written request to the court for an order or other action; the term includes an informal written request to the court, such as a letter.

(i) "Declaration" means a written statement signed by an individual which includes the date and place of signing, and a statement under penalty of perjury that its contents are true and correct.

(j) "Good cause" means circumstances sufficient to justify the requested order or other action, as determined by the judge.

(k) "Mail" means first-class mail with postage fully prepaid, unless stated otherwise.

116.140. The following do not apply in small claims actions:

(a) Subdivision (a) of Section 1013 and subdivision (b) of Section 1005, on the extension of the time for taking action when notice is given by mail.

(b) Title 6.5 (commencing with Section 481.010) of Part 2, on the issuance of prejudgment attachments.

CALIFORNIA CODES
CODE OF CIVIL PROCEDURE
SECTION 116.210-116.270

116.210. In each justice court and each municipal court there shall be a small claims division.

116.220. (a) The small claims court shall have jurisdiction in the following actions:

(1) Except as provided in subdivisions (c), (e), and (f), for recovery of money, if the amount of the demand does not exceed five thousand dollars ($5,000).

(2) Except as provided in subdivisions (c), (e), and (f), to enforce payment of delinquent unsecured personal property taxes in an amount not to exceed five thousand dollars ($5,000), if the legality of the tax is not contested by the defendant.

(3) To issue the writ of possession authorized by Sections 1861.5 and 1861.10 of the Civil Code if the amount of the demand does not exceed five thousand dollars ($5,000).

(4) To confirm, correct, or vacate a fee arbitration award not exceeding five thousand dollars ($5,000) between an attorney and client that is binding or has become binding, or to conduct a hearing de novo between an attorney and client after nonbinding arbitration of a fee dispute involving no more than five thousand dollars ($5,000) in controversy, pursuant to Article 13 (commencing with Section 6200) of Chapter 4 of Division 3 of the Business and Professions Code.

(b) In any action seeking relief authorized by subdivision (a), the court may grant equitable relief in the form of rescission, restitution, reformation, and specific performance, in lieu of, or in addition to, money damages. The court may issue a conditional judgment. The court shall retain jurisdiction until full payment and performance of any judgment or order.

(c) Notwithstanding subdivision (a), the small claims court shall have jurisdiction over a defendant guarantor who is required to respond based upon the default, actions, or omissions of another, only if the demand does not exceed two thousand five hundred dollars ($2,500).

(d) In any case in which the lack of jurisdiction is due solely to an excess in the amount of the demand, the excess may be waived, but any waiver shall not become operative until judgment.

(e) Notwithstanding subdivision (a), in any action filed by a plaintiff incarcerated in a Department of Corrections facility or a Youth Authority facility, the small claims court shall have jurisdiction over a defendant only if the plaintiff has alleged in the complaint that he or she has exhausted his or her administrative remedies against that department, including compliance with Sections 905.2 and 905.4 of the Government Code. The final administrative adjudication or determination of the plaintiff's administrative claim by the department may be attached to the complaint at the time of filing in lieu of that allegation.

(f) In any action governed by subdivision (e), if the plaintiff fails to provide proof of compliance with the requirements of subdivision (e) at the time of trial, the judicial officer shall, at his or her discretion, either dismiss the action or continue the action to give the plaintiff an opportunity to provide such proof.

(g) For purposes of this section, "department" includes an employee of a department against whom a claim has been filed under this chapter arising out of his or her duties as an employee of that department.

116.230. (a) A fee of twenty dollars ($20) shall be charged and collected for the filing of a claim if the number of claims previously filed by the party in each court within the previous 12 months is 12 or less; and a fee of thirty-five dollars ($35) shall be collected for the filing of any additional claims.

(b) A fee to cover the actual cost of court service by mail, adjusted upward to the nearest dollar, shall be charged and collected for each defendant to whom the court clerk mails a copy of the claim under Section 116.340.

(c) The number of claims filed by a party during the previous 12 months shall be determined by a declaration by the party stating the number of claims so filed and submitted to the clerk with the current claim.

(d) Five dollars ($5) of the fees authorized in subdivision (a) shall be deposited upon collection in the special account in the county treasury established pursuant to subdivision (b) of Section 68085 of the Government Code, and transmitted there from monthly to the Controller for deposit in the Trial Court Trust Fund.

116.231. (a) Except as provided in subdivision (d), no person may file more than two small claims actions in which the amount demanded exceeds two thousand five hundred dollars ($2,500), anywhere in the state in any calendar year.

(b) Except as provided in subdivision (d), if the amount demanded in any small claims action exceeds two thousand five hundred dollars ($2,500), the party making the demand shall file a declaration under penalty of perjury attesting to the fact that not more than two small claims actions in which the amount of

the demand exceeded two thousand five hundred dollars ($2,500) have been filed by that party in this state within the calendar year.

(c) The Legislature finds and declares that the pilot project conducted under the authority of Chapter 1196 of the Statutes of 1991 demonstrated the efficacy of the removal of the limitation on the number of actions public entities may file in the small claims courts on claims exceeding two thousand five hundred dollars ($2,500).

(d) The limitation on the number of filings exceeding two thousand five hundred dollars ($2,500) does not apply to filings where the claim does not exceed five thousand dollars ($5,000) which are filed by a city, county, city and county, school district, county office of education, community college district, local district, or any other local public entity. If any small claims action is filed by a city, county, city and county, school district, county office of education, community college district, local district, or any other local public entity pursuant to this section, and the defendant informs the court either in advance of the hearing by written notice or at the time of the hearing, that he or she is represented in the action by legal counsel, the action shall be transferred to the municipal court. A city, county, city and county, school district, county office of education, community college district, local district, or any other local public entity may not file a claim within the small claims division if the amount of the demand exceeds five thousand dollars ($5,000).

116.240. With the consent of the parties who appear at the hearing, the court may order a case to be heard by a temporary judge who is a member of the State Bar, and who has been sworn and empowered to act until final determination of the case.

116.250. (a) Sessions of the small claims court may be scheduled at any time and on any day, including Saturdays, but excluding other judicial holidays. They may also be scheduled at any public building within the judicial district, including places outside the courthouse.

(b) Each small claims division of a municipal court with four or more judicial officers shall conduct at least one night session or Saturday session each month. The term "session" includes, but is not limited to, a proceeding conducted by a member of the State Bar acting as a mediator or referee.

116.260. In each county, individual assistance shall be made available to advise small claims litigants and potential litigants without charge as provided in Section 116.940 and by rules adopted by the Judicial Council.

116.270. Any small claims division may use law clerks to assist the judge with legal research of small claims cases.

116.310. (a) No formal pleading other than the claim described in Section 116.320 or 116.380, is necessary to initiate a small claims action.

(b) The pretrial discovery procedures described in subdivision (a) of Section 2019 are not permitted in small claims actions.

116.320. (a) A plaintiff may commence an action in the small claims court by filing a claim under oath with the clerk of the small claims court in person or by mail.

(b) The claim form shall be a simple nontechnical form approved or adopted by the Judicial Council. The claim form shall set forth a place for (1) the name and address of the defendant, if known; (2) the amount and the basis of the claim; (3) that the plaintiff, where possible, has demanded payment and, in applicable cases, possession of the property; (4) that the defendant has failed or refused to pay, and, where applicable, has refused to surrender the property; and (5) that the plaintiff understands that the judgment on his or her claim will be conclusive and without a right of appeal.

(c) The form or accompanying instructions shall include
information that the plaintiff (1) may not be represented by an attorney, (2) has no right of appeal, and (3) may ask the court to waive fees for filing and serving the claim on the ground that the plaintiff is unable to pay them, using the forms approved by the Judicial Council for that purpose.

116.330. (a) When a claim is filed, the clerk shall schedule the case for hearing in accordance with subdivision (c) and shall issue an order directing the parties to appear at the time set for the hearing with witnesses and documents to prove their claim or defense.

(b) In lieu of the method of setting the case for hearing
described in subdivision (a), at the time a claim is filed the clerk may do all of the following:

(1) Cause a copy of the claim to be mailed to the defendant by any form of mail providing for a return receipt.

(2) On receipt of proof that the claim was served as provided in paragraph (1), issue an order scheduling the case for hearing in accordance with subdivision (c) and directing the parties to appear at the time set for the hearing with witnesses and documents to prove their claim or defense.

(3) Cause a copy of the order setting the case for hearing and directing the parties to appear, to be served upon the parties by any form of mail providing for a return receipt.

(c) If the defendant resides in the county in which the action is filed, the case shall be scheduled for hearing at least 15 days but not more than 40 days from the date of the order. If the defendant resides outside the county in which the action is filed, the case shall be scheduled for hearing at least 30 days but not more than 70 days from the date of the order.

(d) If there are two or more defendants and one or more of them resides outside the county in which the action is filed, the date for the appearance of all the defendants shall be at least 30 days but not more than 70 days from the date of the order.

(e) A public entity, as defined in Section 811.2 of the Government Code, which files more than 10 claims at one time may request a date for the appearance of the defendant later than that otherwise specified in this section, and the clerk may set the case for hearing at that later date subject to the following limits:

(1) If all defendants reside in the county in which the action is filed, the date for appearance shall not be more than 70 days from the date of the order.

(2) In other cases, the date for appearance shall not be more than 90 days from the date of the order.

116.340. (a) Service of the claim and order on the defendant may be made by any one of the following methods:

(1) The clerk may cause a copy of the claim and order to be mailed to the defendant by any form of mail providing for a return receipt.

(2) The plaintiff may cause a copy of the claim and order to be delivered to the defendant in person.

(3) The plaintiff may cause service of a copy of the claim and order to be made by substituted service as provided in subdivision (a) or (b) of Section 415.20 without the need to attempt personal service on the defendant. For these purposes, substituted service as provided in subdivision (b) of Section 415.20 may be made at the office of the sheriff or marshal who shall deliver a copy of the claim and order to any person authorized by the defendant to receive service, as provided in Section 416.90, who is at least 18 years of age, and thereafter mailing a copy of the claim and order to the defendant's usual mailing address.

(4) The clerk may cause a copy of the claim to be mailed, the order to be issued, and a copy of the order to be mailed as provided in subdivision (b) of Section 116.330.

(b) Service of the claim and order on the defendant shall be completed at least 10 days before the hearing date if the defendant resides within the county in which the action is filed, or at least 15 days before the hearing date if the defendant resides outside the county in which the action is filed.

(c) Service by the methods described in subdivision (a) shall be deemed complete on the date that the defendant signs the mail return receipt, on the date of the personal service, as provided in Section 415.20, or as established by other competent evidence, whichever applies to the method of service used.

(d) Service shall be made within this state, except as provided in subdivisions (e) and (f).

(e) The owner of record of real property in California who resides in another state and who has no lawfully designated agent in California for service of process may be served by any of the methods described in this section if the claim relates to that property.

(f) A nonresident owner or operator of a motor vehicle involved in an accident within this state may be served pursuant to the provisions on constructive service in Sections 17450 to 17461, inclusive, of the Vehicle Code without regard to whether the defendant was a nonresident at the time of the accident or when the claim was filed. Service shall be made by serving both the Director of the California Department of Motor Vehicles and the defendant, and may be made by any of the methods authorized by this chapter or by registered mail as authorized by Section 17454 or 17455 of the Vehicle Code.

(g) If an action is filed against a principal and his or her guaranty or surety pursuant to a guarantor or suretyship agreement, a reasonable attempt shall be made to complete service on the principal. If service is not completed on the principal, the action shall be transferred to the court of appropriate jurisdiction.

116.360. (a) The defendant may file a claim against the plaintiff in the same action in an amount not to exceed the jurisdictional limits stated in Sections 116.220 and 116.231. The claim need not relate to the same subject or event as the plaintiff's claim.

(b) The defendant's claim shall be filed and served in the manner provided for filing and serving a claim of the plaintiff under Sections 116.330 and 116.340.

(c) The defendant shall cause a copy of the claim and order to be served on the plaintiff at least five days before the hearing date, unless the defendant was served 10 days or less before the hearing date, in which event the defendant shall cause a copy of the defendant's claim and order to be served on the plaintiff at least one day before the hearing date.

116.370. (a) Venue in small claims actions shall be the same as in other civil actions.

(b) A defendant may challenge venue by writing to the court and mailing a copy of the challenge to each of the other parties to the action, without personally appearing at the hearing.

(c) In all cases, including those in which the defendant does not either challenge venue or appear at the hearing, the court shall inquire into the facts sufficiently to determine whether venue is proper, and shall make its determination accordingly.

(1) If the court determines that the action was not commenced in the proper venue, the court, on its own motion, shall dismiss the action without prejudice unless all defendants are present and agree that the action may be heard.

(2) If the court determines that the action was commenced in the proper venue, the court may hear the case if all parties are present. If the defendant challenged venue and all parties are not present, the court shall postpone the hearing for at least 15 days and shall notify all parties by mail of the court's decision and the new hearing date, time, and place.

116.390. (a) If a defendant has a claim against a plaintiff that exceeds the jurisdictional limits stated in Sections 116.220 and 116.231, and the claim relates to the contract, transaction, matter, or event which is the subject of the plaintiff's claim, the defendant may commence an action against the plaintiff in a court of competent jurisdiction and request the small claims court to transfer the small claims action to that court.

(b) The defendant may make the request by filing with the small claims court in which the plaintiff commenced the action, at or before the time set for the hearing of that action, a declaration stating the facts concerning the defendant's action against the plaintiff with a true copy of the complaint so filed by the defendant against the plaintiff and the sum of one dollar ($1) for a transmittal fee. The defendant shall cause a copy of the declaration and complaint to be personally delivered to the plaintiff at or before the time set for the hearing of the small claims action.

(c) In ruling on a motion to transfer, the small claims court may do any of the following: (1) render judgment on the small claims case prior to the transfer; (2) not render judgment and transfer the small claims case; (3) refuse to transfer the small claims case on the grounds that the ends of justice would not be served. If the small claims action is transferred prior to judgment, both actions shall be tried together in the transferee court.

(d) When the small claims court orders the action transferred, it shall transmit all files and papers to the transferee court.

(e) The plaintiff in the small claims action shall not be required to pay to the clerk of the transferee court any transmittal, appearance, or filing fee unless the plaintiff appears in the transferee court, in which event the plaintiff shall be required to pay the filing fee and any other fee required of a defendant in the transferee court. However, if the transferee court rules against the plaintiff in the action filed in that court, the court may award to the defendant in that action the costs incurred as a consequence of
the transfer, including attorney's fees and filing fees.

CALIFORNIA CODES
CODE OF CIVIL PROCEDURE
SECTION 116.410-116.430

116.410. (a) Any person who is at least 18 years of age and mentally competent may be a party to a small claims action.

(b) A minor or incompetent person may appear by a guardian ad litem appointed by a judge of the court in which the action is filed.

116.420. (a) No claim shall be filed or maintained in small claims court by the assignee of the claim.

(b) This section does not prevent the filing or defense of an action in the small claims court by (1) a trustee in bankruptcy in the exercise of the trustee's duties as trustee, or (2) by the holder of a security agreement, retail installment contract, or lien contract subject to the Unruh Act (Chapter 1 (commencing with Section 1801) of Title 2 of Part 4 of Division 3 of the Civil Code) or the Automobile Sales Finance Act (Chapter 2b (commencing with Section 2981) of Title 14 of Part 4 of Division 3 of the Civil Code), purchased by the holder for the holder's portfolio of investments, provided that the holder is not an assignee for the purpose of collection.

(c) This section does not prevent the filing in small claims court by a local government which is self-insured for purposes of workers' compensation and is seeking subrogation pursuant to Section 3852 of the Labor Code.

116.430. (a) If the plaintiff operates or does business under a fictitious business name and the claim relates to that business, the claim shall be accompanied by the filing of a declaration stating that the plaintiff has complied with the fictitious business name laws by executing, filing, and publishing a fictitious business name statement as required.

(b) A small claims action filed by a person who has not complied with the applicable fictitious business name laws by executing, filing, and publishing a fictitious business name statement as required shall be dismissed without prejudice.

(c) For purposes of this section, "fictitious business name" means the term as defined in Section 17900 of the Business and Professions Code, and "fictitious business name statement" means the statement described in Section 17913 of the Business and Professions Code.

CALIFORNIA CODES
CODE OF CIVIL PROCEDURE
SECTION 116.510-116.570

116.510. The hearing and disposition of the small claims action shall be informal, the object being to dispense justice promptly, fairly, and inexpensively.

116.520. (a) The parties have the right to offer evidence by witnesses at the hearing or, with the permission of the court, at another time.

(b) If the defendant fails to appear, the court shall still require the plaintiff to present evidence to prove his or her claim.

(c) The court may consult witnesses informally and otherwise investigate the controversy with or without notice to the parties.

116.530. (a) Except as permitted by this section, no attorney may take part in the conduct or defense of a small claims action.

(b) Subdivision (a) does not apply if the attorney is appearing to maintain or defend an action (1) by or against himself or herself, (2) by or against a partnership in which he or she is a general partner and in which all the partners are attorneys, or (3) by or against a professional corporation of which he or she is an officer or director and of which all other officers and directors are attorneys.

(c) Nothing in this section shall prevent an attorney from (1) providing advice to a party to a small claims action, either before or after the commencement of the action; (2) testifying to facts of which he or she has personal knowledge and about which he or she is competent to testify; (3) representing a party in an appeal to the superior court; and (4) representing a party in connection with the enforcement of a judgment.

116.531. Nothing in this article shall prevent a representative of an insurer or other expert in the matter before the small claims court from rendering assistance to a party in the litigation except during the conduct of the hearing, either before or after the commencement of the action, unless otherwise prohibited by law; nor shall anything in this article prevent those individuals from testifying to facts of which they have personal knowledge and about which they are competent to testify.

116.540. (a) Except as permitted by this section, no individual other than the plaintiff and the defendant may take part in the conduct or defense of a small claims action.

(b) A corporation may appear and participate in a small claims action only through a regular employee, or a duly appointed or elected officer or director, who is employed, appointed, or elected for purposes other than solely representing the corporation in small claims court.

(c) A party who is not a corporation or a natural person may appear and participate in a small claims action only through a regular employee, or a duly appointed or elected officer or director, or in the case of a partnership, a partner, engaged for purposes other than solely representing the party in small claims court.

(d) If a party is an individual doing business as a sole proprietorship, the party may appear and participate in a small claims action by a representative and without personally appearing if both of the following conditions are met:

(1) The claim can be proved or disputed by evidence of an account that constitutes a business record as defined in Section 1271 of the Evidence Code, and there is no other issue of fact in the case.

(2) The representative is a regular employee of the party for purposes other than solely representing the party in small claims actions and is qualified to testify to the identity and mode of preparation of the business record.

(e) A plaintiff is not required to personally appear, and may submit declarations to serve as evidence supporting his or her claim or allow another individual to appear and participate on his or her behalf, if (1) the plaintiff is serving on active duty in the United States armed forces outside this state, (2) the plaintiff was assigned to his or her duty station after his or her claim arose, (3) the assignment is for more than six months, (4) the representative is serving without compensation, and (5) the representative has appeared in small claims actions on behalf of others no more than four times during the calendar year. The defendant may file a claim in the same action in an amount not to exceed the jurisdictional limits stated in Sections 116.220 and 116.231.

(f) A party incarcerated in a county jail, a Department of Corrections facility, or a Youth Authority facility is not required to personally appear, and may submit declarations to serve as evidence supporting his or her claim, or may authorize another individual to appear and participate on his or her behalf if that individual is serving without compensation and has appeared in small claims actions on behalf of others no more than four times during the calendar year.

(g) A defendant who is a nonresident owner of real property may defend against a claim relating to that property without personally appearing by (1) submitting written declarations to serve as evidence supporting his or her defense, (2) allowing another individual to appear and participate on his or her behalf if that individual is serving without compensation and has appeared in small claims actions on behalf of others no more than four times during the calendar year, or (3) taking the action described in both (1) and (2).

(h) A party who is an owner of rental real property may appear and participate in a small claims action through a property agent under contract with the owner to manage the rental of that property, if (1) the owner has retained the property agent principally to manage the rental of that property and not principally to represent the owner in small claims court, and (2) the claim relates to the rental property.

(i) At the hearing of a small claims action, the court shall require any individual who is appearing as a representative of a party under subdivisions (b) to (h), inclusive, to file a declaration stating (1) that the individual is authorized to appear for the party, and (2) the basis for that authorization. If the representative is appearing under subdivision (b), (c), (d), or (h), the declaration also shall state that the individual is not employed solely to represent the party in small claims court. If the representative is appearing under subdivision (e), (f), or (g), the declaration also shall state that

the representative is serving without compensation, and has appeared in small claims actions on behalf of others no more than four times during the calendar year.

(j) A husband or wife who sues or who is sued with his or her spouse may appear and participate on behalf of his or her spouse if (1) the claim is a joint claim, (2) the represented spouse has given his or her consent, and (3) the court determines that the interests of justice would be served.

(k) If the court determines that a party cannot properly present his or her claim or defense and needs assistance, the court may in its discretion allow another individual to assist that party.

(l) Nothing in this section shall operate or be construed to authorize an attorney to participate in a small claims action except as expressly provided in Section 116.530.

116.541. (a) Notwithstanding Section 116.540 or any other provision of law, the Department of Corrections or the Department of the Youth Authority may appear and participate in a small claims action through a regular employee, who is employed or appointed for purposes other than solely representing that department in small claims court.

(b) Where the Department of Corrections or the Department of the Youth Authority is named as a defendant in small claims court, the representative of the department is not required to personally appear to challenge the plaintiff's compliance with the pleading requirements and may submit pleadings or declarations to assert that challenge.

(c) At the hearing of a small claims action, the court shall require any individual who is appearing as a representative of the Department of Corrections or the Department of the Youth Authority under subdivision (a) to file a declaration stating (1) that the individual is authorized to appear for the party, (2) the basis for that authorization, and (3) that the individual is not employed solely to represent the party in small claims court.

(d) Nothing in this section shall operate or be construed to authorize an attorney to participate in a small claims action except as expressly provided in Section 116.530.

(e) For purposes of this section, all references to the Department of Corrections or the Department of the Youth Authority include an employee thereof, against whom a claim has been filed under this chapter arising out of his or her duties as an employee of that department.

116.550. (a) If the court determines that a party does not speak or understand English sufficiently to comprehend the proceedings or give testimony, and needs assistance in so doing, the court may permit another individual (other than an attorney) to assist that party.

(b) Each small claims court shall make a reasonable effort to maintain and make available to the parties a list of interpreters who are able and willing to aid parties in small claims actions either for no fee, or for a fee which is reasonable considering the nature and complexity of the claims. The list shall include interpreters for all languages that require interpretation before the court, as determined by the court in its discretion and in view of the court's experience.

(c) Failure to maintain a list of interpreters, or failure to include an interpreter for a particular language, shall not invalidate any proceedings before the court.

(d) If a court interpreter or other competent interpreter is not available to aid a party in a small claims action, at the first hearing of the case the court shall postpone the hearing one time only to allow the party the opportunity to obtain another individual (other than an attorney) to assist that party. Any additional continuances shall be at the discretion of the court.

116.560. (a) Whenever a claim that is filed against a person operating or doing business under a fictitious business name relates to the defendant's business, the court shall inquire at the time of the hearing into the defendant's correct legal name and the name or names under which the defendant does business. If the correct legal name of the defendant, or the name actually used by the defendant, is other than the name stated on the claim, the court shall amend the claim to state the correct legal name of the defendant, and the name or names actually used by the defendant.

(b) The plaintiff may request the court at any time, whether before or after judgment, to amend the plaintiff's claim or judgment to include both the correct legal name and the name or names actually used by the defendant. Upon a showing of good cause, the court shall amend the claim or judgment to state the correct legal name of the defendant, and the name or names actually used by the defendant.

(c) For purposes of this section, "fictitious business name" means the term as defined in Section 17900 of the Business and Professions Code.

116.570. (a) Any party may submit a written request for postponement of a hearing date.

(1) The written request may be made either by letter or on a form adopted or approved by the Judicial Council.

(2) On the date of making the written request, the requesting party shall mail or personally deliver a copy to each of the other parties to the action.

(3) If the court finds that the interests of justice would be served by postponing the hearing, the court shall postpone the hearing, and shall notify all parties by mail of the new hearing date, time, and place.

(4) The court shall provide a prompt response by mail to any person making a written request for postponement of a hearing date under this subdivision.

(b) If service of the claim and order upon the defendant is not completed within the number of days before the hearing date required by subdivision (b) of Section 116.340, and the defendant has not personally appeared and has not requested a postponement, the court shall postpone the hearing for at least 15 days. If a postponement is ordered under this subdivision, the clerk shall promptly notify all parties by mail of the new hearing date, time, and place.

(c) Nothing in this section limits the inherent power of the court to order postponements of hearings in appropriate circumstances.

(d) A fee of ten dollars ($10) shall be charged and collected for the filing of a request for postponement and rescheduling of a hearing date after timely service pursuant to subdivision (b) of Section 116.340 has been made upon the defendant.

CALIFORNIA CODES
CODE OF CIVIL PROCEDURE
SECTION 116.610-116.630

116.610. (a) The small claims court shall give judgment for damages, or equitable relief, or both damages and equitable relief, within the jurisdictional limits stated in Sections 116.220 and 116.231, and may make such orders as to time of payment or otherwise as the court deems just and equitable for the resolution of the dispute.

(b) The court may, at its discretion or on request of any party, continue the matter to a later date in order to permit and encourage the parties to attempt resolution by informal or alternative means.

(c) The judgment shall include a determination whether the judgment resulted from a motor vehicle accident on a California highway caused by the defendant's operation of a motor vehicle, or by the operation by some other individual, of a motor vehicle registered in the defendant's name.

(d) If the defendant has filed a claim against the plaintiff, or if the judgment is against two or more defendants, the judgment, and the statement of decision if one is rendered, shall specify the basis for and the character and amount of the liability of each of the parties, including, in the case of multiple judgment debtors, whether the liability of each is joint or several.

(e) If specific property is referred to in the judgment, whether it be personal or real, tangible or intangible, the property shall be identified with sufficient detail to permit efficient implementation or enforcement of the judgment.

(f) In an action against several defendants, the court may, in its discretion, render judgment against one or more of them, leaving the action to proceed against the others, whenever a several judgment is proper.

(g) The prevailing party is entitled to the costs of the action, including the costs of serving the order for the appearance of the defendant.

(h) When the court renders judgment, the clerk shall promptly deliver or mail notice of entry of the judgment to the parties, and shall execute a certificate of personal delivery or mailing and place it in the file.

(i) The notice of entry of judgment shall be on a form approved or adopted by the Judicial Council.

116.620. (a) The judgment debtor shall pay the amount of the judgment either immediately or at the time and upon the terms and conditions, including payment by installments, which the court may order.

(b) The court may at any time, for good cause, upon motion by a party and notice by the clerk to all affected parties at their last known address, amend the terms and conditions for payment of the judgment to provide for payment by installment. The determination shall be made without regard to the nature of the underlying debt and without regard to whether the moving party appeared before entry of the judgment.

(c) In determining the terms and conditions of payment, the court may consider any factors which would be relevant to a claim of exemption under Chapter 4 (commencing with Section 703.010) of Division 2 of Title 9 of Part 2.

116.630. The court may, at any time after judgment, for good cause, upon motion by a party and notice by the clerk to all affected parties at their last known address, amend the name of any party to include both the correct legal name and the actually used name or names of that party.

CALIFORNIA CODES
CODE OF CIVIL PROCEDURE
SECTION 116.710-116.795

116.710. (a) The plaintiff in a small claims action shall have no right to appeal the judgment on the plaintiff's claim, but a plaintiff who did not appear at the hearing may file a motion to vacate the judgment in accordance with Section 116.720.

(b) The defendant with respect to the plaintiff's claim, and a plaintiff with respect to a claim of the defendant, may appeal the judgment to the superior court in the county in which the action was heard.

(c) With respect to the plaintiff's claim, the insurer of the defendant may appeal the judgment to the superior court in the county in which the matter was heard if the judgment exceeds two thousand five hundred dollars ($2,500) and the insurer stipulates that its policy with the defendant covers the matter to which the judgment applies.

(d) A defendant who did not appear at the hearing has no right to appeal the judgment, but may file a motion to vacate the judgment in accordance with Section 116.730 or 116.740 and also may appeal the denial of that motion.

116.720. (a) A plaintiff who did not appear at the hearing in the small claims court may file a motion to vacate the judgment with the clerk of the small claims court. The motion shall be filed within 30 days after the clerk has mailed notice of entry of the judgment to the parties.

(b) The clerk shall schedule the hearing on the motion to vacate for a date no earlier than 10 days after the clerk has mailed written notice of the date, time, and place of the hearing to the parties.

(c) Upon a showing of good cause, the small claims court may grant the motion. If the defendant is not present, the court shall hear the motion in the defendant's absence.

(d) If the motion is granted, and if all parties are present and agree, the court may hear the case without rescheduling it. If the defendant is not present, the judge or clerk shall reschedule the case and give notice in accordance with Section 116.330.

116.725. Nothing in this chapter shall be construed to prevent a court from correcting a clerical error in a judgment or from setting aside and vacating a judgment on the ground of an incorrect or erroneous legal basis for the decision.

116.730. (a) A defendant who did not appear at the hearing in the small claims court may file a motion to vacate the judgment with the clerk of the small claims court. The motion shall be filed within 30 days after the clerk has mailed notice of entry of the judgment to the parties.

(b) The defendant shall appear at any hearing on the motion, or submit written justification for not appearing together with a declaration in support of the motion.

(c) Upon a showing of good cause, the court may grant the motion to vacate the judgment. If the plaintiff is not present, the court shall hear the motion in the plaintiff's absence.

(d) If the motion is granted, and if all parties are present and agree, the court may hear the case without rescheduling it. If the plaintiff is not present, the judge or clerk shall reschedule the case and give notice in accordance with Section 116.330.

(e) If the motion is denied, the defendant may appeal to the superior court only on the denial of the motion to vacate the judgment. The defendant shall file the notice of appeal with the clerk of the small claims court within 10 days after the small claims court has mailed or delivered notice of the court's denial of the motion to vacate the judgment.

(f) If the superior court determines that the defendant's motion to vacate the judgment should have been granted, the superior court may hear the claims of all parties without rescheduling the matter, provided that all parties are present and the defendant has previously complied with this article, or may order the case transferred to the small claims court for a hearing.

116.740. (a) If the defendant was not properly served as required by Section 116.330 or 116.340 and did not appear at the hearing in the small claims court, the defendant may file a motion to vacate the judgment with the clerk of the small claims court. The motion shall be accompanied by a supporting declaration, and shall be filed within 180 days after the defendant discovers or should have discovered that judgment was entered against the defendant.

(b) The court may order that the enforcement of the judgment shall be suspended pending a hearing and determination of the motion to vacate the judgment.

(c) Upon a showing of good cause, the court may grant the motion to vacate the judgment. If the plaintiff is not present, the court shall hear the motion in the plaintiff's absence.

(d) Subdivisions (d), (e), and (f) of Section 116.730 apply to any motion to vacate a judgment.

116.745. The clerk shall charge and collect fees for the filing of a motion to vacate, as provided by Section 26830 of the Government Code.

116.750. (a) An appeal from a judgment in a small claims action is taken by filing a notice of appeal with the clerk of the small claims court.

(b) A notice of appeal shall be filed not later than 30 days after the clerk has delivered or mailed notice of entry of the judgment to the parties. A notice of appeal filed after the 30-day period is ineffective for any purpose.

(c) The time for filing a notice of appeal is not extended by the filing of a request to correct a mistake or by virtue of any subsequent proceedings on that request, except that a new period for filing notice of appeal shall begin on the delivery or mailing of notice of entry of any modified judgment.

116.760. (a) The appealing party shall pay the same superior court filing fee that is required for an appeal of a civil action from a justice or municipal court.

(b) A party who does not appeal shall not be charged any fee for filing any document in the superior court.

116.770. (a) The appeal to the superior court shall consist of a new hearing.

(b) The hearing on an appeal to the superior court shall be conducted informally. The pretrial discovery procedures described in subdivision (a) of Section 2019 are not permitted, no party has a right to a trial by jury, and no tentative decision or statement of decision is required.

(c) Article 5 (commencing with Section 116.510) on hearings in the small claims court applies in hearings on appeal in the superior court, except that attorneys may participate.

(d) The scope of the hearing shall include the claims of all parties who were parties to the small claims action at the time the notice of appeal was filed. The hearing shall include the claim of a defendant which was heard in the small claims court.

(e) The clerk of the superior court shall schedule the hearing for the earliest available time and shall mail written notice of the hearing to the parties at least 14 days prior to the time set for the hearing.

(f) The Judicial Council may prescribe by rule the practice and procedure on appeal and the time and manner in which the record on appeal shall be prepared and filed.

116.780. (a) The judgment of the superior court after a hearing on appeal is final and not appealable.

(b) Article 6 (commencing with Section 116.610) on judgments of the small claims court applies to judgments of the superior court after a hearing on appeal, except as provided in subdivisions (c) and (d).

(c) For good cause and where necessary to achieve substantial justice between the parties, the superior court may award a party to an appeal reimbursement of (1) attorney's fees actually and reasonably incurred in connection with the appeal, not exceeding one hundred fifty dollars ($150), and (2) actual loss of earnings and expenses of transportation and lodging actually and reasonably incurred in connection with the appeal, not exceeding one hundred fifty dollars ($150).

(d) Upon the expiration of 10 days following the completion of the appeal process, the superior court shall order the appeal and any judgment transferred to the small claims court in which the action was originally filed for purposes of enforcement and other proceedings under Article 8 (commencing with Section 116.810) of this chapter.

116.790. If the superior court finds that the appeal was without substantial merit and not based on good faith, but was intended to harass or delay the other party, or to encourage the other party to abandon the claim, the court may award the other party (a) attorney's fees actually and reasonably incurred in connection with the appeal, not exceeding one thousand dollars ($1,000), and (b) any actual loss of earnings and any expenses of transportation and lodging actually and reasonably incurred in connection with the appeal, not exceeding one thousand dollars ($1,000), following a hearing on the matter.

116.795. (a) The superior court may dismiss the appeal if the appealing party does not appear at the hearing or if the appeal is not heard within one year from the date of filing the notice of appeal with the clerk of the small claims court.

(b) Upon dismissal of an appeal by the superior court, the small claims court shall thereafter have the same jurisdiction as if no appeal had been filed.

CALIFORNIA CODES
CODE OF CIVIL PROCEDURE
SECTION 116.810-116.880

116.810. (a) Enforcement of the judgment of a small claims court, including the issuance or recording of any abstract of the judgment, is automatically suspended, without the filing of a bond by the defendant, until the expiration of the time for appeal.

(b) If an appeal is filed as provided in Article 7 (commencing with Section 116.710), enforcement of the judgment of the small claims court is suspended unless (1) the appeal is dismissed by the superior court pursuant to Section 116.795, or (2) the superior court determines that the small claims court properly denied the defendant's motion to vacate filed under Section 116.730 or 116.740. In either of those events, the judgment of the small claims court may be enforced.

(c) The scope of the suspension of enforcement under this section and, unless otherwise ordered, of any suspension of enforcement ordered by the court, shall include any enforcement procedure described in Title 9 (commencing with Section 680.010) of Part 2 and in Sections 674 and 1174.

116.820. (a) The judgment of a small claims court may be enforced as provided in Title 9 (commencing with Section 680.010) of Part 2 and in Sections 674 and 1174 on the enforcement of judgments of other courts. A judgment of the superior court after a hearing on appeal, and after transfer to the small claims court under subdivision (d) of Section 116.780, may be enforced like other judgments of the small claims court, as provided in Title 9 (commencing with Section 680.010) of Part 2 and in Sections 674 and 1174 on the enforcement of judgments of other courts.

(b) Fees as provided in Sections 26828, 26830, and 26834 of the Government Code shall be charged and collected by the clerk for the issuance of a writ of execution, an order of examination of a judgment debtor, or an abstract of judgment.

(c) The prevailing party in any action subject to this chapter is entitled to the costs of enforcing the judgment and accrued interest.

116.830. (a) At the time judgment is rendered, or notice of entry of the judgment is mailed to the parties, the clerk shall deliver or mail to the judgment debtor a form containing questions regarding the nature and location of any assets of the judgment debtor.

(b) Within 30 days after the clerk has mailed notice of entry of the judgment, unless the judgment has been satisfied, the judgment debtor shall complete the form and cause it to be delivered to the judgment creditor.

(c) In the event a motion is made to vacate the judgment or a notice of appeal is filed, a judgment debtor shall complete and deliver the form within 30 days after the clerk has delivered or mailed notice of denial of the motion to vacate, or notice of dismissal of or entry of judgment on the appeal, whichever is applicable.

(d) In case of the judgment debtor's willful failure to comply with subdivision (b) or (c), the judgment creditor may request the court to apply the sanctions, including arrest and attorney's fees, as provided in Section 708.170, on contempt of court.

(e) The Judicial Council shall approve or adopt the form to be used for the purpose of this section.

116.840. (a) At the option of the judgment debtor, payment of the judgment may be made either (1) to the judgment creditor in accordance with Section 116.850, or (2) to the court in which the judgment was entered in accordance with Section 116.860.

(b) The small claims court may order entry of satisfaction of judgment in accordance with subdivisions (c) and (d) of Section 116.850, or subdivision (b) of Section 116.860.

116.850. (a) If full payment of the judgment is made to the judgment creditor or to the judgment creditor's assignee of record, then immediately upon receipt of payment, the judgment creditor or assignee shall file with the clerk of the court an acknowledgment of satisfaction of the judgment.

(b) Any judgment creditor or assignee of record who, after receiving full payment of the judgment and written demand by the judgment debtor, fails without good cause to execute and file an acknowledgment of satisfaction of the judgment with the clerk of the court in which the judgment is entered within 14 days after receiving the request, is liable to the judgment debtor or the judgment debtor's grantees or heirs for all damages sustained by reason of the failure and, in addition, the sum of fifty dollars ($50).

(c) The clerk of the court shall enter a satisfaction of judgment at the request of the judgment debtor if the judgment debtor either (1) establishes a rebuttable presumption of full payment under subdivision (d), or (2) establishes a rebuttable presumption of partial payment under subdivision (d) and complies with subdivision (c) of Section 116.860.

(d) A rebuttable presumption of full or partial payment of the judgment, whichever is applicable, is created if the judgment debtor files both of the following with the clerk of the court in which the judgment was entered:

(1) Either a canceled check or money order for the full or partial amount of the judgment written by the judgment debtor after judgment and made payable to and endorsed by the judgment creditor, or a cash receipt for the full or partial amount of the judgment written by the judgment debtor after judgment and signed by the judgment creditor.

(2) A declaration stating that (A) the judgment debtor has made full or partial payment of the judgment including accrued interest and costs; (B) the judgment creditor has been requested to file an acknowledgment of satisfaction of the judgment and refuses to do so, or refuses to accept subsequent payments, or the present address of the judgment creditor is unknown; and (C) the documents identified in

and accompanying the declaration constitute evidence of the judgment creditor's receipt of full or partial payment.

116.860. (a) A judgment debtor who desires to make payment to the court in which the judgment was entered may file a request to make payment, which shall be made on a form approved or adopted by the Judicial Council.

(b) Upon the filing of the request to make payment and the payment to the clerk of the amount of the judgment and any accrued interest and costs after judgment, plus any required fee authorized by this section, the clerk shall enter satisfaction of the judgment and shall remit payment to the judgment creditor as provided in this section.

(c) If partial payment of the judgment has been made to the judgment creditor, and the judgment debtor files the declaration and evidence of partial payment described in subdivision (d) of Section 116.850, the clerk shall enter satisfaction of the judgment upon receipt by the clerk of the balance owing on the judgment, including any accrued interest and costs after judgment, and the fee required by this section.

(d) If payment is made by means other than money order, certified or cashier's check, or cash, entry of satisfaction of the judgment shall be delayed for 30 days.

(e) The clerk shall notify the judgment creditor, at his or her last known address, that the judgment debtor has satisfied the judgment by making payment to the court. The notification shall explain the procedures which the judgment creditor has to follow to receive payment.

(f) For purposes of this section, "costs after judgment" consist of only those costs itemized in a memorandum of costs filed by the judgment creditor or otherwise authorized by the court.

(g) Payments that remain unclaimed shall go to the local agency pursuant to Sections 50050 to 50056, inclusive, of the Government Code.

(h) The board of supervisors shall set a fee, not to exceed the actual costs of administering this section, up to a maximum of twenty-five dollars ($25), which shall be paid by the judgment debtor.

116.870. Sections 16250 to 16381, inclusive, of the Vehicle Code, regarding the suspension of the judgment debtor's privilege to operate a motor vehicle for failing to satisfy a judgment, apply if the judgment (1) was for damage to property in excess of five hundred dollars ($500) or for bodily injury to, or death of, any person in any amount, and (2) resulted from the operation of a motor vehicle upon a California highway by the defendant, or by any other person for whose conduct the defendant was liable, unless the liability resulted from the defendant's signing the application of a minor for a driver's license.

116.880. (a) If the judgment (1) was for five hundred dollars ($500) or less, (2) resulted from a motor vehicle accident occurring on a California highway caused by the defendant's operation of a motor vehicle, and (3) has remained unsatisfied for more than 90 days after the judgment became final, the judgment creditor may file with the Department of Motor Vehicles a notice requesting a suspension of the judgment debtor's privilege to operate a motor vehicle.

(b) The notice shall state that the judgment has not been satisfied, and shall be accompanied by (1) a fee set by the department, (2) the judgment of the court determining that the judgment resulted from a motor vehicle accident occurring on a California highway caused by the judgment debtor's operation of a motor vehicle, and (3) a declaration that the judgment has not been satisfied. The fee shall be used by the department to finance the costs of administering this section and shall not exceed the department's actual costs.

(c) Upon receipt of a notice, the department shall attempt to notify the judgment debtor by telephone, if possible, otherwise by certified mail, that the judgment debtor's privilege to operate a motor vehicle will be suspended for a period of 90 days, beginning 20 days after receipt of notice by the department from the judgment creditor, unless satisfactory proof, as provided in subdivision (e), is provided to the department before that date.

(d) At the time the notice is filed, the department shall give the judgment creditor a copy of the notice, which shall indicate the filing fee paid by the judgment creditor, and shall include a space to be signed by the judgment creditor acknowledging payment of the judgment by the judgment debtor. The judgment creditor shall mail or deliver a signed copy of the acknowledgment to the judgment debtor once the judgment is satisfied.

(e) The department shall terminate the suspension, or the suspension proceedings, upon the occurrence of any of the following:

(1) Receipt of proof that the judgment has been satisfied, either (A) by a copy of the notice required by this section signed by the judgment creditor acknowledging satisfaction of the judgment, or (B) by a declaration of the judgment debtor stating that the judgment has been satisfied.

(2) Receipt of proof that the judgment debtor is complying with a court-ordered payment schedule.

(3) Proof that the judgment debtor had insurance covering the accident sufficient to satisfy the judgment.

(4) A deposit with the department of the amount of the unsatisfied judgment, if the judgment debtor presents proof, satisfactory to the department, of inability to locate the judgment creditor.

(5) At the end of 90 days.

(f) When the suspension has been terminated under subdivision (e), the action is final and may not be reinstituted. Whenever the suspension is terminated, Section 14904 of the Vehicle Code shall apply. Money deposited with the department under this section shall be handled in the same manner as money deposited under subdivision

(d) of Section 16377 of the Vehicle Code.

(g) No public agency is liable for any injury caused by the suspension, termination of suspension, or the failure to suspend any person's privilege to operate a motor vehicle as authorized by this section.

CALIFORNIA CODES
CODE OF CIVIL PROCEDURE
SECTION 116.910-116.950

116.910. (a) Except as provided in this chapter (including, but not limited to, Section 116.230), no fee or charge shall be collected by any officer for any service provided under this chapter.

(b) All fees collected under this chapter shall be deposited with the treasurer of the city and county or county in whose jurisdiction the court is located.

(c) Six dollars ($6) of each fifteen dollar ($15) fee and fourteen dollars ($14) of each thirty dollar ($30) fee charged and collected under subdivision (a) of Section 116.230 shall be deposited by each county in a special account. Of the money deposited in this account:

(1) In counties with a population of less than 4,000,000, a minimum of 50 percent shall be used to fund the small claims adviser service described in Section 116.940. The remainder of these funds shall be used for court and court-related programs. Records of these moneys shall be available for inspection by the public on request.

(2) In counties with a population of at least 4,000,000, not less than five hundred thousand dollars ($500,000) shall be used to fund the small claims adviser service described in Section 116.940. That amount shall be increased each fiscal year by an amount equal to the percentage increase in revenues derived from small claims court filing fees over the prior fiscal year. The remainder of these funds shall be used for court and court-related programs. Records of these moneys shall be available for inspection by the public on request.

(d) This section and Section 116.940 shall not be applied in any manner that results in a reduction of the level of services, or the amount of funds allocated for providing the services described in Section 116.940, that are in existence in each county during the fiscal year 1989-90. Nothing in this section shall preclude the county from procuring other funding, including state court block grants, to comply with the requirements of Section 116.940.

116.920. (a) The Judicial Council shall provide by rule for the practice and procedure and for the forms and their use in small claims actions. The rules and forms so adopted shall be consistent with this chapter.

(b) The Judicial Council, in consultation with the Department of Consumer Affairs, shall adopt rules to ensure that litigants receive adequate notice of the availability of assistance from small claims advisors, to prescribe other qualifications and the conduct of advisors, to prescribe training standards for advisors and for temporary judges hearing small claims matters, to prescribe, where appropriate, uniform rules and procedures regarding small claims actions and judgments, and to address other matters that are deemed necessary and appropriate.

116.930. (a) Each small claims division shall provide in each courtroom in which small claims actions are heard a current copy of a publication describing small claims court law and the procedures that are applicable in the small claims courts, including the law and procedures that apply to the enforcement of judgments. The Small Claims Court and Consumer Law California Judge's Bench Book developed by the California Center for Judicial Education and Research is illustrative of a publication that satisfies the requirement of this subdivision.

(b) Each small claims division may formulate and distribute to litigants and the public a manual on small claims court rules and procedures. The manual shall explain how to complete the necessary forms, how to determine the proper court in which small claims actions may be filed, how to present and defend against claims, how to appeal, how to enforce a judgment, how to protect property that is exempt from execution, and such other matters that the court deems necessary or desirable.

(c) If the Department of Consumer Affairs determines there are sufficient private or public funds available in addition to the funds available within the department's current budget, the department, in cooperation with the Judicial Council, shall prepare a manual or information booklet on small claims court rules and procedures. The department shall distribute copies to the general public and to each small claims division.

(d) If funding is available, the Judicial Council, in cooperation with the Department of Consumer Affairs, shall prepare and distribute to each judge who sits in a small claims court a bench book describing all state and federal consumer protection laws reasonably likely to apply in small claims actions.

116.940. (a) Except as otherwise provided in this section or in rules adopted by the Judicial Council, the characteristics of the small claims advisory service required by Section 116.260 shall be determined by each county in accordance with local needs and conditions.

(b) Each advisory service shall provide the following services:

(1) Individual personal advisory services, in person or by telephone, and by any other means reasonably calculated to provide timely and appropriate assistance.

(2) Recorded telephone messages may be used to supplement the individual personal advisory services, but shall not be the sole means of providing advice available in the county.

(3) Adjacent counties may provide advisory services jointly.

(c) In any county in which the number of small claims actions filed annually is 1,000 or less as averaged over the immediately preceding two fiscal years, the county may elect to exempt itself from the requirements set forth in subdivision (b). This exemption shall be formally noticed through the adoption of a resolution by the board of supervisors. If a county so exempts itself, the county shall nevertheless provide the following minimum advisory services in accordance with rules adopted by the Judicial Council:

(1) Recorded telephone messages providing general information relating to small claims actions filed in the county shall be provided during regular business hours.

(2) Small claims information booklets shall be provided in each municipal and justice court clerk's office, the county administrator's office, other appropriate county offices, and in any other location that is convenient to prospective small claims litigants in the county.

(d) The advisory service shall operate in conjunction and cooperation with the small claims division, and shall be administered so as to avoid the existence or appearance of a conflict of interest between the individuals providing the advisory services and any party to a particular small claims action or any judicial officer deciding small claims actions.

(e) Advisors may be volunteers, and shall be members of the State Bar, law students, paralegals, or persons experienced in resolving minor disputes, and shall be familiar with small claims court rules and procedures. Advisors shall not appear in court as an advocate for any party.

(f) Advisors and other court employees and volunteers have the immunity conferred by Section 818.9 of the Government Code with respect to advice provided under this chapter.

116.950. (a) This section shall become operative only if the Department of Consumer Affairs determines that sufficient private or public funds are available in addition to the funds available in the department's current budget to cover the costs of implementing this section.

(b) There shall be established an advisory committee, constituted as set forth in this section, to study small claims practice and procedure, with particular attention given to the improvement of procedures for the enforcement of judgments.

(c) The members of the advisory committee shall serve without compensation, but shall be reimbursed for expenses actually and necessarily incurred by them in the performance of their duties. The advisory committee shall report its findings and recommendations to the Judicial Council and the Legislature.

(d) The advisory committee shall be composed as follows:

(1) The Attorney General or a representative.

(2) Two consumer representatives from consumer groups or agencies, appointed by the Secretary of the State and Consumer Services Agency.

(3) One representative appointed by the Speaker of the Assembly and one representative appointed by the President pro Tempore of the Senate.

(4) Two representatives, appointed by the Board of Governors of the State Bar.

(5) Two representatives of the business community, appointed by the Secretary of the Trade and Commerce Agency.

(6) Six judges of the municipal court or justice court who have had extensive experience as judges of small claims court, appointed by the Judicial Council.

(7) One representative appointed by the Governor.

(8) Two clerks of the court, appointed by the Judicial Council.

(e) Staff assistance to the advisory committee shall be provided by the Department of Consumer Affairs, with the assistance of the Judicial Council, as needed.

APPENDIX B
JUDICIAL COUNCIL FORMS

The Judicial Council of the State of California furnishes many mandatory forms to be used in the state courts. The list of forms is extensive. All of the mandated Judicial Council small claims court forms are provided in this appendix, as well as many of the mandatory forms that can be used in a court of any jurisdiction and are often used in small claims court. The Council also "approves" forms and the use of approved forms is optional by the state. Forms designated with * are local forms used in some of the courts. Nevertheless, some local courts may require you to use forms that are optional with the state.

You can photocopy the forms for your own use. You can also obtain copies from the small claims court where you intend to file your action. These will often have the name and address of the court already filled in. It is important to check with your local court to find out if there are any specific local forms that must be used in addition to the Judicial Counsel forms.

You can also obtain copies of Judicial Counsel forms at law libraries. They can also be either printed or downloaded from the internet at http://www.courtinfo.ca.gov/forms.

Also included is a Department of Motor Vehicles form designated with **. You will use this form to take steps to have the driver's license of the debtor suspended. (See chapter 9.)

Some hints:

1. Make a rough draft first. This means making at least two copies in advance.

2. Type. Handwriting looks sloppy. Most courthouses have typewriters available and so do most libraries.

3. Most of the forms are self-explanatory. If you have questions that have not been answered by this book, call the small claims advisor in your county. (See appendix F.) Don't leave blanks. You can also ask the small claims clerk for help in filling out the forms. Remember, they cannot give legal advice.

4. Only sign the form(s) you plan to submit to the court. If you have signed copies of drafts lying around, you will end up getting confused. Make three copies of the original, and ask the court to "conform" the copies. Have an envelope prepared with sufficient postage in case the procedure in the local court is to mail the conformed copies.

LIST OF FORMS

INFORMATION FOR THE SMALL CLAIMS PLAINTIFF

This information sheet is written for the person who sues in the small claims court. It explains some of the rules of and some general information about the small claims court. It may also be helpful for the person who is sued.

WHAT IS SMALL CLAIMS COURT?

Small claims court is a special court where disputes are resolved quickly and inexpensively. The rules are simple and informal. The person who sues is the **plaintiff.** The person who is sued is the **defendant.** In small claims court, you may ask a lawyer for advice before you go to court, but you cannot have a lawyer in court. Your claim cannot be for more than $5,000 (*see below).* If you have a claim for more than this amount, you may sue in the civil division of the municipal court or you may sue in the small claims court and give up your right to the amount over $5,000. You cannot, however, file more than two cases in small claims court for more than $2,500 each during a calendar year.

WHO CAN FILE A CLAIM?

1. You must be at least *18 years old* to file a claim. If you are not yet 18, you may ask the court to appoint a **guardian ad litem**. This is a person who will act for you in the case. The guardian ad litem is usually a parent, a relative, or an adult friend.

2. A person who sues in small claims court must first make a **demand** if possible. This means that you have asked the defendant to pay, and the defendant has refused. If your claim is for possession of property, you must ask the defendant to give you the property.

3. Unless you fall within two technical exceptions, you must be the **original owner** of the claim. This means that if the claim is assigned, the buyer cannot sue in the small claims court. **You must also appear at the small claims hearing yourself unless you filed the claim for a corporation or other entity that is not a natural person.**

4. If a corporation files a claim, an employee, officer, or director must act on its behalf. If the claim is filed on behalf of an association or other entity that is not a natural person, a regularly employed person of the entity must act on its behalf. A person who appears on behalf of a corporation or other entity must not be employed or associated solely for the purpose of representing the corporation or other entity in the small claims court. **You must file a declaration with the court to appear in any of these instances.**

WHERE CAN YOU FILE YOUR CLAIM?

You must sue in the right court and **judicial district.** This rule is called **venue.**

If you file your claim in the wrong court, the court will dismiss the claim unless all defendants personally appear at the hearing and agree that the claim may be heard.

The right district may be any of these:

1. Where the defendant lives or where the business involved is located;
2. Where the damage or accident happened;
3. Where the contract was signed or carried out;
4. If the defendant is a corporation, where the contract was broken;
5. For a retail installment account or sales contract or a motor vehicle finance sale:
   a. Where the buyer lives;
   b. Where the buyer lived when the contract was entered into;
   c. Where the buyer signed the contract;
   d. Where the goods or vehicle are permanently kept.

SOME RULES ABOUT THE DEFENDANT (including government agencies)

1. You must sue using the defendant's *exact legal name.* If the defendant is a business or a corporation and you do not know the exact legal name, check with: the state or local licensing agency; the county clerk's office; or the Office of the Secretary of State, corporate status unit. Ask the clerk for help if you do not know how to find this information. If you do not use the defendant's exact legal name, the court may be able to correct the name on your claim at the hearing or after the judgment.

2. If you want to sue a government agency, you must first file a claim with the agency before you can file a lawsuit in court. Strict time limits apply. If you are in a Department of Corrections or Youth Authority facility, you must prove that the agency denied your claim. Please attach a copy of the denial to your claim.

HOW DOES THE DEFENDANT FIND OUT ABOUT THE CLAIM?

You must make sure the defendant finds out about your lawsuit. This has to be done according to the rules or your case may be dismissed or delayed. The correct way of telling the defendant about the lawsuit is called **service of process.** This means giving the defendant a copy of the claim. **YOU CANNOT DO THIS YOURSELF**. Here are four ways to serve the defendant:

1. **Service by a law officer** — You may ask the marshal or sheriff to serve the defendant. A fee will be charged.

2. **Process server** — You may ask anyone who is *not a party* in your case and who is at least *18 years old* to serve the defendant. The person is called a **process server** and must personally give a copy of your claim to the defendant. The person must also sign a proof of service form showing when the defendant was served. Registered process servers will do this for you for a fee. You may also ask a friend or relative to do it.

3. **Certified mail** — You may ask the clerk of the court to serve the defendant by certified mail. The clerk will charge a fee. You should check back with the court prior to the hearing to see if the receipt for certified mail was returned to the court. **Service by certified mail must be done by the clerk's office except in motor vehicle accident cases involving out-of-state defendants.**

4. **Substituted service** — This method lets you serve another person instead of the defendant. You must follow the procedures carefully. You may also wish to use the marshal or sheriff or a registered process server.

* The $5,000 limit does not apply, and a $2,500 limit applies, if a "defendant guarantor . . . is required to respond based upon the default, actions, or omissions of another."

(Continued on reverse)

Form Adopted by the
Judicial Council of California
SC-150 [Rev. January 1, 1998]

INFORMATION FOR THE PLAINTIFF
(Small Claims)

Cal. Rules of Court, rule 982.7;
Code of Civil Procedure, § 116.110 et seq.

4. Substituted service *(continued)*

A copy of your claim must be left
— at the defendant's business with the person in charge; **OR**
— at the defendant's home with a competent person who is at least 18 years old. The person who receives the claim must be told about its contents. Another copy must be mailed, first class, postage prepaid, to the defendant at the address where the paper was left. The service is not complete until *10 days* after the copy is mailed.

No matter which method of service you choose, the defendant must be served by a certain date or the trial will be postponed. If the defendant lives in the county, service must be completed at least *10 days* before the trial date. This period is *15 days* if the defendant lives outside the county.

The person who serves the defendant must sign a court paper showing when the defendant was served. This paper is called a *Proof of Service* (form SC-104). It must be signed and returned to the court clerk as soon as the defendant has been served.

WHAT IF THE DEFENDANT ALSO HAS A CLAIM?

Sometimes the person who was sued (the **defendant**) will also have a claim against the person who filed the lawsuit (the **plaintiff**). This claim is called the *Defendant's Claim*. The defendant may file this claim in the same lawsuit. This helps to resolve all of the disagreements between the parties at the same time.

If the defendant decides to file the claim in the small claims court, the claim may not be for more than $5,000 (*see reverse*). If the value of the claim is more than this

amount, the defendant may either give up the amount over $5,000 and sue in the small claims court or file a motion to transfer the case to the appropriate court for the full value of the claim.

The defendant's claim must be served on the plaintiff at least *5 days* before the trial. If the defendant received the plaintiff's claim *10 days* or less before the trial, then the claim must be served at least *1 day* before the trial. Both claims will be heard by the court at the same time.

WHAT HAPPENS AT THE TRIAL?

Be sure you are on time for the trial. The small claims trial is informal. You must bring with you all witnesses, books, receipts, and other papers or things to prove your case. You may ask the witnesses to come to court voluntarily. You may also ask the clerk of the court to issue a **subpena**. A subpena is a court order that *requires* the witness to go to trial. The witness has a right to charge a fee for going to the trial. If you do not have the records or papers to prove your case, you may also get a court order prior to the trial date requiring the papers to be brought to the trial.

This order is called a *Civil Subpena Duces Tecum* (form 982(a)(15)).

If you settle the case before the trial, you must file a **dismissal** form with the clerk.

The court's decision is usually mailed to you after the trial. It may also be hand delivered to you when the trial is over and after the judge has made a decision. The decision appears on a form called the *Notice of Entry of Judgment* (form SC-130).

WHAT HAPPENS AFTER JUDGMENT?

The court may have ordered one party to pay money to the other party. The party who wins the case and collects the money is called the **judgment creditor**. The party who loses the case and owes the money is called the **judgment debtor**. Enforcement of the judgment is **postponed** until the time for appeal ends or until the appeal is decided. This means that the judgment creditor cannot collect any

money or take any action until this period is over. Generally both parties may be represented by lawyers after judgment. More information about your rights after judgment is available on the back of the *Notice of Entry of Judgment* form. The clerk may also have this information on a separate sheet.

HOW TO GET HELP WITH YOUR CASE

1. **Lawyers** — Both parties may ask a lawyer about the case, but a lawyer may not represent either party in court at the small claims trial. Generally, after judgment and on appeal, both parties may be represented by a lawyer.

2. **Interpreters** — If you do not speak English, you may take a family member or friend to court with you. The court should keep a list of interpreters who will interpret for you. Some interpreters charge a reasonable or no fee. If an interpreter is not available, the court must postpone the hearing one time only so that you have time to get one.

3. **Waiver of fees** — The court charges fees for some of its procedures. Fees are also charged for serving the defendant with the claim. The court may excuse you from paying these fees if you cannot afford them. Ask the clerk for the *Information Sheet on Waiver of Court Fees and Costs* (form 982(a)(A)) to find out if you meet the requirements so that you do not have to pay the fees.

4. **Night and Saturday court** — If you cannot go to court during working hours, ask the clerk if the court has trials at **night** or on **Saturdays**.

5. **Parties who are in jail** — If you are in jail, the court may excuse you from going to the trial. Instead, you may ask another person who is not an attorney to go to the trial for you. You may mail written declarations to the court to support your case.

6. **Accommodations** — If you have a disability and need assistance, please ask the court immediately to help accommodate your needs. If you are hearing impaired and need assistance, please notify the court immediately.

7. **Small claims advisors** — The law requires each county to provide assistance in small claims cases free of charge. *(Small claims advisor information)*:

INFORMATION FOR THE PLAINTIFF
(Small Claims)

Name and Address of Court:

SC-100

SMALL CLAIMS CASE NO.:

<table>
<tr>
<td>

— NOTICE TO DEFENDANT —
YOU ARE BEING SUED BY PLAINTIFF

To protect your rights, you must appear in this court on the trial date shown in the table below. You may lose the case if you do not appear. The court may award the plaintiff the amount of the claim and the costs. Your wages, money, and property may be taken without further warning from the court.
</td>
<td>

— AVISO AL DEMANDADO —
A USTED LO ESTAN DEMANDANDO

Para proteger sus derechos, usted debe presentarse ante esta corte en la fecha del juicio indicada en el cuadro que aparece a continuación. Si no se presenta, puede perder el caso. La corte puede decidir en favor del demandante por la cantidad del reclamo y los costos. A usted le pueden quitar su salario, su dinero, y otras cosas de su propiedad, sin aviso adicional por parte de esta corte.
</td>
</tr>
</table>

PLAINTIFF/DEMANDANTE *(Name, street address, and telephone number of each):*

DEFENDANT/DEMANDADO *(Name, street address, and telephone number of each):*

Telephone No.:

Telephone No.:

Telephone No.:

Telephone No.:

Fict. Bus. Name Stmt. No.   Expires:

☐ See attached sheet for additional plaintiffs and defendants.

PLAINTIFF'S CLAIM

1. a. ☐ Defendant owes me the sum of: $, not including court costs, because *(describe claim and date)*:

   b. ☐ I have had an **arbitration of an attorney-client fee dispute.** *(Attach Attorney-Client Fee Dispute form (see form SC-101).)*
2. ☐ This claim is against a government agency, and I filed a claim with the agency. My claim was denied by the agency, or the agency did not act on my claim before the legal deadline. *(See form SC-150.)*
3. a. ☐ I have asked defendant to pay this money, but it has not been paid.
   b. ☐ I have NOT asked defendant to pay this money because *(explain)*:
4. This court is the proper court for the trial because ☐ *(In the box at the left, insert one of the letters from the list called "Venue Table" on the back of this sheet. If you select D, E, or F, specify additional facts in this space)*:

5. I ☐ have ☐ have not   filed more than one other small claims action anywhere in California during this calendar year in which the amount demanded is more than $2,500.
6. I ☐ have ☐ have not   filed more than 12 small claims, including this claim, during the previous 12 months.
7. I understand that
   a. I may talk to an attorney about this claim, but I cannot be represented by an attorney at the trial in the small claims court.
   b. I must appear at the time and place of trial and bring all witnesses, books, receipts, and other papers or things to prove my case.
   c. **I have no right of appeal on my claim,** but I may appeal a claim filed by the defendant in this case.
   d. If I cannot afford to pay the fees for filing or service by a sheriff, marshal, or constable, I may ask that the fees be waived.
8. I have received and read the information sheet explaining some important rights of plaintiffs in the small claims court.

I declare under penalty of perjury under the laws of the State of California that the foregoing is true and correct.

Date:

▶

....
(TYPE OR PRINT NAME)   (SIGNATURE OF PLAINTIFF)

ORDER TO DEFENDANT

You must appear in this court on the trial date and at the time LAST SHOWN IN THE BOX BELOW if you do not agree with the plaintiff's claim. Bring all witnesses, books, receipts, and other papers or things with you to support your case.

TRIAL DATE	DATE	DAY	TIME	PLACE	COURT USE
FECHA DEL JUICIO	1.				
	2.				
	3.				

Filed on *(date)*:   Clerk, by_____, Deputy

— The county provides small claims advisor services free of charge. Read the information on the reverse. —

Form Adopted by the
Judicial Council of California
SC-100 [Rev. January 1, 1998]

PLAINTIFF'S CLAIM AND ORDER TO DEFENDANT
(Small Claims)

Cal. Rules of Court, rule 982.7;
Code of Civil Procedure,
§ 116.110 et seq.

INFORMATION FOR DEFENDANT

1. **What is the small claims court?** The small claims court is a special court in which disagreements are resolved quickly and cheaply. A small claim must be for $5,000 (*see below*) or less. With some exceptions no party may file more than two small claims actions in which the amount demanded is more than $2,500 anywhere in the state in a calendar year. The party who sues is called a **plaintiff**. The party who is sued is called a **defendant**. Neither party can be represented by a lawyer at the trial, but either party may talk to a lawyer about the case.

2. **What can you do if you are sued in the small claims court?**
   a. **SETTLE** — You may settle your case before the trial. If you do, be sure that the plaintiff files a dismissal form with the court. If you would like help in settling your case, ask the small claims advisor (see No. 5, below) to refer you to an alternative dispute resolution provider.
   b. **DEFAULT** — If you do not go to the trial, it is called a **default**. The plaintiff may win the amount of the claim and costs. The plaintiff may then be able to use legal procedures to take your money or property to pay the judgment.
   c. **APPEAR AND CONTEST** — You may go to the trial and disagree with the plaintiff's claim. If you do, bring all witnesses, books, receipts, and other papers or things to prove your case. You may ask the witnesses in your case to go to the trial or, before the trial, you may ask the clerk of the court to issue a **subpena**. A subpena is a court order that requires the witness to go to the trial.
   d. **APPEAR AND REQUEST PAYMENTS** — You may agree with the plaintiff's claim, but you may be unable to pay the money all at once. You may then choose to go to the trial and ask the court to order payments you can afford.
   e. **POSTPONE** — If you live in the county where the claim was filed, you must be served with a copy of the claim *10 days before the trial*. If you live outside the county, you must be served *15 days before the trial*. If you did not receive the claim within these time limits, you may ask the court for a postponement. (No fee charged.)
      If you cannot attend the hearing on the date scheduled, write to the court before the hearing date and tell why, and ask the court to postpone the hearing. (Fee charged.)
   f. **CHALLENGE VENUE** — If you believe the plaintiff's claim was filed in the wrong court (see Venue Table, below), write to the court before the hearing date, explain why you think so, and ask the court to dismiss the claim. Mail a copy to the plaintiff and file a proof of mailing with the court. For information about proof of mailing, see the small claims advisor.

3. **What can you do if you also have a claim against the person who sued you?** A claim against the person who sued you is called a *Defendant's Claim* (form SC-120). Ask the clerk for this form to file your claim. The claim must not be for more than $5,000.* If you received your copy of the plaintiff's claim *less than 10 days* before the trial date, you must have the plaintiff served with your claim *at least 1 day* before the trial date. If you received your claim *more than 10 days* before the trial date, you must have the plaintiff served with your claim *at least 5 days* before the trial date. The court will hear both claims at the same time.

4. **What happens after trial?** The court will deliver or mail to you a copy of a form called the *Notice of Entry of Judgment* (form SC-130). This form tells you how the case was decided. If you disagree with the court's decision, you may appeal the judgment on the plaintiff's claim. You may not appeal your own claim. If you appeared at the trial, you must begin your appeal by filing a *Notice of Appeal* (form SC-140) and pay the required fees within *30 days* after the date the *Notice of Entry of Judgment* was mailed or handed to you. If you did not appear at the trial, you must first ask the court to vacate or cancel the judgment. To make this request, you must file a *Motion to Vacate the Judgment* (form SC-135) and pay the required fees within *30 days* after the date the *Notice of Entry of Judgment* was mailed or handed to you. If your request is denied, you then have *10 days* from the date the notice of denial was mailed or handed to you to file an appeal.

5. **How can you get help with your case?**
   a. **MINORS** — If you are under 18 years old, you should tell the clerk. You are too young to act for yourself in the case. You must ask the court to appoint someone to act for you. That person is called a **guardian ad litem**.
   b. **INTERPRETERS** — If you do not speak English, you may take a family member or friend to court with you. The court should keep a list of interpreters who will interpret for you. Some interpreters charge a reasonable or no fee. If an interpreter is not available, the court must postpone the hearing one time only so that you have time to get one.
   c. **ACCOMMODATIONS** — If you have a disability and need assistance, please ask the court immediately to help accommodate your needs. If you are hearing impaired and need assistance, please notify the court immediately.
   d. **SMALL CLAIMS ADVISORS** — The law requires each county to provide assistance in small claims cases free of charge. *(Small claims advisor information)*:

VENUE TABLE

The plaintiff must file the claim in the proper court and geographical area. This rule is called **venue**. Below are possible reasons for filing the claim in this court. *If you are the plaintiff, insert the proper letter from the list below in item 4 on the other side of this sheet and specify additional facts for D, E, or F.* **This court is the proper court for the trial of this case because**

A. a defendant lives in this judicial district or a defendant corporation or unincorporated association has its principal place of business in this judicial district.

B. a person was injured or personal property was damaged in this judicial district.

C. a defendant signed or entered into a contract in this judicial district, a defendant lived in this judicial district when the contract was entered into, a contract or obligation was to be performed in this judicial district, or, if the defendant was a corporation, the contract was breached in this judicial district.

D. the claim is on a retail installment account or contract subject to Civil Code section 1812.10. *(Specify facts on the other side of this sheet.)*

E. the claim is on a vehicle finance sale subject to Civil Code section 2984.4. *(Specify facts on the other side of this sheet.)*

F. other. *(Specify facts on the other side of this sheet.)*

---

* The $5,000 limit does not apply, and a $2,500 limit applies, if a "defendant guarantor . . . is required to respond based upon the default, actions or omissions of another."

SC-100 [Rev. January 1, 1998]

PLAINTIFF'S CLAIM AND ORDER TO DEFENDANT
(Small Claims)

Page two

Name, address and telephone no. of attorney(s)	This space for court clerk only

Attorney(s) for

PETITION AND APPOINTMENT OF GUARDIAN AD LITEM	IN THE MUNICIPAL COURT OF	Case Number

....

....vs...
Plaintiff(s)   Defendant(s)

Petition of Minor (If age 14 or over)

I am the...in the above-entitled action. I am a minor of the age of ....
          (plaintiff - defendant)
years, and by reason thereof, it is necessary that a guardian ad litem be appointed for me in said action.

....is my...
              (name of proposed guardian)   (parent - relative - friend)
and a qualified and proper person to be appointed such guardian ad litem.

Appointment of said guardian ad litem is necessary because I have no general guardian.

Wherefore, I request that said...be appointed guardian
                                         (name of proposed guardian)
ad litem for me in this action.

Dated ....   --
                                                                    (petitioner)

Consent of Proposed Guardian

I consent to the appointment of myself as guardian ad litem for...
in the above-entitled action.   (name of minor)

Dated ....   --
                                                                    (proposed guardian)

Petition for Appointment as Guardian

I am the...of ....,
          (parent - relative - friend)   (name of minor)
....in the above-entitled action. The said minor is of the age of..........................years,
       (plaintiff - defendant)
and by reason thereof, it is necessary that a guardian ad litem be appointed for said minor.

Appointment of said guardian ad litem is necessary because said minor has no general guardian.

Wherefore, I request that I be appointed guardian ad litem for said minor in the above-entitled action.

Dated ....   --
                                                                    (petitioner)

Order

Proper cause appearing therefor, it is ordered that...
                                                              (name of guardian)
be and is hereby appointed guardian ad litem for the above-named minor in the above-entitled action.

Dated ....   --
                                                                    Judge

NOTE:
If minor is a defendant in a Municipal or Justice Court action, petition must state that copy of summons and complaint has been served upon him; and if minor is a defendant in a Small Claims action, petition must state that copy of affidavit or declaration and order has been served upon him.
If minor is over 14 years of age, minor makes the petition; if minor is under 14 years of age, or fails to apply within 10 days after service of summons, guardian ad litem may make the petition. (See Code Civ. Proc. 373.)

PETITION AND APPOINTMENT OF GUARDIAN AD LITEM

Name and Address of Court:

SMALL CLAIMS CASE NO.:

— INSTRUCTIONS —

A. If you regularly do business in California for profit under a fictitious business name, you must execute, file, and publish a fictitious business name statement. This is sometimes called a "dba" which stands for "doing business as." This requirement applies if you are doing business as an individual, a partnership, a corporation, or an association. The requirement does not apply to nonprofit corporations and associations or certain real estate investment trusts. You must file the fictitious business name statement with the clerk of the county where you have your principal place of business, or in Sacramento County if you have no place of business within the state.

B. If you do business under a fictitious business name and you also wish to file an action in the small claims court, you must declare under penalty of perjury that you have complied with the fictitious business name laws by filling out the form below.

C. If you have not complied with the fictitious business name laws, the court may dismiss your claim. You may be able to refile your claim when you have fulfilled these requirements.

FICTITIOUS BUSINESS NAME DECLARATION

1. I wish to file a claim in the small claims court for a business doing business under the fictitious name of *(specify name and address of business):*

2. The business is doing business as
   ☐ an individual
   ☐ a partnership
   ☐ a corporation
   ☐ an association
   ☐ other *(specify):*

statement in the county of *(specify):*

4. The number of the statement is *(specify):*   and the statement expires on *(date):*

I declare under penalty of perjury under the laws of the State of California that the foregoing is true and correct.

Date:

. . . .   ▶ _____
(TYPE OR PRINT NAME)   (SIGNATURE OF DECLARANT)

Form Approved by the
Judicial Council of California
SC-103 [Rev. January 1, 1992]

FICTITIOUS BUSINESS NAME DECLARATION
(Small Claims)

Rule 982.7(b)
Code of Civil Procedure, § 116.430

INFORMATION SHEET ON WAIVER
OF COURT FEES AND COSTS
(California Rules of Court, rule 985)

If you have been sued or if you wish to sue somebody, and if you cannot afford to pay court fees and costs, you may not have to pay if:

1. You are receiving **financial assistance** under one or more of the following programs:
    * SSI and SSP (Supplemental Security Income and State Supplemental Payments Programs)
    * AFDC (Aid to Families with Dependent Children Program; now TANF, Temporary Aid to Needy Families)
    * The Food Stamps Program
    * County Relief, General Relief (G.R.) or General Assistance (G.A.)

    If you are claiming eligibility for a waiver of court fees and costs based on your receiving financial assistance under one or more of these programs, and you did not provide your social security number, you must produce a letter confirming benefits from a public assistance agency or one of the following documents, except if you are a defendant in an unlawful detainer action:

PROGRAM	VERIFICATION
SSI/SSP	MediCal Card *or* Notice of Planned Action *or* SS Computer Generated Printout *or* Bank Statement Showing SSI Deposit *or* "Passport to Services"
AFDC (now TANF)	MediCal Card *or* Notice of Action *or* Income and Eligibility Verification Form *or* Monthly Reporting Form *or* Electronic Benefit Transfer Card *or* "Passport to Services"
Food Stamp Program	Notice of Action *or* Food Stamp ID Card *or* "Passport to Services"
General Relief/General Assistance	Notice of Action *or* Copy of check stub *or* County voucher

— OR —

2. Your gross **monthly income** is less than the following amounts:

NUMBER IN FAMILY	FAMILY INCOME		NUMBER IN FAMILY	FAMILY INCOME
1	$ 821.92		6	$ 2,238.58
2	1,105.25		7	2,521.92
3	1,388.58		8	2,805.25
4	1,671.92		Each additional	283.33
5	1,955.25			

— OR —

3. Your income is not enough to pay for the common **necessaries** of life for yourself and the people you support and also to pay court fees and costs.

To apply, fill out the Application for Waiver of Court Fees and Costs (form 982(a)(17)) available from the clerk's office. If you claim no income, you may be required to file a declaration under penalty of perjury. Prison and jail inmates may be required to pay up to the full amount of the filing fee.

If you have any questions and cannot afford an attorney, you may wish to consult the legal aid office, legal services office, or lawyer referral service in your county (listed in the yellow pages under "Attorneys").

If you are asking for review of the decision of an administrative body under Code of Civil Procedure section 1094.5 (administrative mandate), you may ask for a transcript of the administrative proceedings at the expense of the administrative body.

— *THIS FORM MUST BE KEPT CONFIDENTIAL* —

ATTORNEY OR PARTY WITHOUT ATTORNEY *(Name and Address)*:	TELEPHONE NO.:	*FOR COURT USE ONLY*

ATTORNEY FOR *(Name)*:

NAME OF COURT:
STREET ADDRESS:
MAILING ADDRESS:
CITY AND ZIP CODE:
BRANCH NAME:

PLAINTIFF or PETITIONER:

DEFENDANT or RESPONDENT:

APPLICATION FOR **WAIVER OF COURT FEES AND COSTS**	CASE NUMBER:

I request a court order so that I do not have to pay court fees and costs.

1. My current street or mailing address is *(if applicable, include city or town, apartment no., if any, and zip code)*:

2. My date of birth is *(specify)*:

3. My occupation, employer, and employer's address are *(specify)*:

4. ☐ I am receiving financial assistance under one or more of the following programs:
   a. ☐ **SSI and SSP:** Supplemental Security Income and State Supplemental Payments Programs
   b. ☐ **AFDC:** Aid to Families with Dependent Children Program (now **TANF:** Temporary Aid to Needy Families)
   c. ☐ **Food Stamps:** The Food Stamps Program
   d. ☐ **County Relief, General Relief (G.R.) or General Assistance (G.A.)**

5. *If you checked box 4 above, you must check and complete* **one or the other box, except if you are a defendant in an unlawful detainer action. Do not check both boxes.**
   a. ☐ *(Optional)* My social security number is *(specify)*: ☐☐☐ – ☐☐ – ☐☐☐☐
      [Federal law does not require that you give your social security number. However, if you don't give your social security number, you must check box b and attach documents to verify the benefits checked in item 4.]
   b. ☐ I am attaching documents to verify receipt of the benefits checked in item 4, above.
      [See the **Information Sheet on Waiver of Court Fees and Costs,** *available from the clerk's office, for a list of acceptable documents.]*

[If you checked box 4 above, skip items 6 and 7, and sign at the bottom of this side.]

6. ☐ My gross monthly income is less than the amount shown on the *Information Sheet on Waiver of Court Fees and Costs* available from the clerk's office.

[If you checked box 6 above, skip item 7, complete items 8 and 9 on the back of this form, and sign at the bottom of this side.]

7. ☐ My income is not enough to pay for the common necessaries of life for me and the people in my family I support and also pay court fees and costs. *[If you checked this box you must complete the back of this form.]*

WARNING: You must immediately tell the court if you become able to pay court fees or costs during this action. You may be ordered to appear in court and answer questions about your ability to pay court fees or costs.

I declare under penalty of perjury under the laws of the State of California that the information on both sides of this form and all attachments are complete, true, and correct.

Date:

. . . .
(TYPE OR PRINT NAME)   (SIGNATURE)

Form Adopted by the
 Judicial Council of California
 982(a)(17) [Rev. February 1, 1997]   **APPLICATION FOR WAIVER OF COURT FEES AND COSTS**
 (In Forma Pauperis)   Government Code, § 68511.3

125

PLAINTIFF:	CASE NUMBER:
DEFENDANT:	

FINANCIAL INFORMATION

8. ☐ My pay changes considerably from month to month. *[If you check this box, each of the amounts reported in item 9 should be your average for the past 12 months.]*

9. My monthly income:

a. My gross monthly pay is: . . . . $ _____

b. My payroll deductions are *(specify purpose and amount)*:

    (1) _____ $ _____
    (2) _____ $ _____
    (3) _____ $ _____
    (4) _____ $ _____

    My TOTAL payroll deduction amount is: $ _____

c. My monthly take-home pay is *(a. minus b.)*: . . . . $ _____

d. Other money I get each month is *(specify source and amount)*:

    (1) _____ $ _____
    (2) _____ $ _____

    The TOTAL amount of other money is: $ _____

e. **MY TOTAL MONTHLY INCOME IS** *(c. plus d.)*: . . . . $ _____

f. **The number of people in my family, including me, supported by this money is:** _____

g. My spouse's gross monthly income is: $ _____

h. My spouse's occupation is: _____

10. a. ☐ I am *not* able to pay any of the court fees and costs.

    b. ☐ I am able to pay *only* the following court fees and costs *(specify)*:

11. My monthly expenses not already listed under item 9, above are:

a. Rent or house payment & maintenance $ _____
b. Food and household supplies. . . . . . . $ _____
c. Utilities and telephone . . . . $ _____
d. Clothing . . . . $ _____
e. Laundry and cleaning . . . . $ _____
f. Medical and dental payments . . . . $ _____
g. Insurance (life, health, accident, etc.) $ _____
h. School, child care . . . . $ _____
i. Child, spousal support (prior marriage) $ _____
j. Transportation and auto expenses (insurance, gas, repair) . . . . $ _____
k. Installment payments *(specify purpose and amount)*:

    (1) _____ $ _____
    (2) _____ $ _____
    (3) _____ $ _____

    The TOTAL amount of monthly installment payments is: . . . . $ _____

l. Amounts deducted due to wage assignments and earnings withholding orders: $ _____

m. Other expenses *(specify)*:

    (1) _____ $ _____
    (2) _____ $ _____
    (3) _____ $ _____
    (4) _____ $ _____
    (5) _____ $ _____
    (6) _____ $ _____

    The TOTAL amount of other monthly expenses is: . . . . $ _____

n. **MY TOTAL MONTHLY EXPENSES ARE** *(add a. through m.)*: . . . . $ _____

12. I own or have an interest in the following property:

a. Cash . . . . $ _____

b. Checking, savings and credit union accounts *(list banks)*:

    (1) _____ $ _____
    (2) _____ $ _____
    (3) _____ $ _____

c. Cars, other vehicles and boat equity *(list make, year of each)*:

    (1) _____ $ _____
    (2) _____ $ _____
    (3) _____ $ _____

d. Real estate *(list address, estimated fair market value, and equity of each property)*:

    (1) _____ $ _____ $ _____
    (2) _____ $ _____ $ _____
    (3) _____ $ _____ $ _____

e. Other personal property — jewelry, furniture, furs, stocks, bonds, etc. *(list separately)*:

    $ _____

13. Other facts which support this application are *(describe unusual medical needs, expenses for recent family emergencies, or other unusual expenses to help the court understand your budget; if more space is needed, attach page labeled attachment 13)*:

WARNING: You must immediately tell the court if you become able to pay court fees or costs during this action. You may be ordered to appear in court and answer questions about your ability to pay court fees or costs.

982(a)(17) [Rev. February 1, 1997]

APPLICATION FOR WAIVER OF COURT FEES AND COSTS
(In Forma Pauperis)

Page two

ATTORNEY OR PARTY WITHOUT ATTORNEY *(Name and Address)*:	TELEPHONE NO.:	**FOR COURT USE ONLY**
ATTORNEY FOR *(Name)*:		

INSERT NAME OF COURT AND NAME OF JUDICIAL DISTRICT AND BRANCH COURT, IF ANY:

PLAINTIFF/PETITIONER:

DEFENDANT/RESPONDENT:

ORDER ON APPLICATION FOR WAIVER OF COURT FEES AND COSTS *(Cal. Rules of Court, rule 985(i))*	CASE NUMBER:

1. The application was filed on *(date)*: ☐ A previous order was issued on *(date)*:
2. The application was filed by *(name)*:
3. ☐ IT IS ORDERED that the application is **granted** ☐ in whole ☐ in part *(see Cal. Rules of Court, rule 985).*
    a. ☐ **No payments**. Payment of all the fees and costs listed in California Rules of Court, rule 985(i), **is waived**.
    b. ☐ **Applicant shall pay** all the fees and costs listed in California Rules of Court, rule 985(i), EXCEPT the following:
       (1) ☐ Filing papers.   (5) ☐ Court-appointed interpreter *(small claims only).*
       (2) ☐ Certification and copying.   (6) ☐ Sheriff, marshal, and constable fees.
       (3) ☐ Issuing process and certification.   (7) ☐ Reporter's fees *(valid for 60 days).*
       (4) ☐ Transmittal of papers.   (8) ☐ Telephone appearance (Gov. Code, § 68070.1(c)).
    c. **Method of payment**. Applicant shall pay all the fees and costs when charged, EXCEPT as follows:
       (1) ☐ Pay *(specify)*:   percent.
       (2) ☐ Pay: $ per month or more until the balance is paid.

    before and be examined by the court no sooner than four months from the date of this order, and not more than once in any four-month period.

    ☐ The applicant is ordered to appear for the court's review of the applicant's financial status as follows:

Date:	Time:	Dept.:	Room:

    e. ☐ *(must be completed if application is granted in part)* Reasons for denial of a requested waiver *(specify)*:

    f. ☐ The clerk is directed to mail a copy of this order to the applicant's attorney or to the applicant if unrepresented, and to the judgment debtor.

    g. **All unpaid fees and costs shall be deemed to be taxable costs if applicant is entitled to costs and shall be a lien on any judgment recovered by the applicant and shall be paid directly to the clerk by the judgment debtor upon such recovery.**

4. ☐ IT IS ORDERED that the application is **denied** for the following reasons *(specify)*:

    a. The applicant shall pay any fees and costs due in this action within 10 days from the date of service of this order or any paper filed by the applicant with the clerk will be of no effect.
    b. The clerk is directed to mail a copy of this order to all parties who have appeared in this action.

5. ☐ IT IS ORDERED that a **hearing** be held.
    a. The substantial evidentiary conflict to be resolved by the hearing is *(specify)*:

    b. **Applicant should be present** at the hearing to be held as follows:

Date:	Time:	Dept.:	Room:

    c. The address of the court is *(specify)*:
    d. The clerk is directed to mail a copy of this order to the applicant only.

Date: ▶

_____
JUDICIAL OFFICER

(Continued on reverse)

Form Adopted by Rule 982
Judicial Council of California
982(a)(18) [Rev. July 1, 1997]

**ORDER ON APPLICATION FOR WAIVER
OF COURT FEES AND COSTS
(In Forma Pauperis)**

Government Code, § 68511.3;
Cal. Rules of Court, rule 985

PLAINTIFF/PETITIONER (Name):	CASE NUMBER:
DEFENDANT/RESPONDENT (Name):	

CLERK'S CERTIFICATE OF MAILING

I certify that I am not a party to this cause and that a true copy of the foregoing was mailed first class, postage prepaid, in a sealed envelope addressed as shown below, and that the mailing of the foregoing and execution of this certificate occurred at (place):

, California,

on (date):

Clerk, by _____ , Deputy

(SEAL)

CLERK'S CERTIFICATE

I certify that the foregoing is a true and correct copy of the original on file in my office.

Date:

Clerk, by _____ , Deputy

**ORDER ON APPLICATION FOR WAIVER
OF COURT FEES AND COSTS
(In Forma Pauperis)**

Page two

PARTY ☐ PLAINTIFF ☐ DEFENDANT *(Name and Address):*	TELEPHONE NO.:	FOR COURT USE ONLY

NAME AND ADDRESS OF COURT:

PLAINTIFF(S):

DEFENDANT(S):

PROOF OF SERVICE (Small Claims)	HEARING DATE:	DAY:	TIME:	DEPT./DIVISION:	CASE NUMBER:

1. At the time of service I was at least 18 years of age and not a party to this action, and **I served copies** of the following:

☐ Plaintiff's Claim   ☐ Order of Examination   ☐ Other *(specify):*
☐ Defendant's Claim   ☐ Subpena Duces Tecum

2. a. Party served *(specify name of party as shown on the documents served):*

   b. Person served: ☐ party in item 2.a.   ☐ other *(specify name and title or relationship to the party named in item 2.a.)*

3. By delivery   ☐ at home   ☐ at business
   a. date:
   b. time:
   c. address:

4. **Manner of service** *(check proper box):*
   a. ☐ **Personal service.** I personally delivered to and left copies with the party served. **(C.C.P. 415.10)**
   b. ☐ **Substituted service on corporation, unincorporated association (including partnership), or public entity.** By leaving, during usual office hours, copies in the office of the person served with the person who apparently was in charge and thereafter mailing (by first-class mail, postage prepaid) copies to the person to be served at the place where the copies were left. **(C.C.P. 415.20(a))**
   c. ☐ **Substituted service on natural person, minor, incompetent, or candidate.** By leaving copies at the dwelling house, usual place of abode, usual place of business, or usual mailing address other than a U. S. Postal Service post office box of the person served in the presence of a competent member of the household or a person apparently in charge of the office or place of business, at least 18 years of age, who was informed of the general nature of the papers, and thereafter mailing (by first-class mail, postage prepaid) copies to the person to be served at the place where the copies were left. **(C.C.P. 415.20(b))**
   d. ☐ **Date of mailing:**   **From** *(city):*

> **Information regarding date and place of mailing is required for services effected in manner *4.b.* and *4.c.* above. Certified mail service may be performed only by the Clerk of the Court in small claims matters.**

5. **Person serving** *(name, address, and telephone number):*
   a. **Fee** for service: $
   b. ☐ Not a registered California process server
   c. ☐ **Exempt** from registration under B&P Section 22350(b)
   d. ☐ **Registered** California process server
     1. ☐ Employee or independent contractor
     2. **Registration Number:**
     3. **County:**

6. ☐ I declare under penalty of perjury under the laws of the State of California that the foregoing is true and correct.
7. ☐ I am a California sheriff, marshal, or constable and I certify that the foregoing is true and correct.

▶

Date: _____

_____
(SIGNATURE OF SERVER)

Form Approved by the
Judicial Council of California
SC-104 [New January 1, 1992]

PROOF OF SERVICE
(Small Claims)

Code of Civil Procedure
§§ 415.10, 415.20

INSTRUCTIONS FOR FILING PROOF OF SERVICE

A.   Print the name and address of the person filing the Proof Of Service.

B.   Print the name and address of the Court in which you are filing.

C.   Print the name of the plaintiff and defendant as it appears on the Plaintiff's Claim.

D.   Date of hearing.

E.   Day of week.

F.   Time in which your case is scheduled to be heard.

G.   Division in which your case is calendared.

H.   **YOUR CASE NUMBER**

1.   X the appropriate box.

2.   a.   Print the name of the party you served (most effective service made is on the defendant directly).

      b.   Print the relationship to the party named in 2a.(if the person you served was not the defendant).

3.   Where the documents were delivered and the address.

4.   Manner of Service (check proper box).
      Indicate how the defendant was served, i.e., **personal or substituted service.**

      If you subserved the defendant, **YOU MUST MAIL A COPY OF THE PLAINTIFF'S CLAIM TO THE DEFENDANT.**

5.   Print the name and address of the person serving the document.
      Check the appropriate box.

6.   **CHECKING THIS BOX INDICATES TO THE COURT THAT ALL YOU HAVE STATED ABOVE IS TRUE AND CORRECT.**

7.   Check this box only if you are a California marshal, etc.

      DATE AND SIGN THE PROOF OF SERVICE BEFORE FILING WITH THE CLERK'S OFFICE. RETURN THE PROOF OF SERVICE TO THE COURT 5 DAYS PRIOR TO THE HEARING DATE.

Name and Address of Court:

SMALL CLAIMS CASE NO.

Names and addresses of additional plaintiffs and defendants:	*Nombres y direcciones de los demandantes y demandados adicionales:*

☐ PLAINTIFF/DEMANDANTE ☐ DEFENDANT/DEMANDADO   ☐ PLAINTIFF/DEMANDANTE ☐ DEFENDANT/DEMANDADO
(Name and address)   *(Name and address)*

☐ PLAINTIFF/DEMANDANTE ☐ DEFENDANT/DEMANDADO   ☐ PLAINTIFF/DEMANDANTE ☐ DEFENDANT/DEMANDADO
(Name and address)   *(Name and address)*

☐ PLAINTIFF/DEMANDANTE ☐ DEFENDANT/DEMANDADO   ☐ PLAINTIFF/DEMANDANTE ☐ DEFENDANT/DEMANDADO
(Name and address)   *(Name and address)*

☐ PLAINTIFF/DEMANDANTE ☐ DEFENDANT/DEMANDADO   ☐ PLAINTIFF/DEMANDANTE ☐ DEFENDANT/DEMANDADO
(Name and address)   *(Name and address)*

When space is not available on a small claims form, this form may be used to list additional plaintiffs and defendants. If this form is used, be sure to attach it to the accompanying small claims form and serve both together on the plaintiffs and defendants as provided by law.

Form Approved by the
Judicial Council of California
SC-160 [New January 1, 1985]

ADDITIONAL PLAINTIFFS AND DEFENDANTS
(Small Claims)

Rule 982.7

_____
_____
_____
_____
_____

REQUEST FOR POSTPONEMENT (CCP 116.570)

Name and Address of Requesting Party	Case Number:
Telephone Number: ( )	
PLAINTIFF: VS DEFENDANT:	

I am the Plaintiff/Defendant in the above entitled action. I declare that:

_____ A $10.00 postponement fee is attached (non-refundable)

_____ A fee waiver for the $10.00 postponement fee has been filed.

I am requesting that my small claims hearing date of _____be postponed and rescheduled to_____for the following reason:

I declare under the penalty of perjury under the laws of the State of California that the foregoing is true and correct.

Date:_____   _____
                                                           SIGNATURE OF DECLARANT

REQUEST FOR POSTPONEMENT

DECLARATION OF SERVICE BY MAIL

I served a copy of the Request for Postponement by depositing a copy thereof enclosed in sealed envelope, with postage prepaid in the United States mail at (city) _____, addressed as follows (name and address of opposing party(s).

I declare under penalty of perjury that the foregoing is true and correct.

Executed on _____ at _____, California.

DATE   PLACE

_____
SIGNATURE OF DECLARANT

_____
TYPE OR PRINT NAME OF DECLARANT

_____
TYPE OR PRINT ADDRESS OF DECLARANT

Name and Address of Court:

SC-120

SMALL CLAIMS CASE NO.

— NOTICE TO PLAINTIFF — YOU ARE BEING SUED BY DEFENDANT	— *AVISO AL DEMANDANTE* — *A USTED LO ESTA DEMANDANDO EL*
To protect your rights, you must appear in this court on the trial date shown in the table below. You may lose the case if you do not appear. The court may award the defendant the amount of the claim and the costs. Your wages, money, and property may be taken without further warning from the court.	*Para proteger sus derechos, usted debe presentarse ante esta corte en la fecha del juicio indicada en el cuadro que aparece a continuación. Si no se presenta, puede perder el caso. La corte puede decidir en favor del deman- dado por la cantidad del reclamo y los costos. A usted le pueden quitar su salario, su dinero, y otras cosas de su propiedad, sin aviso adicional por parte de esta corte.*

PLAINTIFF/DEMANDANTE *(Name, address, and telephone number of each):*

DEFENDANT/DEMANDADO *(Name, address, and telephone number of each):*

Telephone No.:

Telephone No.:

Telephone No.:

Telephone No.:

Fict. Bus. Name Stmt. No.   Expires:

☐ See attached sheet for additional plaintiffs and defendants.

DEFENDANT'S CLAIM

1. Plaintiff owes me the sum of: $ _____ , not including court costs, because *(describe claim and date):*

2. a. ☐ I have asked plaintiff to pay this money, but it has not been paid.
   b. ☐ I have NOT asked plaintiff to pay this money because *(explain):*

3. I ☐ have ☐ have not   filed more than one other small claims action anywhere in California during this calendar year in which the amount demanded is more than $2,500.

4. I understand that
   a. I may talk to an attorney about this claim, but I cannot be represented by an attorney at the trial in the small claims court.
   b. I must appear at the time and place of trial and bring all witnesses, books, receipts, and other papers or things to prove my case.
   c. **I have no right of appeal on my claim,** but I may appeal a claim filed by the plaintiff in this case.
   d. If I cannot afford to pay the fees for filing or service by a sheriff, marshal, or constable, I may ask that the fees be waived.

5. I have received and read the information sheet explaining some important rights of defendants in the small claims court.

I declare under penalty of perjury under the laws of the State of California that the foregoing is true and correct.

Date:

▶

. . . .
(TYPE OR PRINT NAME)   (SIGNATURE OF DEFENDANT)

ORDER TO PLAINTIFF

You must appear in this court on the trial date and at the time LAST SHOWN IN THE BOX BELOW if you do not agree with the defendant's claim. Bring all witnesses, books, receipts, and other papers or things with you to support your case.

TRIAL DATE FECHA DEL JUICIO		DATE	DAY	TIME	PLACE	COURT USE
	1.					
	2.					
	3.					
	4.					

Filed on *(date):*   Clerk, by _____ , Deputy

| — The county provides small claims advisor services free of charge. (Advisor phone number: _____) — |

Form Approved by the
 Judicial Council of California
 SC-120 [Rev. January 1, 1998]

DEFENDANT'S CLAIM AND ORDER TO PLAINTIFF
 (Small Claims)

Cal. Rules of Court, rule 982.7;
 Code of Civil Procedure, § 116.110 et seq.

Name and Address of Court:

SMALL CLAIMS CASE NO. _____

| PLAINTIFF/DEMANDANTE *(Name, address, and telephone number of each)*: | DEFENDANT/DEMANDADO *(Name, address, and telephone number of each)*: |

Telephone No.:

Telephone No.:

Telephone No.:

Telephone No.:

☐ See attached sheet for additional plaintiffs and defendants.

NOTICE TO *(Names)*:

NOTICE OF MOTION FOR *(specify)*:

1. I request the court to make an order to *(specify)*:
2. My request is based on this notice of motion and declaration, the records on file with the court, and any evidence that may be presented at the hearing.

DECLARATION SUPPORTING MY REQUEST FOR THIS MOTION

3. I am the ☐ plaintiff ☐ defendant in this action.

4. The facts supporting this motion are as follows *(specify)*:

☐ Item 4 continued on attached page.

I declare under penalty of perjury under the laws of the State of California that the foregoing is true and correct.

Date:

. . . .
(TYPE OR PRINT NAME) ▶ _____
(SIGNATURE)

5. If you wish to oppose this request you should appear at the court on

HEARING DATE		DATE	DAY	TIME	PLACE
FECHA DEL JUICIO	1.				
	2.				
	3.				
	4.				

CLERK'S CERTIFICATE OF MAILING

I certify that I am not a party to this action. This Notice of Motion was mailed first class, postage prepaid, in a sealed envelope to the responding party at the address shown above. The mailing and this certification occurred

at *(place)*: _____ , California,

on *(date)*:

Clerk, by _____ , Deputy

— The county provides small claims advisor services free of charge. —

Form Approved by the
Judicial Council of California
SC-105 [New January 1. 1992]

NOTICE OF MOTION AND DECLARATION
(Small Claims)

SC-134

Name and Address of Court:

SMALL CLAIMS CASE NO.:

PLAINTIFF/DEMANDANTE *(Name, street address, and telephone number of each):*

DEFENDANT/DEMANDADO *(Name, street address, and telephone number of each):*

Telephone No.:

Telephone No.:

☐ See attached sheet for additional plaintiffs and defendants.

ORDER TO APPEAR FOR EXAMINATION—SMALL CLAIMS

1. TO JUDGMENT DEBTOR *(name):*
2. YOU ARE ORDERED to
   a. pay the judgment and file proof of payment (a canceled check or money order or cash receipt, and a written declaration that shows full payment of the judgment, including post-judgment costs and interest) with the court before the hearing date shown in the box below, **or**
   b. personally appear in this court on the date and time shown in the box below to explain why you did not complete and mail the *Judgment Debtor's Statement of Assets* (form SC-133) to judgment creditor within 30 days after the *Notice of Entry of Judgment* (form SC-130) was mailed or handed to you by the clerk, and to answer questions as to your income and assets.

HEARING DATE / FECHA DEL JUICIO	DATE	DAY	TIME	PLACE	COURT USE
1.					
2.					
3.					

If you fail to appear and have not paid the judgment, including post-judgment costs and interest, a bench warrant may be issued for your arrest, you may be held in contempt of court, and you may be ordered to pay penalties.	Si usted no se presenta y no ha pagado el monto del fallo judicial, inclusive las costas e intereses posteriores al fallo, la corte puede expedir una orden de detención contra usted, declararle en desacato y ordenar que pague multas.

3. This order may be served by a sheriff, marshal, or registered process server.

Date:

▶ _____
(SIGNATURE OF JUDGE)

APPLICATION FOR ORDER TO APPEAR FOR EXAMINATION—SMALL CLAIMS

1. Judgment creditor (the person who won the case) *(name):*   applies for an order requiring
   judgment debtor (the person or business who lost the case and owes money) *(name):*   to
   (a) pay the judgment **or** (b) personally appear in this court to explain why judgment debtor did not pay the judgment or complete and mail the *Judgment Debtor's Statement of Assets* to judgment creditor within 30 days after the *Notice of Entry of Judgment* was mailed or handed to judgment debtor, and to answer questions as to judgment debtor's income and assets.

2. Judgment creditor states the following:
   a. Judgment debtor has not paid the judgment.
   b. Judgment debtor either did not file an appeal or the appeal has been dismissed or judgment debtor lost the appeal.
   c. Judgment debtor either did not file a motion to vacate or the motion to vacate has been denied.
   d. More than 30 days have passed since the *Notice of Entry of Judgment* form was mailed or delivered to judgment debtor.
   e. Judgment creditor has not received a completed *Judgment Debtor's Statement of Assets* form from judgment debtor.

I declare under penalty of perjury under the laws of the State of California that the foregoing is true and correct.
Date:

▶
_____   _____
(TYPE OR PRINT NAME)   (See Instructions on reverse)   (SIGNATURE OF JUDGMENT CREDITOR)

— The county provides small claims advisor services free of charge. —

Form Adopted by the
Judicial Council of California
SC-134 [New January 1, 1998]

APPLICATION AND ORDER TO APPEAR FOR EXAMINATION
(Small Claims)

Cal. Rules of Court, rule 982.7(a);
Code of Civil Procedure,
§§ 116.820, 116.830

INSTRUCTIONS FOR JUDGMENT CREDITOR

1. To set a hearing on an *Application for Order to Appear for Examination—Small Claims*, you must complete this form, present it to the court clerk, and pay the fee. The clerk will set a hearing date and note it on the form and return an original and one copy of the form to you.

2. You must have this form personally served on the judgment debtor by a sheriff, marshal, or registered process server at least 10 calendar days before the date of the hearing, and have a proof of service filed with the court.

3. If the judgment is paid, including all post-judgment costs and interests, you must immediately complete the *Acknowledgment of Satisfaction of Judgment* form on the reverse of the *Notice of Entry of Judgment* (form SC-130) and file a copy with the court.

4. You must attend the hearing unless the judgment has been paid.

Name and Address of Court:

SMALL CLAIMS CASE NO.

PLAINTIFF/DEMANDANTE *(Name, address, and telephone number of each)*:

DEFENDANT/DEMANDADO *(Name, address, and telephone number of each)*:

Telephone No.:

Telephone No.:

Telephone No.:

Telephone No.:

☐ See attached sheet for additional plaintiffs and defendants.

DECLARATION FOR SUBPENA DUCES TECUM

1. I, the undersigned, declare I am the ☐ plaintiff ☐ defendant ☐ judgment creditor ☐ other *(specify)*:
in the above entitled action.
2. This action has been set for hearing on *(date)*:   at *(time)*:   in the above named court.
3. *(Name)*:   has in his or her possession or under his or her control
the following documents relating to *(name of party)*   :
   a. ☐ Payroll receipts, stubs, and other records concerning employment of the party. Receipts, invoices, documents, and other papers or records concerning any and all accounts receivable of the party.
   b. ☐ Bank account statements, canceled checks, and check registers from any and all bank accounts in which the party has an interest.
   c. ☐ Savings account passbooks and statements, savings and loan account passbooks and statements, and credit union share account passbooks and statements of the party.
   d. ☐ Stock certificates, bonds, money market certificates, and any other records, documents, or papers concerning all investments of the party
   e. ☐ California registration certificates and ownership certificates for all vehicles registered to the party.
   f. ☐ Deeds to any and all real property owned or being purchased by the party.
   g. ☐ Other *(specify)*:

These documents are material to the issues involved in this case for the following reasons *(specify)*:

I declare under penalty of perjury under the laws of the State of California that the foregoing is true and correct.

Date:

. . . .
(TYPE OR PRINT NAME)

▶ _____
(SIGNATURE OF JUDGMENT CREDITOR)

Form Approved by the
Judicial Council of California
SC-107 [New January 1, 1992]

DECLARATION FOR SUBPENA DUCES TECUM
(Small Claims)

Code of Civil Procedure, §§ 1985-1987.5

141

ATTORNEY OR PARTY WITHOUT ATTORNEY *(Name and Address)*:	TELEPHONE NO.:	*FOR COURT USE ONLY*

ATTORNEY FOR *(Name)*:

NAME OF COURT:
STREET ADDRESS:
MAILING ADDRESS:
CITY AND ZIP CODE:
BRANCH NAME:

PLAINTIFF/PETITIONER:

DEFENDANT/RESPONDENT:

CIVIL SUBPENA

[ ] **Duces Tecum**

CASE NUMBER:

THE PEOPLE OF THE STATE OF CALIFORNIA, TO (NAME):

1. **YOU ARE ORDERED TO APPEAR AS A WITNESS in this action at the date, time, and place shown in the box below UNLESS you make a special agreement with the person named in item 3:**

   a. Date: Time: [ ] Dept.:   [ ] Div.:   [ ] Room:
   b. Address:

2. AND YOU ARE
   a. [ ] ordered to appear in person.
   b. [ ] not required to appear in person if you produce the records described in the accompanying affidavit and a completed declaration of custodian of records in compliance with Evidence Code sections 1560, 1561, 1562, and 1271. (1) Place a copy of the records in an envelope (or other wrapper). Enclose your original declaration with the records. Seal them. (2) Attach a copy of this subpena to the envelope or write on the envelope the case name and number, your name and date, time, and place from item 1 (the box above). (3) Place this first envelope in an outer envelope, seal it, and mail it to the clerk of the court at the address in item 1. (4) Mail a copy of your declaration to the attorney or party shown at the top of this form.
   c. [ ] ordered to appear in person and to produce the records described in the accompanying affidavit. The **personal attendance** of the custodian or other qualified witness and the production of the original records **is required** by this subpena. The procedure authorized by subdivision (b) of section 1560, and sections 1561 and 1562, of the Evidence Code will not be deemed sufficient compliance with this subpena.

3. **IF YOU HAVE ANY QUESTIONS ABOUT THE TIME OR DATE FOR YOU TO APPEAR, OR IF YOU WANT TO BE CERTAIN THAT YOUR PRESENCE IS REQUIRED, CONTACT THE FOLLOWING PERSON BEFORE THE DATE ON WHICH YOU ARE TO APPEAR:**
   a. Name: b. Telephone number:

4. **Witness Fees:** You are entitled to witness fees and mileage actually traveled both ways, as provided by law, if you request them at the time of service. You may request them before your scheduled appearance from the person named in item 3.

DISOBEDIENCE OF THIS SUBPENA MAY BE PUNISHED AS CONTEMPT BY THIS COURT. YOU WILL ALSO BE LIABLE FOR THE SUM OF FIVE HUNDRED DOLLARS AND ALL DAMAGES RESULTING FROM YOUR FAILURE TO OBEY.

Date issued:

. . . .   ▶ _____
                (TYPE OR PRINT NAME)   (SIGNATURE OF PERSON ISSUING SUBPENA)

_____
(TITLE)

(See reverse for proof of service)

Form Adopted by Rule 982   **CIVIL SUBPENA**   Code of Civil Procedure, §§ 1985, 1986, 1987
Judicial Council of California
982(a)(15) [Rev. January 1, 1991]

PLAINTIFF/PETITIONER:	CASE NUMBER:
DEFENDANT/RESPONDENT:	

PROOF OF SERVICE OF CIVIL SUBPENA

1. I served ☐ Subpena ☐ Subpena Duces Tecum and supporting affidavit   by personally delivering a copy to the person served as follows:

   a. Person served *(name)*:

   b. Address where served:

   c. Date of delivery:

   d. Time of delivery:

   e. Witness fees *(check one)*:
      (1) ☐ were offered or demanded
         and paid. Amount: . . . . . $ _____
      (2) ☐ were not demanded or paid.

   f. Fee for service: . . . . $ _____

2. I received this subpena for service on *(date)*:

3. Person serving:
   a. ☐ Not a registered California process server.
   b. ☐ California sheriff, marshal, or constable.
   c. ☐ Registered California process server.
   d. ☐ Employee or independent contractor of a registered California process server.
   e. ☐ Exempt from registration under Bus. & Prof. Code section 22350(b).
   f. ☐ Registered professional photocopier.
   g. ☐ Exempt from registration under Bus. & Prof. Code section 22451.
   h. Name, address, and telephone number and, if applicable, county of registration and number:

I declare under penalty of perjury under the laws of the State of California that the foregoing is true and correct.

Date:

▶ _____
         (SIGNATURE)

(For California sheriff, marshal, or constable use only)
I certify that the foregoing is true and correct.

Date:

▶ _____
         (SIGNATURE)

ATTORNEY OR PARTY WITHOUT ATTORNEY *(Name and Address)*:

TELEPHONE NO.:

FOR COURT USE ONLY

ATTORNEY FOR *(Name)*:

Insert name of court and name of judicial district and branch court, if any:

PLAINTIFF/PETITIONER:

DEFENDANT/RESPONDENT:

REQUEST FOR DISMISSAL

☐ **Personal Injury, Property Damage, or Wrongful Death**
   ☐ **Motor Vehicle**   ☐ **Other**
☐ **Family Law**
☐ **Eminent Domain**
☐ **Other** *(specify)*:

CASE NUMBER:

— **A conformed copy will not be returned by the clerk unless a method of return is provided with the document.** —

1. **TO THE CLERK:** Please **dismiss** this action as follows:

   a. (1) ☐ With prejudice   (2) ☐ Without prejudice

   b. (1) ☐ Complaint   (2) ☐ Petition
      (3) ☐ Cross-complaint filed by *(name)*:   on *(date)*:
      (4) ☐ Cross-complaint filed by *(name)*:   on *(date)*:
      (5) ☐ Entire action of all parties and all causes of action
      (6) ☐ Other *(specify)*:*

Date:

. . . .
(TYPE OR PRINT NAME OF ☐ ATTORNEY ☐ PARTY WITHOUT ATTORNEY)
* If dismissal requested is of specified parties only, of specified causes of
action only, or of specified cross-complaints only, so state and identify
the parties, causes of action, or cross-complaints to be dismissed.

▶ _____
(SIGNATURE)
Attorney or party without attorney for:

☐ Plaintiff/Petitioner   ☐ Defendant/Respondent
☐ Cross-complainant

2. **TO THE CLERK:** Consent to the above dismissal is hereby given.**
Date:

. . . .
(TYPE OR PRINT NAME OF ☐ ATTORNEY ☐ PARTY WITHOUT ATTORNEY)
** If a cross-complaint—or Response (Family Law) seeking affirmative
relief—is on file, the attorney for cross-complainant (respondent) must
sign this consent if required by Code of Civil Procedure section 581(i)
or (j).

▶ _____
(SIGNATURE)
Attorney or party without attorney for:

☐ Plaintiff/Petitioner   ☐ Defendant/Respondent
☐ Cross-complainant

(To be completed by clerk)

3. ☐ Dismissal entered as requested on *(date)*:
4. ☐ Dismissal entered on *(date)*:   as to only *(name)*:
5. ☐ Dismissal **not entered** as requested for the following reasons *(specify)*:

6. ☐ a. Attorney or party without attorney notified on *(date)*:
      b. Attorney or party without attorney not notified. Filing party failed to provide
         ☐ a copy to conform   ☐ means to return conformed copy

Date: _____   Clerk, by _____, Deputy

Form Adopted by the
Judicial Council of California
982(a)(5) [Rev. January 1, 1997]

REQUEST FOR DISMISSAL

Code of Civil Procedure, § 581 et seq.
Cal. Rules of Court, rules 383, 1233

ATTORNEY OR PARTY WITHOUT ATTORNEY *(Name and Address):*   TELEPHONE NO.:   FOR RECORDER'S USE ONLY

☐ Recording requested by and return to:

☐ ATTORNEY FOR   ☐ JUDGMENT CREDITOR   ☐ ASSIGNEE OF RECORD

NAME OF COURT:

STREET ADDRESS:

MAILING ADDRESS:

CITY AND ZIP CODE:

BRANCH NAME:

PLAINTIFF:

DEFENDANT:

ABSTRACT OF JUDGMENT

CASE NUMBER:

FOR COURT USE ONLY

1. The ☐ judgment creditor ☐ assignee of record
   applies for an abstract of judgment and represents the following:
   a. Judgment debtor's

   Name and last known address

   b. Driver's license No. and state: ☐ Unknown
   c. Social Security No.:   ☐ Unknown
   d. Summons or notice of entry of sister-state judgment was personally served or
      mailed to *(name and address):*

   e. ☐ Additional judgment debtors are shown on reverse.
   Date:

. . . .
(TYPE OR PRINT NAME)

▶ _____
(SIGNATURE OF APPLICANT OR ATTORNEY)

2. a. ☐ I certify that the following is a true and correct
       abstract of the judgment entered in this action.
   b. ☐ A certified copy of the judgment is attached.
3. Judgment creditor *(name):*

   whose **address** appears on this form above the court's name.
4. Judgment debtor *(full name as it appears in judgment):*

6. Total amount of judgment as entered or last renewed:
   $
7. ☐ An ☐ execution ☐ attachment   lien
      is endorsed on the judgment as follows:
   a. Amount: $
   b. In favor of *(name and address):*

[SEAL]

5. a. Judgment entered on
      (date):
   b. Renewal entered on
      (date):
   c. Renewal entered on
      (date):

   This abstract issued on
   (date):

8. A stay of enforcement has
   a. ☐ not been ordered by the court.
   b. ☐ been ordered by the court effective until
      (date):
9. ☐ This judgment is an installment judgment.

Clerk, by _____ , Deputy

Form Adopted by Rule 982
Judicial Council of California
982(a)(1) [Rev. January 1, 1991]

ABSTRACT OF JUDGMENT
(CIVIL)

Code of Civil Procedure, §§ 488.480,
674, 700.190

147

PLAINTIFF:	CASE NUMBER:
DEFENDANT:	

INFORMATION ON ADDITIONAL JUDGMENT DEBTORS

10.   Name and last known address

Driver's license No. & state: ☐ Unknown
Social Security No.:   ☐ Unknown
Summons was personally served at or mailed to (*address*):

11.   Name and last known address

Driver's license No. & state: ☐ Unknown
Social Security No.:   ☐ Unknown
Summons was personally served at or mailed to (*address*):

12.   Name and last known address

Driver's license No. & state: ☐ Unknown
Social Security No.:   ☐ Unknown
Summons was personally served at or mailed to (*address*):

13.   Name and last known address

Driver's license No. & state: ☐ Unknown
Social Security No.:   ☐ Unknown
Summons was personally served at or mailed to (*address*):

14.   Name and last known address

Driver's license No. & state: ☐ Unknown
Social Security No.:   ☐ Unknown
Summons was personally served at or mailed to (*address*):

15.   Name and last known address

Driver's license No. & state: ☐ Unknown
Social Security No.:   ☐ Unknown
Summons was personally served at or mailed to (*address*):

16.   Name and last known address

Driver's license No. & state: ☐ Unknown
Social Security No.:   ☐ Unknown
Summons was personally served at or mailed to (*address*):

17.   Name and last known address

Driver's license No. & state: ☐ Unknown
Social Security No.:   ☐ Unknown
Summons was personally served at or mailed to (*address*):

18. ☐ Continued on attachment 18.

ABSTRACT OF JUDGMENT
(CIVIL)

SC-130

SMALL CLAIMS CASE NO.:

NOTICE TO ALL PLAINTIFFS AND DEFENDANTS: Your small claims case has been decided. If you lost the case, and the court ordered you to pay money, your wages, money, and property may be taken without further warning from the court. Read the back of this sheet for important information about your rights.	***AVISO A TODOS LOS DEMANDANTES Y DEMANDADOS:*** *Su caso ha sido resuelto por la corte para reclamos judiciales menores. Si la corte ha decidido en su contra y ha ordenado que usted pague dinero, le pueden quitar su salario, su dinero, y otras cosas de su propiedad, sin aviso adicional por parte de esta corte. Lea el reverso de este formulario para obtener información de importancia acerca de sus derechos.*

PLAINTIFF/DEMANDANTE *(Name, street address, and telephone number of each)*:

DEFENDANT/DEMANDADO *(Name, street address, and telephone number of each)*:

Telephone No.:

Telephone No.:

Telephone No.:

Telephone No.:

[ ] See attached sheet for additional plaintiffs and defendants.

NOTICE OF ENTRY OF JUDGMENT

Judgment was entered as checked below on *(date)*:

1. [ ] Defendant *(name, if more than one)*:
   shall pay plaintiff *(name, if more than one)*:
   $ _____ principal and $ _____ costs on plaintiff's claim.
2. [ ] Defendant does not owe plaintiff any money on plaintiff's claim.
3. [ ] Plaintiff *(name, if more than one)*:
   shall pay defendant *(name, if more than one)*:
   $ _____ principal and: $ _____ costs on defendant's claim.
4. [ ] Plaintiff does not owe defendant any money on defendant's claim.
5. [ ] Possession of the following property is awarded to plaintiff *(describe property)*:

6. [ ] Payments are to be made at the rate of: $ _____ per *(specify period)*: _____ , beginning on *(date)*: _____
   and on the *(specify day)*: _____ day of each month thereafter until paid in full. If any payment is missed, the entire balance may become due immediately.
7. [ ] Dismissed in court [ ] with prejudice. [ ] without prejudice.
8. [ ] *Attorney-Client Fee Dispute (Attachment to Notice of Entry of Judgment)* (form SC-132) is attached.
9. [ ] Other *(specify)*:

10. [ ] This judgment results from a motor vehicle accident on a California highway and was caused by the judgment debtor's operation of a motor vehicle. If the judgment is not paid, the judgment creditor may apply to have the judgment debtor's driver's license suspended.
11. Enforcement of the judgment is automatically postponed for 30 days or, if an appeal is filed, until the appeal is decided.
12. [ ] This notice was personally delivered to *(insert name and date)*:
13. CLERK'S CERTIFICATE OF MAILING—I certify that I am not a party to this action. This *Notice of Entry of Judgment* was mailed first class, postage prepaid, in a sealed envelope to the parties at the addresses shown above. The mailing and this certification occurred at the place and on the date shown below.

   Place of mailing: _____ , California
   Date of mailing:

   Clerk, by _____ , Deputy

— The county provides small claims advisor services free of charge. Read the information sheet on the reverse. —

Form Adopted by the
Judicial Council of California
SC-130 [Rev. January 1, 1998]

NOTICE OF ENTRY OF JUDGMENT
(Small Claims)

Cal. Rules of Court, rule 982.7;
Code of Civil Procedure, § 116.610

Your small claims case has been decided. The **judgment** or decision of the court appears on the front of this sheet. The court may have ordered one party to pay money to the other party. The person (or business) who won the case and who can collect the money is called the **judgment creditor**. The person (or business) who lost the case and who owes the money is called the **judgment debtor**.

Enforcement of the judgment is **postponed** until the time for appeal ends or until the appeal is decided. This means that the judgment creditor cannot collect any money or take any action until this period is over. Generally, both parties may be represented by lawyers after judgment.

IF YOU LOST THE CASE . . .

1. If you lost the case on your own claim and the court did not award you any money, the court's decision on your claim is **FINAL**. You may not appeal your own claim.

2. If you lost the case and the court ordered you to pay money, your money and property may be taken to pay the claim unless you do one of the following things:

   a. **PAY THE JUDGMENT**
   The law requires you to pay the amount of the judgment. You may pay the judgment creditor directly, or pay the judgment to the court for an additional fee. You may also ask the court to order monthly payments you can afford. Ask the clerk for information about these procedures.

   b. **APPEAL**
   If you disagree with the court's decision, you may appeal the decision *on the other party's claim*. You may not appeal the decision on your own claim. However, if any party appeals, there will be a new trial on *all* the claims. If you appeared at the trial, you *must* begin your appeal by filing a form called a *Notice of Appeal* (form SC-140) and pay the required fees within *30 days* after the date this *Notice of Entry of Judgment* was mailed or handed to you. Your appeal will be in the superior court. You will have a **new trial** and you must present your evidence again. You may be represented by a lawyer.

   c. **VACATE OR CANCEL THE JUDGMENT**
   If you did not go to the trial, you may ask the court to vacate or cancel the judgment. To make this request, you must file a *Motion to Vacate the Judgment* (form SC-135) and pay the required fee *within 30 days* after the date this *Notice of Entry of Judgment* was mailed. If your request is denied, you then have *10 days* from the date the notice of denial was mailed to file an appeal.

   The period to file the *Motion to Vacate the Judgment* is *180 days* if you were *not properly served* with the claim. The 180-day period begins on the date you found out or should have found out about the judgment against you.

IF YOU WON THE CASE . . .

1. If you were sued by the other party and you won the case, then the other party may not appeal the court's decision.

2. If you won the case and the court awarded you money, here are some steps you may take to collect your money or get possession of your property:

   a. **COLLECTING FEES**
   Sometimes fees are charged for filing court papers or for serving the judgment debtor. These extra costs can become part of your original judgment. To claim these fees, ask the clerk for a *Memorandum of Costs*.

   b. **VOLUNTARY PAYMENT**
   Ask the judgment debtor to pay the money. If your claim was for possession of property, ask the judgment debtor to return the property to you. **THE COURT WILL NOT COLLECT THE MONEY OR ENFORCE THE JUDGMENT FOR YOU.**

   c. **STATEMENT OF ASSETS**
   If the judgment debtor does not pay the money, the law requires the debtor to fill out a form called the *Judgment Debtor's Statement of Assets* (form SC-133). This form will tell you what property the judgment debtor has that may be available to pay your claim. If the judgment debtor willfully fails to send you the completed form, you may file an *Application and Order to Appear for Examination (Small Claims)* (form SC-134) and ask the court to give you your attorney's fees and expenses, and other appropriate relief, after proper notice, under Code of Civil Procedure section 708.170.

   d. **ORDER OF EXAMINATION**
   You may also make the debtor come to court to answer questions about income and property. To do this, ask the clerk for an *Application and Order for Appearance and Examination (Enforcement of Judgment)* (form EJ-125) and pay the required fee. There is a fee if a law officer serves the order on the judgment debtor. You may also obtain the judgment debtor's financial records. Ask the clerk for the *Civil Subpena Duces Tecum* (form 982(a)(15)).

   e. **WRIT OF EXECUTION**
   After you find out about the judgment debtor's property, you may ask the court for a *Writ of Execution* (form EJ-130) and pay the required fee. A writ of execution is a court paper that tells a law officer to take property of the judgment debtor to pay your claim. Here are some examples of the kinds of property the officer may be able to take: **wages, bank account, automobile, business property, or rental income**. For some kinds of property, you may need to file other forms. See the law officer for information.

   f. **ABSTRACT OF JUDGMENT**
   The judgment debtor may own land or a house or other buildings. You may want to put a lien on the property so that you will be paid if the property is sold. You can get a lien by filing an *Abstract of Judgment* (form 982(a)(1)) with the county recorder in the county where the property is located. The recorder will charge a fee for the *Abstract of Judgment*.

NOTICE TO THE PARTY WHO WON: As soon as you have been paid in full, you *must* fill out the form below and mail it to the court *immediately* or you may be fined. If an *Abstract of Judgment* has been recorded, you must use another form; see the clerk for the proper form.

SMALL CLAIMS CASE NO.: _____

ACKNOWLEDGMENT OF SATISFACTION OF JUDGMENT
(Do not use this form if an Abstract of Judgment has been recorded.)

To the Clerk of the Court:

I am the ☐ judgment creditor. ☐ assignee of record.

I agree that the judgment in this action has been paid in full or otherwise satisfied.

Date:

▶

_____
(TYPE OR PRINT NAME)

_____
(SIGNATURE)

EXEMPTIONS FROM THE ENFORCEMENT OF JUDGMENTS

The following is a list of assets that may be exempt from levy.

Exemptions are found in the United States Code **(USC)** and in the California codes, primarily in the Code of Civil Procedure **(CCP)**.

Because of periodic changes in the law, the list may not include all exemptions that apply in your case. The exemptions may not apply in full or under all circumstances. Some are not available after a certain period of time. You or your attorney should read the statutes.

If you believe the assets that are being levied on are exempt, file a claim of exemption, which you can get from the levying officer.

Type of Property	Code and Section	Type of Property	Code and Section
Accounts *(See Deposit Accounts)*		Benefit Payments (cont.)	
Appliances	CCP § 704.020	Relocation Benefits	CCP § 704.180
Art and Heirlooms	CCP § 704.040	Retirement Benefits and Contributions—	
Automobiles	CCP § 704.010	Private	CCP § 704.115
BART District Benefits	CCP § 704.110	Public	CCP § 704.110
	Pub Util C § 28896	Segregated Benefit Funds	Ins C § 10498.5
Benefit Payments:		Social Security Benefits	42 USC § 407
BART District Benefits	CCP § 704.110	Strike Benefits	CCP § 704.120
	Pub Util C § 28896	Transit District Retirement	
Charity	CCP § 704.170	Benefits (Alameda &	
Civil Service Retirement		Contra Costa Counties)	CCP § 704.110
Benefits (Federal)	5 USC § 8346		Pub Util C § 25337
County Employees		Unemployment Benefits	
Retirement Benefits	CCP § 704.110	and Contributions	CCP § 704.120
	Govt C § 31452	Veterans Benefits	38 USC § 3101
Disability Insurance Benefits	CCP § 704.130	Veterans Medal of Honor	
Fire Service Retirement		Benefits	38 USC § 562
Benefits	CCP § 704.110	Welfare Payments	CCP § 704.170
	Govt C § 32210		Welf & I C § 17409
Fraternal Organization		Workers Compensation	CCP § 704.160
Funds Benefits	CCP § 704.130	Boats	CCP § 704.060
	CCP § 704.170		CCP § 704.710
Health Insurance Benefits	CCP § 704.130	Books	CCP § 704.060
Irrigation System		Building Materials (Residential)	CCP § 704.030
Retirement Benefits	CCP § 704.110	Business:	
Judges Survivors Benefits		Licenses	CCP § 695.060
(Federal)	28 USC § 376(n)		CCP § 699.720(a)(1)
Legislators Retirement		Tools of Trade	CCP § 704.060
Benefits	CCP § 704.110	Cars and Trucks (including	
	Govt C § 9359.3	proceeds)	CCP § 704.010
Life Insurance Benefits—		Cash	CCP § 704.070
Group	CCP § 704.100	Cemeteries	
Individual	CCP § 704.100	Land Proceeds	Health & S § 7925
Lighthouse Keepers		Plots	CCP § 704.200
Widows Benefits	33 USC § 775	Charity	CCP § 704.170
Longshore & Harbor Workers		Claims, Actions & Awards:	
Compensation or Benefits	33 USC § 916	Personal Injury	CCP § 704.140
Military Benefits—		Worker's Compensation	CCP § 704.160
Retirement	10 USC § 1440	Wrongful Death	CCP § 704.150
Survivors	10 USC § 1450	Clothing	CCP § 704.020
Municipal Utility District		Condemnation Proceeds	CCP § 704.720(b)
Retirement Benefits	CCP § 704.110	County Employees Retirement	
	Pub Util C § 12337	Benefits	CCP § 704.110
Peace Officers Retirement			Govt C § 31452
Benefits	CCP § 704.110	Credit Union Shares	Fin C § 14864
	Govt C § 31913	Damages *(See Personal Injury*	
Pension Plans (and Death		*and Wrongful Death)*	
Benefits)—		Deposit Accounts:	
Private	CCP § 704.115	Escrow or Trust Funds	Fin C § 17410
Public	CCP § 704.110	Social Security Direct	
Public Assistance	CCP § 704.170	Deposits	CCP § 704.080
	Welf & I C § 17409	Direct Deposit Account—	
Public Employees—		Social Security	CCP § 704.080
Death Benefits	CCP § 704.110	Disability Insurance Benefits	CCP § 704.130
Pension	CCP § 704.110	Dwelling House	CCP § 704.740
Retirement Benefits	CCP § 704.110	Earnings	CCP § 704.070
Vacation Credits	CCP § 704.113		CCP § 706.050
Railroad Retirement Benefits	45 USC § 228*l*		15 USC § 1673(a)
Railroad Unemployment		Educational Grant	Ed C § 21116
Insurance	45 USC § 352(e)		

(Continued on reverse)

Approved by the Judicial Council of California
EJ-155 [Rev. January 1, 1985]   **EXEMPTIONS FROM THE ENFORCEMENT OF JUDGMENTS**   CCP 681.030(c) CCP 700.010

151

EXEMPTIONS FROM THE ENFORCEMENT OF JUDGMENTS
(Continued)

Type of Property	Code and Section	Type of Property	Code and Section
Employment Bonds	Lab C § 404	Peace Officers Retirement	
Financial Assistance:		Benefits	CCP § 704.110
Charity	CCP § 704.170		Govt C § 31913
Public Assistance	CCP § 704.170	Personal Effects	CCP § 704.020
	Welf & I C § 17409	Personal Injury Actions	
Student Aid	CCP § 704.190	or Damages	CCP § 704.140
Welfare (See Public		Pension Plans:	
Assistance)		Private	CCP § 704.115
Fire Service Retirement	CCP § 704.110	Public	CCP § 704.110
	Govt C § 32210	Prisoner's Funds	CCP § 704.090
Fraternal Organizations		Property Not Subject to	
Funds and Benefits	CCP § 704.130	Enforcement of Money	
	CCP § 704.170	Judgments	CCP § 704.210
Fuel for Residence	CCP § 704.020	Prosthetic & Orthopedic	
Furniture	CCP § 704.020	Devices	CCP § 704.050
General Assignment for		Provisions (for Residence)	CCP § 704.020
Benefit of Creditors	CCP § 1801	Public Assistance	CCP § 704.170
Health Aids	CCP § 704.050		Welf & I C § 17409
Health Insurance Benefits	CCP § 704.130	Public Employees:	
Home:		Death Benefits	CCP § 704.110
Building Materials	CCP § 704.030	Pension	CCP § 704.110
Dwelling House	CCP § 704.740	Retirement Benefits	CCP § 704.110
Homestead	CCP § 704.720	Vacation Credits	CCP § 704.113
	CCP § 704.730	Railroad Retirement Benefits	45 USC § 228l
Housetrailer	CCP § 704.710	Railroad Unemployment	
Mobilehome	CCP § 704.710	Insurance	45 USC § 352(e)
Homestead	CCP § 704.720	Relocation Benefits	CCP § 704.180
	CCP § 704.730	Retirement Benefits &	
Household Furnishings	CCP § 704.020	Contributions—	
Irrigation System		Private	CCP § 704.115
Retirement Benefits	CCP § 704.110	Public	CCP § 704.110
Insurance:			Ins C § 10498.5
Disability Insurance	CCP § 704.130	Segregated Benefit Funds	Ins C § 10498.6
Fraternal Benefit Society	CCP § 704.110	Social Security	42 USC § 407
Group Life	CCP § 704.100	Social Security	
Health Insurance Benefits	CCP § 704.130	Direct Deposit Account	CCP § 704.080
Individual	CCP § 704.100	Soldiers & Sailors Property	50 USC § 523(b)
Insurance Proceeds —		Strike Benefits	CCP § 704.120
Motor Vehicle	CCP § 704.010	Student Aid	CCP § 704.190
Jewelry	CCP § 704.040	Tools of Trade	CCP § 704.060
Judges Survivors Benefits		Transit District Retirement	
(Federal)	28 USC § 376(n)	Benefits (Alameda & Contra	
Legislators Retirement		Costa Counties)	CCP § 704.110
Benefits	CCP § 704.110		Pub Util C § 25337
	Govt C § 9359.3	Travelers Check Sales Proceeds	Fin C § 1875
Licenses	CCP § 695.060	Unemployment Benefits &	
	CCP § 720(a)(1)	Contributions	CCP § 704.120
Lighthouse Keepers Widows		Uniforms	CCP § 704.060
Benefits	33 USC § 775	Vacation Credits (Public	
Longshore & Harbor Workers		Employees)	CCP § 704.113
Compensation or Benefits	33 USC § 916	Veterans Benefits	38 USC § 3101
Military Benefits:		Veterans Medal of Honor	
Retirement	10 USC § 1440	Benefits	38 USC § 562
Survivors	10 USC § 1450	Wages	CCP § 704.070
Military Personnel — Property	50 USC § 523(b)		CCP § 706.050
Motor Vehicle (including			CCP § 706.051
proceeds)	CCP § 704.010	Welfare Payments	CCP § 704.170
	CCP § 704.060		Welf & I C § 17409
Municipal Utility District		Workers Compensation	
Retirement Benefits	CCP § 704.110	Claims or Awards	CCP § 704.160
	Pub Util C § 12337	Wrongful Death Actions or	
		Damages	CCP § 704.150

Name and Address of Court:

SMALL CLAIMS CASE NO.

| PLAINTIFF/DEMANDANTE *(Name, address, and telephone number of each)*: | DEFENDANT/DEMANDADO *(Name, address, and telephone number of each)*: |

Telephone No.:

Telephone No.:

Telephone No.:

Telephone No.:

☐ See attached sheet for additional plaintiffs and defendants.

NOTICE OF FILING NOTICE OF APPEAL

TO: ☐ Plaintiff *(name)*:
☐ Defendant *(name)*:

| Your small claims case has been APPEALED to the superior court. Do not contact the small claims court about this appeal. The superior court will notify you of the date you should appear in court. The notice of appeal is set forth below. | *La decisión hecha por la corte para reclamos judiciales menores en su caso ha sido APELADA ante la corte superior. No se ponga en contacto con la corte para reclamos judiciales menores acerca de esta apelación. La corte superior le notificará la fecha en que usted debe presentarse ante ella. El aviso de la apelación aparece a continuación.* |

Date: _____ Clerk, by _____ , Deputy

NOTICE OF APPEAL

I appeal to the superior court, as provided by law, from
☐ the small claims judgment **or** ☐ the denial of the motion to vacate the small claims judgment.

| **DATE APPEAL FILED** *(clerk to insert date)*: |

▶ _____
· (SIGNATURE OF APPELLANT OR APPELLANT'S ATTORNEY)
(TYPE OR PRINT NAME)

☐ I am an insurer of defendant *(name)* _____ in this case. The judgment against defendant exceeds $2,500, and the policy of insurance with the defendant covers the matter to which the judgment applies.

▶ _____
· (SIGNATURE OF DECLARANT)
(NAME OF INSURER)

CLERK'S CERTIFICATE OF MAILING

I certify that
1. I am not a party to this action.
2. This Notice of Filing Notice of Appeal and Notice of Appeal were mailed first class, postage prepaid, in a sealed envelope to
☐ plaintiff
☐ defendant
at the address shown above.
3. The mailing and this certification occurred
at *(place)*: _____ , California,
on *(date)*: _____

Clerk, by _____ , Deputy

| Form Adopted by the Judicial Council of California SC-140 [Rev. January 1, 1992] | **NOTICE OF APPEAL** (Small Claims) | Rule 982.7 Code of Civil Procedure, § 116.710 |

153

ATTORNEY OR PARTY WITHOUT ATTORNEY *(Name and Address)*:	TELEPHONE NO.:	**FOR COURT USE ONLY**

ATTORNEY FOR *(Name)*:

INSERT NAME OF COURT, JUDICIAL DISTRICT, AND BRANCH COURT, IF ANY:

PLAINTIFF:

DEFENDANT:

MEMORANDUM OF COSTS (SUMMARY)

CASE NUMBER:

The following costs are requested:　　　　　　　　　　　　**TOTALS**

1. a. ☐ Filing and motion fees . . . . 1a. $ _____

   b. ☐ Jury fees . . . . 1b. $ _____

2. ☐ Jury food and lodging . . . . 2. $ _____

3. ☐ Deposition costs . . . . 3. $ _____

4. ☐ Service of process . . . . 4. $ _____

5. ☐ Attachment expenses. . . . . 5. $ _____

6. ☐ Surety bond premiums . . . . 6. $ _____

7. ☐ Witness fees . . . . 7. $ _____

8. ☐ Court-ordered transcripts . . . . 8. $ _____

9. ☐ Attorney fees authorized by statute, assessed upon motion or by this memorandum . . . . 9. $ _____

10. ☐ Models, blowups, and photocopies of exhibits . . . . 10. $ _____

11. ☐ Other . . . . 11. $ _____

12. TOTAL COSTS . . . . **TOTAL** $ _____

13. I am the attorney, agent, or party who claims these costs. To the best of my knowledge and belief this memorandum of costs is correct and these costs were necessarily incurred in this case.

I declare under penalty of perjury under the laws of the State of California that the foregoing is true and correct.

Date:

. . . .
(TYPE OR PRINT NAME)　　　　　　　　　▶　　　　(SIGNATURE OF DECLARANT)

(Proof of service on reverse)

Form Approved by the
Judicial Council of California
MC-010 [New January 1, 1987]

MEMORANDUM OF COSTS (SUMMARY)

CCP 1032, 1033.5

155

PROOF OF SERVICE

☐ **Personal Service**   ☐ **Mail**

1. At the time of service I was at least 18 years of age and **not a party to this legal action.**

2. I served a copy of the Memorandum of Costs (Summary) as follows *(check either a or b below)*:

   a. ☐ **Personal service.** I personally delivered the Memorandum of Costs (Summary) as follows:
      (1) Name of person served:
      (2) Address where served:

      (3) Date served:
      (4) Time served:

   b. ☐ **Mail.** I deposited the Memorandum of Costs (Summary) in the United States mail, in a sealed envelope with postage fully prepaid. The envelope was addressed as follows:
      (1) Name of person served:
      (2) Address:

      (3) Date of mailing:
      (4) Place of mailing *(city and state)*:
      (5) I am a resident of or employed in the county where the Memorandum of Costs (Summary) was mailed.

   c. My residence or business address is *(specify)*:

   d. My phone number is *(specify)*:

I declare under penalty of perjury under the laws of the State of California that the foregoing is true and correct.

Date:

....
(TYPE OR PRINT NAME)

▶ _____
(SIGNATURE OF DECLARANT)

Name and Address of Court:

SMALL CLAIMS CASE NO.

PLAINTIFF/DEMANDANTE *(Name, address, and telephone number of each):*

DEFENDANT/DEMANDADO *(Name, address, and telephone number of each):*

Telephone No.:

Telephone No.:

Telephone No.:

Telephone No.:

☐ See attached sheet for additional plaintiffs and defendants.

REQUEST TO CORRECT OR VACATE JUDGMENT

FILING THIS REQUEST DOES NOT INCREASE THE TIME FOR FILING A NOTICE OF APPEAL

REQUEST TO ☐ CORRECT ☐ VACATE JUDGMENT

1. I request the court to make an order to ☐ correct ☐ vacate the judgment entered on *(date)*:
2. My request is based on this declaration and the records on file with the court.

DECLARATION SUPPORTING MY REQUEST

3. I am the ☐ plaintiff ☐ defendant in this action.
4. The facts supporting this request
   a. ☐ to correct a clerical error in the judgment
   b. ☐ to set aside or vacate the judgment on the grounds of an incorrect or erroneous legal basis for the decision
   are as follows *(specify facts, statute, rule of court case law, etc.)*:

☐ Item 4 continued on attached page.

I declare under penalty of perjury under the laws of the State of California that the foregoing is true and correct.

Date:

. . . .
(TYPE OR PRINT NAME)

▶

(SIGNATURE)

5. If you wish to oppose this request, please file a response with the court within 15 days and serve a copy on the opposing side.

No hearing will be held unless ordered by the court.

CLERK'S CERTIFICATE OF MAILING

I certify that I am not a party to this action. A copy of this Request was mailed first class, postage prepaid, in a sealed envelope to the responding party at the address shown above. The mailing and this certification occurred
at *(place)*: _____ , California,
on *(date)*:

Clerk, by _____ , Deputy

— The county provides small claims advisor services free of charge. —

Form Approved by the
Judicial Council of California
SC-108 [New January 1, 1994]

REQUEST TO CORRECT OR VACATE JUDGMENT
(Small Claims)

Code of Civil Procedure, § 116.725

ORDER

1. ☐ Request is granted.

2. ☐ Request is denied.

3. ☐ A hearing on this request is scheduled as follows:

DATE	DAY	TIME	PLACE

4. ☐ Other orders:

5. ☐ Comments, if any:

Date: _____

_____

(JUDGE)

Name and Address of Court:

SMALL CLAIMS CASE NO.:

PLAINTIFF/DEMANDANTE *(Name, street address, and telephone number of each)*:

DEFENDANT/DEMANDADO *(Name, street address, and telephone number of each)*:

Telephone No.:

Telephone No.:

Telephone No.:

Telephone No.:

☐ See attached sheet for additional plaintiffs and defendants.

NOTICE TO *(Name)*:

One of the parties has asked the court to CANCEL the small claims judgment in your case. If you disagree with this request, you should appear in this court on the hearing date shown below. If the request is granted, ANOTHER TRIAL may immediately be held. Bring all witnesses, books, receipts, and other papers or things with you to support your case.	*Una de las partes en el caso le ha solicitado a la corte que DEJE SIN EFECTO la decisión tomada en su caso por la corte para reclamos judiciales menores. Si usted está en desacuerdo con esta solicitud, debe presentarse en esta corte en la fecha de la audiencia indicada a continuación. Si se concede esta solicitud, es posible que se efectúe otro juicio inmediatamente. Traiga a todos sus testigos, libros, recibos, y otros documentos o cosas para presentarlos en apoyo de su caso.*

NOTICE OF MOTION TO VACATE (CANCEL) JUDGMENT

1. A hearing will be held in this court at which I will ask the court to **cancel** the judgment entered against me in this case. If you wish to oppose the motion you should appear at the court on

HEARING DATE		DATE	DAY	TIME	PLACE	COURT USE
FECHA DEL JUICIO	1.					
	2.					
	3.					

2. I am asking the court to cancel the judgment for the reasons stated in item 5 below. My request is based on this notice of motion and declaration, the records on file with the court, and any evidence that may be presented at the hearing.

DECLARATION FOR MOTION TO VACATE (CANCEL) JUDGMENT

3. Judgment was entered against me in this case on *(date)*:

4. I first learned of the entry of judgment against me on *(date)*:

5. I am asking the court to cancel the judgment for the following reason:

   a. ☐ I did not appear at the trial of this claim because *(specify facts)*:

   b. ☐ Other *(specify facts)*:

6. I understand that I must bring with me to the hearing on this motion all witnesses, books, receipts, and other papers or things to support my case.

I declare under penalty of perjury under the laws of the State of California that the foregoing is true and correct.

Date:

▶

.... (TYPE OR PRINT NAME) ....   (SIGNATURE)

CLERK'S CERTIFICATE OF MAILING

I certify that I am not a party to this action. This Notice of Motion to Vacate Judgment and Declaration was mailed first class, postage prepaid, in a sealed envelope to the responding party at the address shown above. The mailing and this certification occurred

at *(place)*:   , California,

on *(date)*:

Clerk, by _____ , Deputy

— **The county provides small claims advisor services free of charge.** —

Form Approved by the
Judicial Council of California
SC-135 [Rev. January 1, 1997*]

* NOTE: Continued use of form SC-135 (Rev. January 1, 1992) is authorized through December 31, 1997.

NOTICE OF MOTION TO VACATE JUDGMENT AND DECLARATION
(Small Claims)

Cal. Rules of Court, rule 982.7
Code of Civil Procedure,
§§ 116.720, 116.730, 116.740

_____

_____

_____

(type in name and address of court)

	)	CASE NO._____
	)	
	)	
plaintiff	)	
	)	
	)	**ORDER**
	)	**STAYING PROCEEDINGS**
vs.	)	**ON WRIT**
	)	
	)	
defendant	)	
	)	
	)	
	)	
	)	
_____	)	

TO THE MARSHAL OF THE MUNICIPAL COURT OF _____ _____JUDICIAL DISTRICT (or other Peace Officer holding the writ). ADDRESS of Marshal/Sheriff holding the writ: _____ _____.

A Writ of Execution for the enforcement of the judgment entered above entitled action having been issued on _____ and delivered to you for service, and _____ _____, defendant in the above entitled action, having filed a Motion to Vacate said judgment, and said motion having been set for hearing in Division # _____ on _____ at _____AM/PM, you are hereby ordered to stay all further proceedings for the enforcement of said judgment pursuant to said writ until said motion is heard and determined.

_____   _____
            DATE   JUDGE, MUNICIPAL COURT

Name and Address of Court:

SMALL CLAIMS CASE NO.

PLAINTIFF/DEMANDANTE *(Name and address of each)*:	DEFENDANT/DEMANDADO *(Name and address of each)*:

☐ See attached sheet for additional plaintiffs and defendants.

REQUEST TO PAY JUDGMENT TO COURT

1. **Instead of paying** the judgment directly to the creditor, I want to pay it to the court.
2. Date judgment was entered *(specify)*:
3. **Judgment creditor** *(the person or business you were ordered to pay)*
   a. Full name:
   b. Address *(use last known)*:

4. **I understand** that the amount of money I must pay to get a satisfaction of judgment is the total of the
   a. principal amount of money the court ordered me to pay,
   b. costs (if awarded by the court),
   c. interest accrued on the judgment,
   d. the court's processing fee, and
   e. other charges the court has added to the judgment. *(The court will calculate the total (see reverse).)*
5. **Partial payment** *(Complete this section if you have ALREADY PAID PART of the judgment.)*
   ☐ I have already paid part of the judgment.
   Amount paid: $ *(check one or both of the boxes below)*
   a. ☐ by check or money order. *(Attach a copy of both sides of the canceled check or money order.)*
   b. ☐ by cash. *(Attach a copy of the signed, dated cash receipt.)*
6. I understand that if I pay by personal check, satisfaction of judgment will be delayed 30 days.
7. **I request the court** to calculate the total amount required to enter a satisfaction of judgment, and to enter a satisfaction of judgment after I have paid the total amount to the court.

I declare under penalty of perjury under the laws of the State of California that the foregoing is true and correct.

Date:

▶

....
(TYPE OR PRINT NAME)   (SIGNATURE OF JUDGMENT DEBTOR)

Judgment creditor: See important notice on reverse.

CERTIFICATION	SATISFACTION OF JUDGMENT (for court use only)
I certify that this document is a true and correct copy of the original on file with this court. (Seal) Clerk, by _____, Deputy	(1) ☐ Full satisfaction of judgment entered as to judgment debtor *(name)*: on *(date)*: (2) ☐ Full satisfaction of judgment NOT entered as requested *(state reason)*: Clerk, by _____, Deputy

(Continued on reverse)

Form Adopted by the
Judicial Council of California
SC-145 [New January 1, 1990]

**REQUEST TO PAY
JUDGMENT TO COURT
(Small Claims)**

Rule 982.7

PLAINTIFF:	CASE NUMBER:
DEFENDANT:	

FOR COURT USE ONLY

1. Judgment entered on *(date)*:

2. **Amount to be paid as of date of request** *(specify)*:

   a. Unpaid principal . . . . $

   b. Costs . . . . $

   c. Post judgment costs . . . . $

   d. Credits *(see receipts)* . . . . $

   e. Interest accrued (to date in item 2, above) . . . . $

   f. Processing fee . . . . $

   g. Other *(specify)* . . . . $

   SUBTOTAL $

   Add interest at: $ per day *(from date in item 2)* . . . . $

   TOTAL $ _____

CLERK'S CERTIFICATE OF MAILING

I certify that I am not a party to this action. This Notice to Judgment Creditor was mailed first class, postage prepaid, in a sealed envelope to the address shown in item 3 on the reverse. The mailing and this certification occurred
at *(place)*:   California,
on *(date)*:

Clerk, by _____ , Deputy

NOTICE TO JUDGMENT CREDITOR

1. The judgment debtor has fully satisfied the judgment entered by making payment to the court in the amount shown above.

2. You may claim this money by

   a. presenting this form in person to the court clerk during regular business hours,
   -OR-

   b. mailing this form to the court.

3. Complete the Judgment Creditor's Request for Funds below.

4. Money not claimed within three years becomes the property of the court *(see Government Code sections 50050-50056).*

JUDGMENT CREDITOR'S REQUEST FOR FUNDS

I request the court to pay the money to me by mail at my current address *(specify)*:

(Mail or deliver this form to the court clerk. Keep a photocopy for yourself.)

Date:

▶

. . . .

(TYPE OR PRINT NAME)   (SIGNATURE OF JUDGMENT CREDITOR)

**REQUEST TO PAY
JUDGMENT TO COURT
(Small Claims)**

Name and Address of Court:

SMALL CLAIMS CASE NO.

PLAINTIFF/DEMANDANTE *(Name, address, and telephone number of each):*

DEFENDANT/DEMANDADO *(Name, address, and telephone number of each):*

Telephone No.:

Telephone No.:

Telephone No.:

Telephone No.:

☐ See attached sheet for additional plaintiffs and defendants.

REQUEST TO PAY JUDGMENT IN INSTALLMENTS

1. I request the court to allow me to make installment payments on the judgment entered against me in this case in the amount and manner stated below.

2. My request is based on this declaration, the court records, my completed financial declaration (Form EJ-165—*obtain from court clerk*) attached to this declaration, and any other evidence that may be presented.

   NOTE: YOU MUST ATTACH A COMPLETED FINANCIAL DECLARATION WITH THIS REQUEST TO MAKE INSTALLMENT PAYMENTS.

3. Judgment was entered against me in this matter on *(date)*:   in the amount of *(specify)*: $

4. Payment of the entire amount of the judgment at one time will be a hardship on me because *(specify)*:

5. I can and will make payments toward the judgment in the amount of *(specify)*: $ per ☐ week ☐ month.

6. I request the court to order that I make payments as specified in item 5 and that execution on the judgment be stayed as long as I make payments according to this schedule.

I declare under penalty of perjury under the laws of the State of California that the foregoing is true and correct.

Date:

▶

. . . .
(TYPE OR PRINT NAME)

(SIGNATURE OF JUDGMENT DEBTOR)

NOTICE TO JUDGMENT CREDITOR

The judgment debtor has requested the court to allow payment of the judgment in installments. Complete the following and return this form to the court within 10 days. You will be notified of the court's order, or, if a hearing is necessary, the date of the hearing.

1. I am the judgment creditor, and I have read and considered the judgment debtor's request to make installment payments on the judgment.

2. a. ☐ I am willing to accept the payment schedule the judgment debtor has requested.
   b. ☐ I am willing to accept payments in the amount of *(specify)*: $ per ☐ week ☐ month.
   c. ☐ I am opposed to accepting installment payments because *(specify)*:

I declare under penalty of perjury under the laws of the State of California that the foregoing is true and correct.

Date:

▶

. . . .
(TYPE OR PRINT NAME)

(SIGNATURE OF JUDGMENT CREDITOR)

SEE REVERSE FOR HEARING DATE, IF ANY.

(Continued on reverse)

Form Approved by the
Judicial Council of California
SC-106 [New January 1. 1992]

REQUEST TO PAY JUDGMENT IN INSTALLMENTS
(Small Claims)

Code of Civil Procedure, § 116.620(b)

NOTICE OF MOTION

A hearing will be held on this request as follows:

		DATE	DAY	TIME	PLACE
HEARING DATE	1.				
	2.				
FECHA DEL JUICIO	3.				
	4.				

COURT ORDER

1. ☐ The judgment debtor shall pay the full amount of the judgment immediately.
2. ☐ The judgment debtor may pay the judgment as follows:
   a. *(If initial lump sum ordered)* Pay $ _____ on *(date)*:
   b. Pay $ _____ or more on *(specify)*: _____ of every *(specify)*: _____
      until the judgment is fully paid.
3. *(Missed payments)* On the filing of an affidavit or declaration by the judgment creditor showing that any payment due has not been paid, this order shall be set aside and the clerk may issue a writ of execution immediately, without further order of the court.

Date:

_____
(JUDGE OR COMMISSIONER)

WARNING: IF YOU MISS A PAYMENT, THE BALANCE OWING ON THE JUDGMENT WILL BECOME DUE IMMEDIATELY.

CLERK'S CERTIFICATE OF MAILING—NOTICE TO JUDGMENT CREDITOR

I certify that I am not a party to this action. This Notice to Judgment Creditor was mailed first class, postage prepaid, in a sealed envelope to the responding party at the address shown on the reverse. The mailing and this certification occurred
at *(place)*: _____ , California,
on *(date)*:

Clerk, by _____ , Deputy

CLERK'S CERTIFICATE OF MAILING — NOTICE OF MOTION

I certify that I am not a party to this action. This Notice of Motion was mailed first class, postage prepaid, in a sealed envelope to the responding party at the address shown on the reverse. The mailing and this certification occurred
at *(place)*: _____ , California,
on *(date)*:

Clerk, by _____ , Deputy

CLERK'S CERTIFICATE OF MAILING — COURT ORDER

I certify that I am not a party to this action. This Court Order was mailed first class, postage prepaid, in a sealed envelope to the responding party at the address shown on the reverse. The mailing and this certification occurred
at *(place)*: _____ , California,
on *(date)*:

Clerk, by _____ , Deputy

MAIL TO THE JUDGMENT CREDITOR
DO NOT FILE WITH THE COURT

JUDGMENT CREDITOR (the person or business who won the case) *(name)*:

JUDGMENT DEBTOR (the person or business who lost the case and owes money) *(name)*:

SMALL CLAIMS CASE NO.:

NOTICE TO JUDGMENT DEBTOR: You *must* (1) pay the judgment or (2) appeal or (3) file a motion to vacate. If you fail to pay or take one of the other two actions, you must complete and mail this form to the judgment creditor. If you do not, you may have to go to court to answer questions and may have penalties imposed on you by the court.	**AVISO AL DEUDOR POR FALLO JUDICIAL: Usted debe (1) pagar el monto del fallo judicial, o (2) presentar un recurso de apelación o (3) presentar un recurso de nulidad.** Si usted no paga el fallo o presenta uno de estos dos recursos, deberá llenar y enviar por correo este formulario a su acreedor por fallo judicial. Si no lo hace, es posible que deba presentarse ante la corte para contestar preguntas y pagar las multas que la corte le pueda imponer.

INSTRUCTIONS

The small claims court has ruled that you owe money to the judgment creditor.

1. You may appeal a judgment against you only on the other party's claim. You may *not* appeal a judgment against you on *your* claim.

   a. If you appeared at the trial and you want to appeal, you must file a *Notice of Appeal* (form SC-140) within 30 days after the date the *Notice of Entry of Judgment* (form SC-130) was mailed or handed to you by the clerk.

   b. If you did not appear at the trial, before you can appeal, you must first file a *Notice of Motion to Vacate Judgment and Declaration (form SC-135)* and pay the required fee within 30 days after the date the *Notice of Entry of Judgment* was mailed or handed to you, and the judgment cannot be collected until the motion is decided. If your motion is denied, you then have 10 days after the date the notice of denial was mailed to file your appeal.

2. Unless you **pay the judgment or appeal or file a motion to vacate, you must fill out this form and mail it to the person who won the case** within **30 days** after the *Notice of Entry of Judgment* was mailed or handed to you by the clerk.

3. If you lose your appeal or motion to vacate, you must pay the judgment, including post-judgment costs and interest, and complete and mail this form to the judgment creditor within **30 days** after the date the clerk mails or delivers to you (a) the denial of your motion to vacate, or (b) the dismissal of your appeal, or (c) the judgment against you on your appeal.

4. As soon as the small claims court denies your motion to vacate and the denial is not appealed, or receives the dismissal of your appeal or judgment from the superior court after appeal, the judgment is no longer suspended and may be immediately enforced against you by the judgment creditor.

If you were sued as an individual, skip this box and begin with item 1 below. Otherwise, check the applicable box, attach the documents indicated, and complete item 15 on the reverse.

a. ☐ *(Corporation or partnership)* Attached to this form is a statement describing the nature, value, and exact location of all assets of the corporation or the partners, and a statement showing that the person signing this form is authorized to submit this form on behalf of the corporation or partnership.

b. ☐ *(Governmental agency)* Attached to this form is the statement of an authorized representative of the agency stating when the agency will pay the judgment and any reasons for its failure to do so.

JUDGMENT DEBTOR'S STATEMENT OF ASSETS

EMPLOYMENT

1. What are your sources of income and occupation? *(Provide job title and name of division or office in which you work.)*

2. a. Name and address of your business or employer *(include address of your payroll or human resources department, if different)*:

   b. If not employed, names and addresses of all sources of income *(specify)*:

3. How often are you paid?
   ☐ daily ☐ every two weeks ☐ monthly
   ☐ weekly ☐ twice a month ☐ other *(explain)*:

4. What is your gross pay each pay period? $

5. What is your take-home pay each pay period? $

6. If your spouse earns any income, give the name of your spouse, the name and address of the business or employer, job title, and division or office *(specify)*:

(Continued on reverse)

Form Approved by the
Judicial Council of California
SC-133 [Rev. January 1, 1998]

JUDGMENT DEBTOR'S STATEMENT OF ASSETS
(Small Claims)

Cal. Rules of Court, rule 982.7(a);
Code of Civil Procedure,
§§ 116.620(a), 116.830

167

CASH, BANK DEPOSITS

7. How much money do you have in cash? . . . . $

8. How much other money do you have in banks, savings and loans, credit unions, and other financial institutions either in your own name or jointly *(list):*

Name and address of financial institution	Account number	Individual or joint?	Balance
a.			$
b.			$
c.			$

PROPERTY

9. List all automobiles, other vehicles, and boats owned in your name or jointly:

Make and year	Value	Legal owner if different from registered owner	Amount owed
a.	$		$
b.	$		$
c.	$		$
d.	$		$

10. List all real estate owned in your name or jointly:

Address of real estate	Fair market value		Amount owed
a.	$		$
b.	$		$

OTHER PERSONAL PROPERTY *(Do not list household furniture and furnishings, appliances, or clothing.)*

11. List anything of value not listed above owned in your name or jointly *(continue on attached sheet if necessary):*

Description	Value	Address where property is located
a.	$	
b.	$	
c.	$	

12. Is anyone holding assets for you? ☐ Yes. ☐ No. If yes, describe the assets and give the name and address of the person or entity holding each asset *(specify):*

13. Have you disposed of or transferred any asset within the last 60 days? ☐ Yes. ☐ No. If yes, give the name and address of each person or entity who received any asset and describe each asset *(specify):*

14. If you are not able to pay the judgment in one lump sum, you may be able to make payment arrangements with the person or business who won the case (the judgment creditor). State the amount that you can pay each month: $, beginning on *(date):*   . If you are unable to agree, you may also ask the court for permission to make installment payments by filing a *Request to Pay Judgment in Installments* (form SC-106).

15. I declare under penalty of perjury under the laws of the State of California that the foregoing is true and correct.

Date:

▶

. . . .
(TYPE OR PRINT NAME)   (SIGNATURE)

Mail or deliver this completed form to the judgment creditor at the address shown on the Notice of Entry of Judgment form.

SC-133 [Rev. January 1, 1998]   **JUDGMENT DEBTOR'S STATEMENT OF ASSETS**   Page two
(Small Claims)

168

A Public Service Agency

Certificate of Facts RE Unsatisfied Judgment

(Do not complete or sign until 30 days after finality of judgment unless the court ordered installment payments.) **After completion of this form, please mail it with your check or money order in the amount of $20 to: Financial Responsibility, P.O. Box 942884, Sacramento, CA 94284-0001. DO NOT TAKE IT TO YOUR LOCAL DEPARTMENT OF MOTOR VEHICLES.**

In the _____   Court of _____ _____

Court Code _____

STATE OF _____ CALIFORNIA _____

Plaintiff : _____   Defendant : _____

_____ vs. _____

Case No. : _____   Date Filed : _____

The undersigned Clerk/Judge of the Court hereby certifies as follows:

1. The above judgment was based on a tort claim as a result of a motor vehicle accident.
2. The judgment was entered on _____ 19 ___ , and became final _____ 19 ___ , and remained unsatisfied for thirty days thereafter.
3. Judgment was entered against _____
    _____

    a. Bodily injury _____   d. Costs _____
    b. Damage to property _____   e. Loss of use _____
    c. Wrongful death _____   f. Any other ground _____
    TOTAL _____

4. The court (ordered, did not order) the judgment paid in installments.

    If so ordered, a certified copy of such order must be attached as required by Section 16379 of the Vehicle Code.)

Date _____   SIGNED _____

Official Title _____ CLERK OF THE COURT _____

By _____

Official Title _____

The undersigned creditor/attorney hereby certifies as follows:

5. Date of accident _____
6. Did accident result from the operation of a motor vehicle in California? _____
7. Vehicle involved was owned by _____
8. Vehicle involved was operated by _____
9. Ownership of vehicle resulted in judgment against _____
10. Operation of vehicle resulted in judgment against _____
11. License number of debtor's vehicle involved in the accident _____
12. Identifying information for judgment debtor(s)—enter "unknown", if information not available.
    Full name _____   Former name, or AKA _____
    Current address _____
    Former address _____
    Birthdate or approximate age _____   Calif. Driver License No. _____
    Other information _____

Date _____   Name and address of Judgment Creditor or Attorney

_____   _____

FOR DMV USE ONLY: _____

_____   _____

_____   Signed _____

Court Report of Judgments (Reference 16373 V.C.)

The clerk of a court, or the judge of a court which has no clerk, shall issue upon the request of a judgment creditor, a certified copy of the judgment or a certified copy of the docket entries in an action resulting in a judgment for damages, and a certificate of facts relative to such judgment on a form provided by the Department, the rendering and nonpayment of which judgment requires the Department to suspend the driver license of the judgment debtor. The document shall be forwarded immediately upon the expiration of thirty days after the judgment has become final and when the judgment has not been stayed or satisfied within the amounts specified in this chapter as shown by the records of the court. Department of Motor Vehicles, P.O. Box 942884, Sacramento, CA 94284-0001.

DL 30 (REV 3/93)

ATTORNEY OR PARTY WITHOUT ATTORNEY *(Name and Address)*:

☐ Recording requested by and return to:

TELEPHONE NO.:

FOR RECORDER'S USE ONLY

☐ ATTORNEY FOR ☐ JUDGMENT CREDITOR ☐ ASSIGNEE OF RECORD

NAME OF COURT:

STREET ADDRESS:

MAILING ADDRESS:

CITY AND ZIP CODE:

BRANCH NAME:

PLAINTIFF:

DEFENDANT:

WRIT OF

☐ EXECUTION (Money Judgment)
☐ POSSESSION OF ☐ Personal Property
☐ Real Property
☐ SALE

CASE NUMBER:

FOR COURT USE ONLY

1. **To the Sheriff or any Marshal or Constable of the County of:**

   You are directed to enforce the judgment described below with daily interest and your costs as provided by law.

2. **To any registered process server:** You are authorized to serve this writ only in accord with CCP 699.080 or CCP 715.040.

3. *(Name)*:
   is the ☐ judgment creditor ☐ assignee of record
   whose address is shown on this form above the court's name.

4. **Judgment debtor** *(name and last known address)*:

   ☐ additional judgment debtors on reverse

5. **Judgment entered** on *(date)*:

6. ☐ **Judgment renewed** on *(dates)*:

7. **Notice of sale** under this writ
   a. ☐ has not been requested.
   b. ☐ has been requested *(see reverse)*.

8. ☐ Joint debtor information on reverse.

[SEAL]

9. ☐ See reverse for information on real or personal property to be delivered under a writ of possession or sold under a writ of sale.

10. ☐ This writ is issued on a sister-state judgment.

11. Total judgment . . . . $

12. Costs after judgment (per filed order or memo CCP 685.090) . . . . $

13. Subtotal *(add 11 and 12)* . . . . $ _____

14. Credits . . . . $

15. Subtotal *(subtract 14 from 13)* . . . . . $ _____

16. Interest after judgment (per filed affidavit CCP 685.050) . . . . $

17. Fee for issuance of writ . . . . $

18. **Total** *(add 15, 16, and 17)* . . . . . . $ _____

19. Levying officer:
    (a) Add daily interest from date of writ
        (at the legal rate on 15) of. . . . . $
    (b) Pay directly to court costs included in 11 and 17 (GC 6103.5, 68511.3; CCP 699.520(i)) . . . . $

20. ☐ The amounts called for in items 11-19 are different for each debtor. These amounts are stated for each debtor on Attachment 20.

Issued on *(date)*:

Clerk, by _____, Deputy

— **NOTICE TO PERSON SERVED: SEE REVERSE FOR IMPORTANT INFORMATION.** —

(Continued on reverse)

Form Approved by the
Judicial Council of California
EJ-130 [Rev. January 1, 1997*]

WRIT OF EXECUTION

Code of Civil Procedure, §§ 699.520, 712.010, 715.010

* *See note on reverse.*

— Items continued from the first page —

4. ☐ **Additional judgment debtor** (name and last known address):

7. ☐ **Notice of sale** has been requested by (name and address):

8. ☐ **Joint debtor** was declared bound by the judgment (CCP 989-994)
    a. on (date):
    b. name and address of joint debtor:

    a. on (date):
    b. name and address of joint debtor:

    c. ☐ additional costs against certain joint debtors (itemize):

9. ☐ (Writ of Possession or Writ of Sale) **Judgment** was entered for the following:
    a. ☐ Possession of real property: The complaint was filed on (date):   **(Check (1) or (2)):**
        (1) ☐ The Prejudgment Claim of Right to Possession was served in compliance with CCP 415.46.
            The judgment includes all tenants, subtenants, named claimants, and other occupants of the premises.
        (2) ☐ The Prejudgment Claim of Right to Possession was NOT served in compliance with CCP 415.46.
            (a) $ was the daily rental value on the date the complaint was filed.
            (b) The court will hear objections to enforcement of the judgment under CCP 1174.3 on the following
                dates (specify):
    b. ☐ Possession of personal property
        ☐ If delivery cannot be had, then for the value (itemize in 9e) specified in the judgment or supplemental order.
    c. ☐ Sale of personal property
    d. ☐ Sale of real property
    e. Description of property:

— NOTICE TO PERSON SERVED —
WRIT OF EXECUTION OR SALE. Your rights and duties are indicated on the accompanying Notice of Levy.
WRIT OF POSSESSION OF PERSONAL PROPERTY. If the levying officer is not able to take custody of the property, the levying officer will make a demand upon you for the property. If custody is not obtained following demand, the judgment may be enforced as a money judgment for the value of the property specified in the judgment or in a supplemental order.
WRIT OF POSSESSION OF REAL PROPERTY. If the premises are not vacated within five days after the date of service on the occupant or, if service is by posting, within five days after service on you, the levying officer will remove the occupants from the real property and place the judgment creditor in possession of the property. Except for a mobile home, personal property remaining on the premises will be sold or otherwise disposed of in accordance with CCP 1174 unless you or the owner of the property pays the judgment creditor the reasonable cost of storage and takes possession of the personal property not later than 15 days after the time the judgment creditor takes possession of the premises.
► A Claim of Right to Possession form accompanies this writ (unless the Summons was served in compliance with CCP 415.46).

EJ-130 [Rev. January 1, 1997*]
* NOTE: Continued use of form EJ-130 (Rev. July 1, 1996) is authorized through December 31, 1997.
WRIT OF EXECUTION
Page two

172

[NOT FOR WAGE GARNISHMENT]
[RETURN TO LEVYING OFFICER. DO NOT FILE WITH COURT]

ATTORNEY OR PARTY WITHOUT ATTORNEY *(Name and Address)*:	TELEPHONE NO.:	LEVYING OFFICER *(Name and Address)*:

ATTORNEY FOR *(Name)*:

NAME OF COURT, JUDICIAL DISTRICT OR BRANCH COURT, IF ANY:

PLAINTIFF:

DEFENDANT:

CLAIM OF EXEMPTION (Enforcement of Judgment)	LEVYING OFFICER FILE NO.:	COURT CASE NO.:

Copy all the information required above (except the top left space) from the Notice of Levy. The top left space is for your name or your attorney's name and address. The original and one copy of this form must be filed with the levying officer. DO NOT FILE WITH THE COURT.

1. My name is *(specify)*:
2. Papers should be sent to
   ☐ me.
   ☐ my attorney (I have filed with the court and served on the judgment creditor a request that papers be sent to my attorney and my attorney has consented in writing on the request to receive these papers.)
   at the address ☐ shown above ☐ following *(specify)*:

3. ☐ I am not the judgment debtor named in the notice of levy. The name and last known address of the judgment debtor is *(specify)*:

4. The property I claim to be exempt is *(describe)*:

5. The property is claimed to be exempt under the following code and section *(specify)*:

6. The facts which support this claim are *(describe)*:

7. ☐ The claim is made pursuant to a provision exempting property to the extent necessary for the support of the judgment debtor and the spouse and dependents of the judgment debtor. **A Financial Statement form is attached to this claim.**

8. ☐ The property claimed to be exempt is
   a. ☐ a motor vehicle, the proceeds of an execution sale of a motor vehicle, or the proceeds of insurance or other indemnification for the loss, damage, or destruction of a motor vehicle.
   b. ☐ tools, implements, materials, uniforms, furnishings, books, equipment, a commercial motor vehicle, a vessel, or other personal property used in the trade, business or profession of the judgment debtor or spouse.
   c. all other property of the same type owned by the judgment debtor, either alone or in combination with others, is *(describe)*:

9. ☐ The property claimed to be exempt consists of the loan value of unmatured life insurance policies (including endowment and annuity policies) or benefits from matured life insurance policies (including endowment and annuity policies). All other property of the same type owned by the judgment debtor or the spouse of the judgment debtor, either alone or in combination with others, is *(describe)*:

I declare under penalty of perjury under the laws of the State of California that the foregoing is true and correct.

Date:

▶

· ·
(TYPE OR PRINT NAME)

_____
(SIGNATURE OF CLAIMANT)

Form Approved by the Judicial Council of California EJ-160 [New July 1, 1983]	**CLAIM OF EXEMPTION** (Enforcement of Judgment)	CCP 703.520

173

ATTORNEY OR PARTY WITHOUT ATTORNEY *(Name and Address)*:	TELEPHONE NO.:	LEVYING OFFICER *(Name and Address)*:

ATTORNEY FOR *(Name)*:

NAME OF COURT, JUDICIAL DISTRICT OR BRANCH COURT, IF ANY:

PLAINTIFF
:

DEFENDANT:

CLAIM OF EXEMPTION (Wage Garnishment)	LEVYING OFFICER FILE NO.:	COURT CASE NO.:

—READ THE EMPLOYEE INSTRUCTIONS BEFORE COMPLETING THIS FORM—

for your name or your attorney's name and address. The original and one copy of this form with the Financial Statement attached must be filed with the levying officer. **DO NOT FILE WITH THE COURT.**

1. I need the following earnings to support myself or my family *(check a or b)*:
   a. ☐ All earnings.
   b. ☐ $ _____ each pay period.

2. Please send all papers to
   ☐ me
   ☐ my attorney
   at the address ☐ shown above ☐ following *(specify)*:

3. I am willing for the following amount to be withheld from my earnings **each pay period** during the withholding period. **I under-stand that the judgment creditor can accept this offer by not opposing the Claim of Exemption, which will result in the following sum being withheld each pay period** *(check a or b)*:
   a. ☐ None
   b. ☐ Withhold $ _____ each pay period.

4. I am paid
   ☐ daily ☐ every two weeks ☐ monthly
   ☐ weekly ☐ twice a month ☐ other *(specify)*:

NOTE: *You must attach a properly completed Financial Statement form to this Claim of Exemption.*
The Financial Statement form is available without charge from the levying officer.

I declare under penalty of perjury under the laws of the State of California that the foregoing is true and correct.

Date:

. . . .   ▶ _____
(TYPE OR PRINT NAME)   *(SIGNATURE OF DECLARANT)*

Form Adopted by the
Judicial Council of California
982.5(5) [Rev. July 1, 1983]

CLAIM OF EXEMPTION
(Wage Garnishment)

CCP 706.124

ATTORNEY OR PARTY WITHOUT ATTORNEY *(Name and Address)*:	TELEPHONE NO.:	*FOR COURT USE ONLY*
ATTORNEY FOR *(Name)*:		

NAME OF COURT, JUDICIAL DISTRICT OR BRANCH COURT, IF ANY:

PLAINTIFF:

DEFENDANT:

NOTICE OF HEARING ON CLAIM OF EXEMPTION **(Wage Garnishment—Enforcement of Judgment)**	LEVYING OFFICER FILE NO.:	COURT CASE NO.:

1. **TO:**

Name and address of levying officer

Name and address of judgment debtor

☐ Claimant, if other than judgment debtor *(name and address)*:

☐ Judgment debtor's attorney *(name and address)*:

2. **A hearing to determine the claim of exemption of**
   ☐ judgment debtor
   ☐ other claimant
   will be held as follows:

   a. date: time: ☐ dept.:   ☐ div.:   ☐ rm.:

   b. address of court:

3. ☐ **The judgment creditor will not appear at the hearing and submits the issue on the papers filed with the court.**

Date:

▶

. . . .
(TYPE OR PRINT NAME)   *(SIGNATURE OF JUDGMENT CREDITOR OR ATTORNEY)*

If you do not attend the hearing, the court may determine your claim based on the Claim of Exemption, Financial Statement (when one is required), Notice of Opposition to Claim of Exemption, and other evidence that may be presented.

(Proof of service on reverse)

Form Adopted by the
Judicial Council of California
982.5(8), EJ-175 [Rev. July 1, 1983]

NOTICE OF HEARING ON CLAIM OF EXEMPTION
(Wage Garnishment—Enforcement of Judgment)

CCP 703.550,
706.105

177

SHORT TITLE:	LEVYING OFFICER FILE NO.:	COURT CASE NO.:

PROOF OF SERVICE BY MAIL

I am over the age of 18 and not a party to this cause. I am a resident of or employed in the county where the mailing occurred. My residence or business address is *(specify)*:

I served the attached Notice of Hearing on Claim of Exemption and the attached Notice of Opposition to Claim of Exemption by enclosing true copies in a sealed envelope addressed to each person whose name and address is given below and depositing the envelope in the United States mail with the postage fully prepaid.

(1) Date of deposit: (2) Place of deposit *(city and state)*:

NAME AND ADDRESS OF EACH PERSON TO WHOM NOTICE WAS MAILED

I declare under penalty of perjury under the laws of the State of California that the foregoing is true and correct.

Date:

▶

. . . .   _____
(TYPE OR PRINT NAME)   *(SIGNATURE OF DECLARANT)*

PROOF OF SERVICE—PERSONAL DELIVERY

I am over the age of 18 and not a party to this cause. My residence or business address is *(specify)*:

I served the attached Notice of Hearing on Claim of Exemption and the attached Notice of Opposition to Claim of Exemption by personally delivering copies to the person served as shown below.

PERSONS SERVED

Name   **Delivery At**
                            Date: Time: Address:

I declare under penalty of perjury under the laws of the State of California that the foregoing is true and correct.

Date:

▶

. . . .   _____
(TYPE OR PRINT NAME)   *(SIGNATURE OF DECLARANT)*

ATTORNEY OR PARTY WITHOUT ATTORNEY *(Name and Address)*:

TELEPHONE NO.:

FOR COURT USE ONLY

ATTORNEY FOR *(Name)*:

NAME OF COURT:
STREET ADDRESS:
MAILING ADDRESS:
CITY AND ZIP CODE:
BRANCH NAME:

PLAINTIFF:

DEFENDANT:

LEVYING OFFICER FILE NO.: | COURT CASE NO.:

NOTICE OF OPPOSITION TO CLAIM OF EXEMPTION
(Enforcement of Judgment)

— *DO NOT USE THIS FORM FOR WAGE GARNISHMENTS* —

The original of this form and a Notice of Hearing on Claim of Exemption must be filed with the court.

A copy of this Notice of Opposition and the Notice of Hearing *must* be filed with the levying officer.

A copy of this Notice of Opposition and the Notice of Hearing must be served on the judgment debtor and other claimant at least 10 days *before* the hearing.

TO THE LEVYING OFFICER:

1. Name and address of judgment creditor

2. Name and address of judgment debtor

Social Security Number *(if known)*:

3. ☐ Name and address of claimant *(if other than judgment debtor)*

4. The notice of filing claim of exemption states it was mailed on *(date)*:

5. The item or items claimed as exempt are
   a. ☐ not exempt under the statutes relied upon in the Claim of Exemption.
   b. ☐ not exempt because the judgment debtor's equity is greater than the amount provided in the exemption.
   c. ☐ other *(specify)*:

6. The facts necessary to support item 5 are
   ☐ continued on the attachment labeled Attachment 6.
   ☐ as follows:

I declare under penalty of perjury under the laws of the State of California that the foregoing is true and correct.

Date:

....
(TYPE OR PRINT NAME)

▶

_____
(SIGNATURE OF DECLARANT)

Form Approved by the
Judicial Council of California
EJ-170 [New July 1, 1983]

NOTICE OF OPPOSITION TO CLAIM OF EXEMPTION
(Enforcement of Judgment)

CCP 703.550

179

ATTORNEY OR PARTY WITHOUT ATTORNEY *(Name and Address)*:   TELEPHONE NO.:

FOR COURT USE ONLY

ATTORNEY FOR *(Name)*:

NAME OF COURT, JUDICIAL DISTRICT OR BRANCH COURT, IF ANY:

PLAINTIFF:

DEFENDANT:

NOTICE OF OPPOSITION TO CLAIM OF EXEMPTION
(Wage Garnishment)

LEVYING OFFICER FILE NO.:   COURT CASE NO.:

TO THE LEVYING OFFICER:

1. Name and address of judgment creditor

2. Name and address of employee

Social Security Number *(if known)*:

3. The Notice of Filing Claim of Exemption states it was mailed on
(date):

4. The earnings claimed as exempt are
   a. ☐ not exempt.
   b. ☐ partially exempt. The amount *not* exempt per month is
   $

5. The judgment creditor opposes the claim of exemption because
   a. ☐ the judgment was for the following common necessaries of life *(specify)*:

   b. ☐ the following expenses of the debtor are *not* necessary for the support of the debtor or the debtor's family *(specify)*:

   c. ☐ other *(specify)*:

6. ☐ The judgment creditor will accept $ per pay period for payment on account of this debt.

I declare under penalty of perjury under the laws of the State of California that the foregoing is true and correct.

Date:

. . . .
(TYPE OR PRINT NAME)

▶ _____
(SIGNATURE OF DECLARANT)

F 0328-245 (6/83)

Form Adopted by the
Judicial Council of California
982.5(7) (Rev. July 1, 1983)

NOTICE OF OPPOSITION TO CLAIM OF EXEMPTION
(Wage Garnishment)

CCP 706.128

181

ATTORNEY OR PARTY WITHOUT ATTORNEY *(Name and Address)*:

TELEPHONE NO.:

FOR COURT USE ONLY

ATTORNEY FOR *(Name)*:

PLAINTIFF:

DEFENDANT:

ORDER DETERMINING CLAIM OF EXEMPTION (Wage Garnishment–Enforcement of Judgment)	LEVYING OFFICER FILE NO.:	COURT CASE NO.:

1. The application of *(name)*:

for an order determining the Claim of Exemption of *(name)*:

was heard on *(date)*:
(Check boxes to indicate personal presence)

☐ Judgment Creditor *(name)*:   ☐ Attorney *(name)*:

☐ Judgment Debtor *(name)*:   ☐ Attorney *(name)*:

2. The court considered the evidence in support of and in opposition to the Claim of Exemption.

3. IT IS ORDERED

a. ☐ The judgment debtor's Claim of Exemption is denied.

b. ☐ The judgment debtor's Claim of Exemption is granted.

c. ☐ The levying officer is directed to release any earnings held to the **judgment debtor**.

d. ☐ The levying officer is directed to release any earnings held to the **judgment creditor** for payment on the **judgment.**

e. ☐ Other orders *(specify)*:

f. The clerk shall transmit a certified copy of this order to the levying officer. The levying officer shall notify **the employer** of any change in the Earnings Withholding Order and release any retained sums as provided in this order.

Date: _____   ▶ _____

(SIGNATURE OF JUDGE)

[SEAL]

CLERK'S CERTIFICATION

I certify that the foregoing is a true and correct copy of the original on file in my office.

Date: _____   Clerk, by _____ , **Deputy**

F051-2728.2

Form Adopted by the
Judicial Council of California
982.5(9) [Rev. July 1, 1983]

ORDER DETERMINING CLAIM OF EXEMPTION
(Wage Garnishment–Enforcement of Judgment)

CCP 706.105

ATTORNEY OR PARTY WITHOUT ATTORNEY *(Name and Address):*

TELEPHONE NO.:

FOR RECORDER'S OR SECRETARY OF STATE'S USE ONLY

ATTORNEY FOR *(Name):*

NAME OF COURT:

STREET ADDRESS:

MAILING ADDRESS:

CITY AND ZIP CODE:

BRANCH NAME:

PLAINTIFF:

DEFENDANT:

ACKNOWLEDGMENT OF SATISFACTION OF JUDGMENT

☐ FULL   ☐ PARTIAL   ☐ MATURED INSTALLMENT

CASE NUMBER:

FOR COURT USE ONLY

1. Satisfaction of the judgment is acknowledged as follows *(see footnote* before completing):*
   a. ☐ Full satisfaction
      (1) ☐ Judgment is satisfied in full.
      (2) ☐ The judgment creditor has accepted payment or performance other than that specified in the judgment in full satisfaction of the judgment.
   b. ☐ Partial satisfaction
      The amount received in partial satisfaction of the judgment is
      $
   c. ☐ Matured installment
      All matured installments under the installment judgment have been satisfied as of *(date):*

2. Full name and address of judgment creditor:

3. Full name and address of assignee of record, if any:

4. Full name and address of judgment debtor being fully or partially released:

5. a. Judgment entered on *(date):*
      ☐ (1) in judgment book volume no.:   (2) page no.:
   b. ☐ Renewal entered on *(date):*
      ☐ (1) in judgment book volume no.:   (2) page no.:

6. ☐ An ☐ abstract of judgment ☐ certified copy of the judgment has been recorded as follows *(complete all information for each county where recorded):*

COUNTY	DATE OF RECORDING	BOOK NUMBER	PAGE NUMBER

7. ☐ A notice of judgment lien has been filed in the office of the Secretary of State as file number *(specify):*

NOTICE TO JUDGMENT DEBTOR: If this is an acknowledgment of full satisfaction of judgment, it will have to be recorded in each county shown in item 6 above, if any, in order to release the judgment lien, and will have to be filed in the office of the Secretary of State to terminate any judgment lien on personal property.

▶

Date:

_____
(SIGNATURE OF JUDGMENT CREDITOR OR ASSIGNEE OF CREDITOR OR ATTORNEY)

*The names of the judgment creditor and judgment debtor must be stated as shown in any Abstract of Judgment which was recorded and is being released by this satisfaction. **A separate notary acknowledgment must be attached for each signature.**

Form Approved by the
Judicial Council of California
EJ-100 [Rev. July 1, 1983] (Cor. 7/84)

ACKNOWLEDGMENT OF SATISFACTION OF JUDGMENT

CCP 724.060, 724.120,
724.250

Name and Address of Court:

SMALL CLAIMS CASE NO.:

ATTORNEY-CLIENT FEE DISPUTE (ATTACHMENT TO PLAINTIFF'S CLAIM)
(Attach to Plaintiff's Claim)

1. **Parties**. At the arbitration hearing, plaintiff was ☐ attorney ☐ client. the

2. **Arbitration award**. The award made after the arbitration hearing
   a. ☐ requires the ☐ attorney ☐ client   to pay the other party this amount: $
   b. ☐ requires neither the attorney nor the client to pay the other anything.

3. **Amount in dispute**. The amount of fees and costs in dispute is *(may not exceed $5,000)*: $

4. ☐ **Binding award**. The award made after the arbitration hearing was binding because *(check at least one box)*:
   a. ☐ the attorney and client agreed in writing to have binding arbitration. *(Attach a copy.)*
   b. ☐ the award document was mailed on *(date)*:   , and more than 30 days have passed since then.

5. ☐ **Nonbinding award**. The award made after the arbitration hearing was NOT binding because
   a. the attorney and client did NOT agree in writing *after* the dispute arose to have binding arbitration; and
   b. thirty days have NOT passed since the award document was mailed on *(date)*:

6. **Plaintiff's request**.
   a. ☐ *(Trial after arbitration)* I reject the arbitration award and request a TRIAL ("hearing de novo") in small claims court to resolve the dispute. *(NOTE: Do NOT check a box unless you also checked item 5, "Nonbinding award," above.)*
      (1) ☐ I appeared at the arbitration hearing.
      (2) ☐ I did not appear at the arbitration hearing, but the award does not contain a finding that my failure to appear was willful.
      (3) A court action (case) involving this attorney-client fee dispute
         (i) ☐ is not pending.
         (ii) ☐ is pending. *(Your request for a trial must be filed in that court using the same case number.)*

   (NOTE: Do not check boxes b, c, or d, unless you also checked item 4, "Binding award," above.)
   b. ☐ *(Correct award)* I request that the court correct the award as follows:
      (1) Reason award should be corrected *(specify in this box a letter from item 3 on page three)*: ☐
      (2) Change requested *(specify)*:

   c. ☐ *(Vacate award)* I request that the award be vacated ("canceled") as follows:
      (1) Reason award should be vacated *(specify in this box a letter from item 4 on page three)*: ☐
      (2) Explain the circumstances *(specify)*:

      (3) I ☐ do not ☐ do   request a new arbitration hearing.
   d. ☐ *(Confirm award)* I request that the award be confirmed.

7. **Copy of award**. A copy of the arbitration award is attached. *(Attach a copy and check this box: ☐)*

▶

. . . .
(TYPE OR PRINT NAME)   (SIGNATURE OF PLAINTIFF)

| — The county provides small claims advisor services free of charge. Read the information on the reverse. — |

ATTORNEY-CLIENT FEE DISPUTE (ATTACHMENT TO PLAINTIFF'S CLAIM)
(Small Claims)

Form Adopted by the
Judicial Council of California
SC-101 [New January 1, 1997]

Page one of three
Cal. Rules of Court, rule 982.7
Code of Civil Procedure, §§ 116.220(a)(4), 1280 et seq.
Business & Professions Code, § 6200 et seq.

INFORMATION
ATTORNEY-CLIENT FEE DISPUTE CASES IN SMALL CLAIMS COURT

1. **Rights After Nonbinding Arbitration**

   A. **What are my rights if the arbitration award is nonbinding?**

   If the arbitration award is nonbinding, you may have a right to a trial in court. If you did not appear at your fee arbitration hearing, however, you will have to prove to the court that you had a good reason for not being there. If a court determines that your failure to appear was willful, you may not be entitled to a trial after arbitration.

   If you are not satisfied with the award, you should follow the instructions below to protect your rights.

   B. **How long do I have to act?**

   If you want a trial in court, you must act within 30 days after the date the arbitration award was mailed to you. The date the arbitration award was mailed is written at the end of the notice you received with the award.

   C. **What must I do to get a trial in court?**

   You must file papers in the proper court within the 30-day limit.

   D. **What papers must I file? In what court must I file them?**

   That depends. Has a lawsuit about the fees already been filed?

   (1) *YES—lawsuit already filed*

   If a lawsuit about the fees has already been filed, then you must file in that same court. You may need a lawyer's help to file your complaint if it is not a small claims court.

   (2) *NO—lawsuit not yet filed*

   If no lawsuit about the fees has been filed, then you must file your own lawsuit in the proper court. The small claims court is not the proper court if the amount in dispute is more than $5,000. Also consult the Venue Table on the back of the Plaintiff's Claim *(form SC-100)*.

   E. **What if I am satisfied with the award?**

   If you are satisfied with the award, do nothing. The award will become binding if the other party does not file papers for a trial in court within the 30-day limit.

   F. **What are my rights if the award becomes binding?** *(Read item 2 below.)*

2. **Rights After Binding Arbitration**

   A. **What are my rights if the arbitration award is binding?**

   If the arbitration award is binding, you must abide by it. There is no appeal from a binding award. Even so, a binding award can be corrected or "vacated" (overturned) by a court, but only in rare cases.

   Please read on to learn more about your rights after a binding arbitration.

   B. **What if I am dissatisfied with the award?**

   A court has the power to "vacate" (overturn) an arbitration award, but only on very narrow grounds. *(See item 4 on page three.)* A court can also correct obvious mistakes in the award, like an arithmetic mistake. *(See item 3 on page three.)*

   If you think you are entitled to correct or vacate the arbitration award, please follow the instructions below to protect your rights.

   (1) *What must I do to vacate or correct the arbitration award?*

   You must file a petition in the proper court within the 100-day limit.

   (2) *How long do I have to act?*

   (a) If you want to correct or vacate the award, you must act within 100 days after the date the arbitration award was mailed to you. The date the award was mailed is at the end of the notice mailed with the award.

   (b) If, however, you receive notice from a court that the other side has filed a petition to confirm the award, you no longer have 100 days to file your petition. You must then respond by filing your petition to vacate or correct the award within the time stated on the notice from the court.

   (3) *What is a petition?*

   A petition is a technical legal document that tells the court what you want and why you are entitled to it.

   (4) *In what court do I file my petition?*

   That depends. Has a lawsuit about the fees already been filed?

   (a) *YES—lawsuit already filed*

   If a lawsuit about the fees has already been filed, you will file your petition to vacate or correct with that same court.

   (b) *NO—lawsuit not yet filed*

   If no lawsuit about the fees has been filed, then you will file your petition with the court that has jurisdiction over the amount of the arbitration award. The small claims court is not the proper court if the amount of the arbitration award exceeds $5,000. For awards over $5,000, the municipal court or the superior court (over $25,000) is the proper court.

(Continued on page three)

ATTORNEY-CLIENT FEE DISPUTE (ATTACHMENT TO PLAINTIFF'S CLAIM)
(Small Claims)

C. What if I am satisfied with the arbitration award?

If the arbitration award says that you are owed money, you should write the other party a letter and demand payment. If you are not paid, and you are the client and your arbitration request was filed on or after January 1, 1994, you have the right to ask the State Bar to assist you. If you want the State Bar to assist you and

(1) 100 days have passed from service of the award and the award is binding, or

(2) the award has become a final judgment after a trial following arbitration or after a petition to vacate, correct, or confirm the award, you can reach the State Bar at

> **Mandatory Fee Arbitration**
> **100 Van Ness Avenue, 28th Floor**
> **San Francisco, CA 94102**
> **(415) 241-2020**

D. How do I confirm the arbitration award?

Any party who is owed money has the right to request court orders allowing that party to take property or money from the other party's paycheck and/or bank accounts. To get those court orders, you must first confirm the arbitration award.

(1) *How do I confirm the arbitration award?*

To confirm the arbitration award, you must petition for confirmation with the proper court.

(a) What is a petition for confirmation?

A petition for confirmation is a legal document that tells the court what you want and why you are entitled to it. In small claims court, request confirmation by checking box 6d on page one.

(b) What is the proper court?

That depends on the amount you are owed. If it is $5,000 or less, you may choose to file in small claims court or municipal court. If it is $25,000 or less, the municipal court is the proper court. File in superior court if you are owed more than $25,000.

(2) *How long do I have to file my petition for confirmation?*

You must file your petition for confirmation within four years of the date the arbitration award is mailed to you. That date appears at the end of the notice mailed with the award.

(3) *What are my rights after the arbitration award is confirmed?*

When the arbitration award is confirmed, it becomes a judgment of the court. Once you have a judgment, you have a right to enforce the judgment. That means you can get court orders allowing you to collect your money. Enforcing judgments can be very technical and very complicated. The court has forms to use for this procedure.

E. What if the arbitration award says I owe money?

If you owe money, pay it. If you do not, the other party has a right to get court orders allowing him or her to collect the debt by taking and selling your property and by taking money from your paycheck and your bank account.

---

3. Reasons to Correct the Award *(See item 6b(1) on page one)*

A. The numbers were not calculated correctly or a person, thing, or property was not described correctly.

B. The arbitrators exceeded their authority.

C. The award is imperfect as a matter of form.

---

4. Reasons to "Vacate" (Cancel) the Award *(See item 6c(1) on page one)*

A. The award was obtained by corruption, fraud, or other unfair means.

B. One or more of the arbitrators was corrupt.

C. The misconduct of a neutral arbitrator substantially prejudiced my rights.

D. The arbitrators exceeded their authority and the award cannot be fairly corrected.

E. The arbitrators unfairly refused to postpone the hearing or to hear evidence useful to settle the dispute.

F. An arbitrator should have disqualified himself or herself after I made a demand to do so.

Name and Address of Court:

SMALL CLAIMS CASE NO.:

ATTORNEY-CLIENT FEE DISPUTE (ATTACHMENT TO NOTICE OF ENTRY OF JUDGMENT)
(Attach to Notice of Entry of Judgment)

1. ☐ **Trial after arbitration**. A trial after arbitration of an attorney-client fee dispute
    a. ☐ is denied because
       (1) ☐ the arbitration award is binding.
       (2) ☐ plaintiff willfully failed to appear at the arbitration hearing.

    b. ☐ is granted, and a trial
       (1) ☐ was held on *(date)*:
       (2) ☐ will be held on *(date)*:

2. ☐ **Correction of award**. The arbitration award is
    a. corrected as follows *(specify)*:

    b. ☐ and in all other respects the award is confirmed as indicated below in item 4b.

3. ☐ **Vacation of award**. The arbitration award is vacated ("canceled").
    a. ☐ A new arbitration hearing is ordered before
       (1) ☐ new arbitrators. *(See Code of Civil Procedure section 1287.)*
       (2) ☐ the original arbitrators. *(See Code of Civil Procedure section 1287.)*
      The attorney and client are both ordered to appear at the new arbitration hearing.

    b. ☐ No new arbitration hearing is ordered.

4. ☐ **Confirmation of award**. The arbitration award is
    a. ☐ not confirmed.
       (1) ☐ The award is vacated under item 3 above.
       (2) ☐ The case is dismissed. *(See Code of Civil Procedure section 1287.2.)*

    b. ☐ confirmed
       (1) ☐ as made by the arbitrators. *(A copy of the award is attached.)*
       (2) ☐ as corrected in item 2 above. *(A copy of the award is attached.)*

5. **Payment**.
    a. ☐ The ☐ plaintiff ☐ defendant shall pay to ☐ plaintiff ☐ defendant
       (i) ☐ disputed fees and costs of: $
       (ii) ☐ costs of this proceeding of: $

    b. ☐ Neither the plaintiff nor the defendant shall pay the other anything.

— The county provides small claims advisor services free of charge. —

Form Adopted by the
Judicial Council of California
SC-132 [New January 1, 1997]

**ATTORNEY-CLIENT FEE DISPUTE
(ATTACHMENT TO NOTICE OF ENTRY OF JUDGMENT)
*(Small Claims)***

Cal. Rules of Court, rule 982.7
Code of Civil Procedure, §§ 116.220(a)(4),
1280 et seq.
Business & Professions Code, § 6200 et seq.

Appendix C
Demand Letters

The following are samples of the types of demand letters you need to send to someone before filing suit. Use these as guides for writing your own letter.

Via Certified Mail

May 1, 1999

123 Main Street
(555)555-5555

Mr. Warren Tee, Manager
Magnets R' Us
5000 Elm Street
Anytown, California

Re: defective magnets

Dear Mr. Tee:

On January 12, 1999 I purchased 12 refrigerator magnets in the shapes of various items of food from your store. I paid $3.95 for each magnet for a total of $47.40 plus $3.56 tax for a total of $50.96. I paid in cash, and received a receipt, a copy of which is enclosed. The person who sold me the magnets was wearing a name tag which said Suzanne.

While admiring the magnets, I told Suzanne that I would love to purchase them but that I was afraid that they wouldn't stick to my brushed steel refrigerator. Suzanne assured me that the refrigerator magnets will stay put on any refrigerator.

When I got home from your store, I took all of the magnets out of their wrapping and tried to put them on my refrigerator. Every one of them fell and broke into several pieces.

As you know, I returned to the store the next day to return the broken magnets and get my money back. You told me that you would only refund my money on one magnet, for a total of $3.95 plus tax. You told me that I should not have taken the 11 other magnets out of their packages or attempted to put them on the refrigerator until I was sure that the first one would stay on the refrigerator. As I told you then, I tried them all out because Suzanne had assured me that they would stay on any refrigerator.

Your salesperson sold me a product which did not work the way she said it would. This constitutes a breach of the warranty of fitness for a particular purpose.

The purpose of this letter is to let you know that I intend to file a claim against you in small claims court in the amount of $50.96 plus costs unless you refund the money I paid for the magnets within 7 days.

Please call me to discuss this matter to see if we can resolve it without the additional time and expense of a lawsuit.

Sincerely,

Dee Straught

Via Certified Mail

February 1, 1999

124 Main Street
(555)555-5555

Mr. Red Handid
111 Hwy 100
Anytown, California

Re: Return of Security Deposit

Dear Mr. Handid:

On November 30, 1998, I notified you by mail that I would be moving out of the premises known as 12 East 14th Street, Unit 12C in Any town, California on December 31, 1998. I had been a resident on a month-to-month rental agreement since January 12, 1995.

On December 31, 1998, I cleaned and vacated the unit. I still have not received the return of my security deposit of $400.00, nor have I received an itemized list of any deductions.

Section 1950.5 of the California Civil Code states that a landlord must return all deposits no later than three weeks after vacating. Furthermore, you may be subject to an additional $600.00 in damages if you are determined to have retained my deposit in bad faith.

I would appreciate a response and a check in the mail from you within five working days after your receipt of this letter so that there will be no need for my to institute legal proceedings.

Sincerely,

M.T. Pockets

<u>Claim Against the City of Anytown, California</u>

Joe Tenashus hereby makes claim against Charles Blind, employee, and the City of Anytown for damages sustained when Claimant was hit by a city owned vehicle while crossing the street at the corner of Pine and 4th Street at 7 a.m. on October 31, 1998.

Claimant's address is   Joseph T. Tenashus
                         67 W. Pine Avenue
                         Anytown, California, 12345-6789
                         3-333-333-3333

Notices concerning this claim should be sent to claimant at the address above.

The occurrence giving rise to this claim is as follows:

On October 31, 1998, claimant, dressed as an escaped convict in celebration of Halloween, was walking to his job as a teller at the Bank of Anytown located at 12 Civic Center Drive from his residence at 67 W. Pine. Upon arriving at the pedestrian walkway at the intersection of Pine and 4th Street, claimant entered the crosswalk and was thereafter hit by City police vehicle license # E33333, driven by Officer Charles Blind, Shield # 3333 who negligently failed to stop at the stop sign and hit claimant as claimant was trying to move out of the path of the vehicle.

As a result of the collision, Claimant was forced to seek medical attention for a sprained wrist and was absent from work for 3 days. Claimant is requesting compensation in the amount of $6,000.00 as follows: $ 100.00 medical treatment
                         300.00 lost wages
                         100.00 property damage to costume
                         1000.00 for false arrest
                         3500.00 pain & suffering

The names of the public employees causing this claimant's injuries Officer Charles Blind and other unknown employees. Claimant claims that the City of Anytown failed to properly hire, supervise and train its personnel, thereby causing the above damages to claimant.

Date _____   _____
                                     Joseph T. Tenashus

APPENDIX D
QUESTIONS FOR
JUDGMENT DEBTOR

Use these questions in case you must ask the defendant about his or her property to collect your judgment.

What is your full legal name?

Have you been known by any other names?

Social Security Number?

What is your home address?

What is your home telephone number? Business? Cellular? Fax?

Driver's license number, expiration?

Spouse name, address, phone number, ss#, driver's license number, other names?

Vehicles owned or leased, including boats, motorcycles, trucks, autos, recreational vehicles, etc? Descriptions? Amount owed and to whom?

Names, addresses, telephone number and employer of any former spouse?

Do you pay any or receive child support, family support, or alimony? Details?

Is your residence owned by you?

Who lives in the home with you?

Does anyone who lives in the home pay rent or board to you? Details?

Is residence or contents insured? Details?

Do you own any other residences?

Who are the other co-owners of your residence?

Is there any equity in your residence?

Who are the mortgage holders?

How long have you lived at your current address?

Do you pay your rent by check? Cash? Money Order?

Who do you make your rent checks out to?

Who owns the residence where you live?

Who is the manager?

Are your rent payments current?

What was prior address if less than one year?

Do you own any rental property?

Do you own any other real estate, either in California or anywhere else?

Do you own any mobile homes?

Are you a member of a partnership that owns any real property?

Property you own?

Are there any liens on any of your property? Details?

Are you or spouse employed? Name, address, location etc.?

Salary? Commission? Advances? Bonuses? Expense Accounts?

Does your employer owe you any money?

Do you have any checking accounts, savings accounts, money market accounts, CDs?

Names of banks, account numbers, balances, dates of last deposit or withdrawal? Do you own any 401, 453 or IRA accounts? Details?

Any bank accounts in children's names?

Do you have any credit cards? Details?

Have you ever filed for bankruptcy? Details?

Have you ever applied for credit and been turned down?

Do you own any stock, bonds?

Name, address, telephone number of broker?

Do you own any life insurance or disability policies? Details?

Who prepared your last income tax forms?

Have you had an accountant or service prepare your income tax return within the last three years? Details?

Do you own a business?

Name, locations, phone numbers?

What cities do you have business licenses?

Fictitious name statements filed? Where?

Sole proprietorship, partnership, corporation, what kind?

How long have you owned it? Co-owners?

Type of accounting system used? Software?

Type of business, creditors? Main customers? Methods of payment? When?

Name of bookkeeper?

Other bank accounts not mentioned yet?

Any credit cards not mentioned yet?

Separate tax return?

How many employees? Payroll current? When employees paid? Which account?

Professional licenses current? Details?

Own an interest in anyone else's business?

Do you owe any money other than to credit card companies and mortgage? Details?

Have you loaned any money to anyone in the last five years? Details?

Do you have any children in college? How is college paid for?

Do you own any antiques, furnishings, collections, artwork? Details?

Have you inherited anything within the last ten years?

Do you have any cash?

How much money do you have with you right now?

How much money does your spouse have right now?

APPENDIX E
LIST OF RELEVANT
CONSUMER STATUTES

The following is a listing of significant California and federal consumer laws. There are many more than those listed below. A more complete list can be obtained by writing or calling:

California Department of Consumer Affairs
400 R Street
Sacramento, CA 95814
phone (800) 952-5210

or at their web site located at:

http://www.dca.ca.gov/legal/m-1.html

Abbreviations:

B&P = Business & Professions Code

Cal. Const. = California Constitution

CC = Civil Code

CCP = Code of Civil Procedure

CFR = Code of Federal Regulations

Com. Code = Commercial Code

PC = Penal Code

PUC = Public Utilities Code

VC = Vehicle Code

Appliances: B&P 22410 et seq, B&P 9800 et seq.

As-Is Sales: CC 1791.3, 1792.4, 1792.5, 1670.5, 1770(s), 15 USC 2308, 16 CFR 455.2, Com. Code 2316

Attorney Fee Agreements: B&P 6146 et seq.

Attorneys Fees: CC 1717, 1717.5

Automobiles Financing: CC 2982.5

Automobile Leasing: CC 2985.7, 15 USC 1667 et seq.

Automobile Rescission: CC 2986 et seq.

Automobile Lemon Law: CC 1793.22 - 1793.25

Bad Check Law: CC 1719

Baggage Claims: CC 2194 et seq.

Civil Liability for Petty Theft: PC 490.5

Consumer Credit Contracts: CC 1799.90(re co-signing)

Consumer Warranty Act, (Song-Beverly):CC 1790

Contractor's License Law: B&P 7000 et seq.

Credit Card Act (Song-Beverly): CC 1747-1748.7

Credit Repair Agencies: CC 1789.10 et seq.

Dance Studio Contracts: CC 1812.50 et seq.

Dating Services: CC 1694 et seq.

Disasters Home Repair: CC 1689.6 et seq.

Disasters: Price Gouging: PC 396

Door-to-Door Solicitation: B&P 17510 et seq., 16 CFR Part 429, CC 1689.5

Employment Agencies: CC 1812.500 et seq.

Fair Debt Collection Practices: CC 1788 et seq., 15 USC 1692 et seq.

False and Deceptive Advertising: B&P 17500, 17508

Gender Based Price Discrimination: CC 51.6

Gifts or Prizes: B&P 17533.8, 17537

Health Studio Contracts: CC 1812.80 et seq.

Identification for Paying by Check or Credit Card: CC 1725 and CC 1747.8

Inducements to Visit Locations or Attend Sales Presentations: B&P 17537.1

Layaways: CC 1749

Made in U.S.A.: B&P 17537.1

Magnuson-Moss (Federal Warranty) Act: 15 USC 2301--2312, 16 CFR Part 703

Misrepresentation: CC 1770

Mobile Home Warranties: CC 1797-1797.5

Parking Lots: CC 1630, 1630.5

Rent to Own: CC 1812.600 et seq.

Return Policies: CC 1723

Scalping Tickets: PC 346

Self-Service Storage: B&P 21700 et seq.

Seminar Sales: CC 1689.24

Senior Citizens (enhanced penalties): CC 1780 (b), 3345, B&P 17206.1

Service Contracts: CC 1794.4, 1794.41 B&P 9855.1 et seq.

Sports Memorabilia: B&P 21670 et seq, CC 1739.7

Structural Pest Control Operators: B&P 8500 et seq.

Swap Meets: B&P 21660 et seq.

Swimming Pool Construction: B&P 7165-7168

Tanning Facilities: B&P 22700 et seq.

Telemarketing and Consumer Fraud and Abuse Prevention Act: 15 USC 6101 et seq. 16 CFR part 310

Timeshare Contracts: B &P 11024, 11003.5

Towing: CC 3068 et seq., VC 22658(i), VC 22513, VC 22651.1

Travel Consumer Restitution Fund: B&P 17550.36, 17550.37, 17500.47

Universal Product Code: CC 7100 et seq.

Unpaid Wages: LC 203, 227.3

Unruh Retail Sales Act: CC 1801-1812.20

Used Merchandise (disclosure): B&P 17531, CC 1770 (f)

Vocational Schools: EC 94312 et seq.

Warranties (express): CC 1791.2, 1793, 1793.1, 1793.2, Com. Code 2313, 2314,2315, 2316

Warranties (implied): CC 1791.1, 1792-1792.4, Com. Code 2314,2315, 2316

Water Treatment Devices: B&P 17577 et seq.

Weight Loss: CC 1694.5 et seq

APPENDIX F
SMALL CLAIMS ADVISORS

California requires each county to provide free help to all plaintiffs and defendants in small claims actions. The list below contains the name, address and phone number of the Small Claims Court Advisor for each county, where available. Although almost all of them offer help by telephone, some counties provide walk-in service or help by appointment. One or two have small group workshops or videos. Some have very limited hours, others are available during regular business hours, at night and on weekends. Orange County has a twenty-four hour "teletip" phone service.

The advisors are not permitted to dispense legal advice, however they will explain the rules, help in filling out the forms, and provide general information about preparing for the hearing. They also will explain how to collect your money after you've won or how to make periodic payments. The advisors are also an invaluable source of information on how to use the law library, where you can find an attorney to advise you, where you can find a copy or fax machine, and the location of the best coffee close to the courthouse.

The best way to avail yourself of the services of the advisor is first call the county where you plan to file your lawsuit to find out the extent of services offered and whether there are procedures unique to that county. Plan to spend some time on the phone winding your way through voice mail options or finding the information you requested.

Since there is probably more than one county which provides the correct venue for your lawsuit, it makes sense to contact the advisor from all of them to determine whether there are any advantages to filing in one county over the other. For example, one county may convene small claims court at night so you won't have to miss work on the day of the hearing. One county's small claims advisor may be more knowledgeable or helpful than another. Or maybe you want to choose a county that has a better mediation program.

Alameda County

Ruby Sutton
Small Claims Advisor
Alameda County Bar Association
661 Washington Street Dept.20 2nd Floor
Oakland, CA 94612
510-763-9282

Alpine County

Small Claims Advisor
El Dorado County Public Defenders
1360 Johnson Blvd., Ste. 106
South Lake Tahoe, CA 96150
916-573-3115

Amador County

Small Claims Advisor
c/o McGeorge School of Law
301 Bicentennial Circle, 3rd Floor
Sacramento, CA 95826
800-858-3057

Butte County

Doug Day
Small Claims Advisor Director
Community Legal Information Center
830 West 2nd Street
Chico, CA 95928
916-899-2280

Calaveras County

(rotating volunteer attorneys)
209-754-1443

Colusa County

(Contact Colusa Court for information)
Small Claims Advisor
Colusa Court
532 Oak Street
Colusa, CA 95932
916-458.5149
916-473-2811

Contra Costa County

Michael D. Farr,
Deputy County Counsel
Small Claims Advisor
651 Pine Street, 9th Floor
Martinez, CA 94533
510-372-0292

Del Norte County

Dana Avila, Deputy Clerk
Del Norte County Municipal Court
Small Claims Division
450 H Street, Room 182
Crescent City, CA 95531
707-464-7205

El Dorado County

Renee Schauble
Small Claims Advisor
P.O. Box 13086
South Lake Tahoe, CA 96151
916-573-3045
916-541-8787

Fresno County

Denise Kerner
Small Claims Advisor's Office
Fresno Downtown Plaza Building
2220 Tulare, 8th Floor
Fresno, CA 93721
209-262-4291

Glenn County

Penny Arnold
Small Claims Advisor
Glenn County Counsel
525 W. Sycamore St.
Willows, CA 95988
916-934-6455

Humboldt County

Christopher G. Metzger
Small Claims Advisor
930 3rd Street, #207
Eureka, CA 95501
707-441-1185

Imperial County

Lyla Corfman
Small Claims Advisor
Imperial Superior Court
939 Main Street
El Centro, CA 92243
619-339-4374

Inyo County

Small Claims Advisor
c/o McGeorge School of Law
301 Bicentennial Circle, 3rd Floor
Sacramento, CA 95826
800-858-3057

Kern County
Kelley Smith
Small Claims Advisor
1215 Truxtun Avenue, 1st Floor
Bakersfield, CA 93301
805-861-3323

Kings County
Cheryl Lane
Small Claims Advisor
1400 W. Lacey Blvd.
Hanford, CA 93230
209-582-3211, extension 4430

Lake County
Small Claims Advisor
c/o McGeorge School of Law
301 Bicentennial Circle, 3rd Floor
Sacramento, CA 95826
800-858-3057

Lassen County
Small Claims Advisor
County Counsel Office
707 Nevada Street
Susanville, CA 96130
916-251-8334

Los Angeles County
Muriel Jones
Supervisor/Program Director
Los Angeles County Department of Consumer Affairs
500 W. Temple St., Room B-96
Los Angeles, CA 90012
213-974-9759

Madera County
Small Claims Advisor
c/o McGeorge School of Law
301 Bicentennial Circle, 3rd Floor
Sacramento, CA 95826
800-858-3057

Marin County
Stan Pierce
Marin County Small Claims Advisor
Marin County Mediation Services
4 Mt. Lassen Drive
San Rafael, CA 94903
415-499-7454

Mariposa County
Richard Gimblin, Attorney at Law
Small Claims Advisor
P.O. Box 105
Mariposa, CA 95338
209-966-3627

Mendocino County
Small Claims Advisor
c/o McGeorge School of Law
301 Bicentennial Circle, 3rd Floor
Sacramento, CA 95826
800-858-3057

Merced County
Jack Uren
Small Claims Advisor
P.O. Box 1566
Merced, CA 95341
209-722-3279

Modoc County
Wendy J. Dier, Attorney at Law
Small Claims Advisor
201 S. Street, #28
Alturas, CA 96101
916-233-2008

Mono County
Small Claims Advisor
c/o McGeorge School of Law
301 Bicentennial Circle, 3rd Floor
Sacramento, CA 95826
800-858-3057

Monterey County
Candice C. Chin
Small Claims Advisor
District Attorney
Consumer Protection Division
P.O. Box 1369
Salinas, CA 93902
408-755-5073

Napa County
Small Claims Advisor
Napa County Counsel's Office
1195 3rd Street, Room 305
Napa, CA 94559
707-253-4524

Nevada County

Truckee Division
(Contact Truckee Court for information)
10075 Levon Ave., Ste 301
Truckee, CA 96161
916-582-7834 or 5

Connie Savelly
Small Claims Advisor
Nevada City Division
916-265-0192

Orange County

Stan Machado and Carol Hatch
Small Claims Advisors
Community Service Agency
1300 S. Grand Avenue,
Santa Ana, CA 92705
714-567-5006
recorded information
714-567-7475

Placer County

Kathleen Berdon
Small Claims Advisor
Office of the Public Defender
2422 Lindbergh
Auburn, CA 95603
916-885-2422

Plumas County

Liz Cortez
Small Claims Advisor
County Counsel
Small Claims Advisor Program
P.O. Box 10388
Quincy, CA 95971
916-283-6240

Riverside County

Ward Albert
Small Claims Advisor
P.O. Box 892
Temecula, CA 92593
800-244-8898 and
909-695-7012

Sacramento County

Small Claims Advisor
c/o McGeorge School of Law
301 Bicentennial Circle, 3rd Floor
Sacramento, CA 95826
800-858-3057

San Benito County

Small Claims Advisor
c/o McGeorge School of Law
301 Bicentennial Circle, 3rd Floor
Sacramento, CA 95826
800-858-3057

San Bernadino County

Tel-Law
909-824-2300

San Diego County

Elliot G. Lande Director
Larry Steorts, Attorney at Law
Judy Crowley and Thomas Kelly
Small Claims Advisor
233 A Street, Rm. 1010
San Diego, CA 92101
619-236-2700

San Francisco County

Small Claims Legal Advisor
The Municipal Court
Small Claims Division
575 Polk Street
San Francisco, CA 94102
Telephone advisor 415-292-2124

San Joaquin County

Joan Schroeder and Peggy Mouriski
Small Claims Advisors
209-468-2986
800-8342201

San Luis Obispo County

The Small Claims and Consumer Advisory
Office of the District Attorney
County Government Center, Room 235 (walk-in)
1050 Montgomery Street, Room 235 (mail)
San Luis Obispo, CA 93408
805-781-5856

San Mateo County

Leslie Airola
Small Claims Advisor
800 N. Humboldt St.
San Mateo, CA 94401

Santa Barbara County

Tony Lorian
Small Claims Advisor
County Counsel's Office
105 East Anapamu St., Room 201
Santa Barbara, CA 93101
805-568-2984

Santa Clara County

Patti McRae and Myrna Cohen
Small Claims Advisors
Santa Clara District Attorney
Consumer Protection Unit
70 W. Hedding St.,Lower Level, West Wing
San Jose, CA 95110
408-299-7400

Santa Cruz County

Legal Aid Society of Santa Cruz County
Small Claims Advisors
21 Carr St.
Watsonville, CA 95076
408-724-2253

Shasta County

Jerry Larrea
800-795-8136

Sierra County

No program available

Siskiyou County

Small Claims Advisor
c/o McGeorge School of Law
301 Bicentennial Circle, 3rd Floor
Sacramento, CA 95826
800-858-3057

Solano County

707-421-7478

Sonoma County

E. Gregory Schrader
Small Claims Advisor
Hall of Justice
600 Administration Drive, Room 107J
Santa Rosa, CA 95403
707-524-7349

Stanislaus County

Kathleen Aguilar
Small Claims Advisor
P.O. Box 74
Modesto, CA 95353

Sutter County

Susan Townsend
Small Claims Advisor
Yuba-Sutter Legal Center
725 D Street
Maryville, CA 95901
916-742-8289

Tehama County

No program available

Trinity County

Peter Navarro Paralegal Service
Small Claims Advisor
P.O. Box 991288/1416 West Street
Redding, CA 96099-1388
916-241-7726

Tulare County

Walter McArthur, Attorney at Law
Small Claims Advisor
1809 W. Main Street, Suite F
P.O. Box 2563
Visalia, CA 93279
209-625-4300

Tuolumne County

Small Claims Advisor
c/o McGeorge School of Law
301 Bicentennial Circle, 3rd Floor
Sacramento, CA 95814
800-858-3057

Ventura County

Melodianne Duffy
Small Claims Advisor
District Attorney's Office
Consumer Protection Unit
800 S. Victoria Avenue
Ventura, CA 93009
805-654-5054

Yolo County

Small Claims Advisor
c/o McGeorge School of Law
301 Bicentennial Circle, 3rd Floor
Sacramento, CA 95826
800-858-3057

Yuba County

Susan Townsend
Small Claims Advisor
Yuba-Sutter Legal Center
725 D Street
Marysville, CA 95901
916-742-8289

APPENDIX G
STATUTES OF LIMITATION

Below is a list of the most common Statutes of Limitation. They are listed for your convenience, but understand that this is an area of the law that is extremely complicated and there are many exceptions to the rules below.

The safest thing to do is to file your lawsuit as soon as possible. If you think you may have missed the deadline, check with a lawyer or do the legal research yourself. In some situations, the statute may have been "tolled." For example, the statute does not run if the defendant was out of state when the injury occurred or while you are under eighteen in most circumstances, or if you were in jail, or insane when the injury occurred. (The decision as to whether you were insane is not yours to make.) In other situations, you may not have characterized the injury correctly. For example it is very easy to mis-characterize *patent* and *latent* construction defects. (See the glossary for definitions of these terms.) When in doubt as to whether you missed the statute, file your case and let the judge decide if you missed the statute.

Personal injury—including false imprisonment, seduction of a person below the age of legal consent, wrongful death—one year from the date of the incident or three years based on professional negligence against a medical provider. (You must also provide ninety days notice to the medical provider that you plan to file a lawsuit.) If you fell on the steps of the hospital, that is not professional negligence.

Libel and Slander—one year from the date of injury

Construction defects causing injury to person or property—Patent defects—four years

Construction defects causing injury to person or property—Latent Defects—ten years

Oral Contract and Rescission of Oral Contract—two years from the breach

An Action on an Oral Lease—two years from the breach

Written Contract and Rescission of Written Contract—four years from the breach

Damage to Real and Personal Property—three years from the date the damage occurred

Action for Slander of Tile to real property—three years

An action against a Notary or a notary's bond holder—three years

Fraud and mistake—three years from the date of discovery

Minors—the statute doesn't start to run until they are no longer minors. For example, if a child was injured when he was thirteen years old, he could file a lawsuit until his nineteenth birthday.

Government entities—six months after the claim was rejected (almost all government claims are rejected) or if you do not receive a letter of rejection, you must file within two years from the date of the incident.

Government claims—must be submitted to the correct government entity within six months (180 days from the date of incident) or within one year on a contract. There is also a procedure for filing a late claim. The government entity you are suing will probably have its own claim form. However, you can adapt the one in appendix C, but make sure you pay attention to detail.

Appendix H
Mediation Programs
by County

This appendix contains the names and addresses of the mediation services available throughout the state. These can help you settle your dispute without going through with the trial.

Alameda

Conciliation Forum of Oakland
663 13th Street
Oakland, CA 94612
510-763-2117

Berkeley Dispute Resolution Program Service
1769 Alcatraz
Berkeley, CA 94703
510-428-1811

Family Violence Law Center
P.O. Box 2529
Berkeley, CA 94702
510-540-5370

Victim Offender Reconciliation Program
443 Jefferson Street
Oakland, CA 94607
510-8345656

Contra Costa

Contra Costa Conflict Resolution Panel
P.O. Box 23227
Pleasant Hill, CA 94523-0227
West County 510-754-3729
East County 510 234-5010

Battered Women's Alternatives
P.O. Box 6406
Concord, CA 94524
510-930-8300

Catholic Charities Diocese of Oakland
433 Jefferson Street
Oakland, CA 94607
510-754-3729

Contra Costa County Human Relations Commission
2425 Bisso Lane
Concord, CA 94520
510-646-5322

California Community Dispute Services
30 Hotaling Place #302
San Francisco, CA 94111
415-865-2520

Fresno

Better Business Bureau Dispute Settlement Center
2519 W. Shaw Street
Fresno, CA 93711
209-222-8111

Humboldt

Humboldt Mediation Services
940 Samoa Blvd., Room 205
Arcata, CA 95521
707-826-1066

Inyo

Center for Settlement Services
P.O. Box 3034
Mammoth Lakes, CA 93546
619-934-7539

Los Angeles

Dispute Resolution Service
617 S. Olive, 6th Floor
P.O. Box 55020
Los Angeles, CA 90014
213-896-6533

Claremont Dispute Resolution Center
333 W. Foothill Blvd.
Glendora, CA 91741
909-625-6632

California Lawyers for the Arts
1549 11th Street, Suite 200
Santa Monica, CA 90401
301-395-8893

Norwalk Consumer-Rental Mediation Board
11929 Alondra Blvd
Norwalk, CA 90650
310-864-3785

The Center for Conflict Resolution
1800 North Highland Ave. #507
Hollywood, CA 90028
213-467-3331

Martin Luther King, Jr. Dispute Resolution Center
4182 S. Western Avenue
Los Angeles, CA 90062
213-290-4132

Los Angeles County Dispute Settlement Services
500 West Temple Street, #B-96
Los Angeles CA 90012
213-974-0825

Los Angeles County Community and Senior
        Citizens Services
3175 W. 6th Street
Los Angeles, CA 90020
213-738-2621

Marin

Mediation Services
County of Marin
Jody Becker and Eleanor Spater
3501 Civic Center Drive
Room 278
San Rafael, CA 94903
415-499-7454

Marin Fair Housing Program
88 Belvedere Street, #A-1
San Rafael, CA 94901
415-457-5025

Mono

Center for Settlement Services
P.O. Box 3034
Mammoth Lakes, CA 93546
619-934-7539

Monterey County

Conflict Resolution and Mediation Center of
Monterey County
814 Airport Road
Monterey, CA 93940
408-649-6219

Orange County

St. Vincent de Paul
Institute for Conflict Management
2525 N. Grand Ave, Ste. L & N
Orange, CA 92705
562-425-0199

Southern California Mediation Association
Orange County Mediation Roundtable
c/o Vickie Lester
P.O. Box 517
Long Beach, CA 90815

Sacramento

Sacramento Mediation Center
1220 H Street, Suite 102
Sacramento, CA 95814
916-441-7979

Sacramento Valley Apartment Association
221 Lathrop Way, Suite M
Sacramento, CA 95815
916-920-1120

San Bernadino

Inland Mediation Board
1005 Begonia Avenue
Ontario, CA 91762
909-984-2254

San Diego

San Diego Mediation Center
Community Mediation Program of San Diego
625 Broadway, Suite 1221
San Diego, CA 92101
619-238-2400

San Francisco

Community Boards of San Francisco
1540 Market Street, Room 490
San Francisco, CA 84102
415-863-6100

California Community Dispute Services
699 8th Street, Suite 3125A
San Francisco, CA 94103
415-865-2520

California Lawyers for the Arts
Fort Mason Center
Building C-255
San Francisco, CA 94123
415-775-7200

San Luis Obispo

SLO Municipal Court Small Claims Mediation
Project
805-549-0442

San Mateo

San Mateo County Mediation Program
300 Bradford Street
Redwood City, CA 94063
650-373-3496

Peninsula Conflict Resolution Center
3 Waters Park Drive, Suite 206
San Mateo, CA 94403
650-373-3490

Santa Barbara

City of Santa Barbara Rental Housing Mediation
Task Force
423 West Victoria Street
Santa Barbara, CA 93101
805-730-1523

Isla Vista Mediation Project
970 Embarcadero Del Mar, Suite C
Isla Vista, CA 93117
805-968-5158

Community Mediation Program
906 Garden Street
Santa Barbara, CA 93101
805-963-6765

Santa Clara

Office of Human Relations Dispute Resolution
Program Services, County of Santa Clara
San Jose: 408-299-2206

Los Altos Mediation Program
650-949-5267

Consumer Protection Unit
District Attorney's Office,
County of Santa Clara
408-792-2880

Santa Cruz

Community Boards of Monterey Peninsula
207 Monterey Street
Santa Cruz, CA 95060
408-423-2793

Conflict Resolution Program
200 7th Avenue, Suite 100
Santa Cruz, CA 95062
408-475-8277

Sonoma

Recourse Mediation Services
707-525-8545

Ventura

Office of the District Attorney
Consumer Mediation Section
800 S. Victoria Avenue
Ventura, CA 93009
805-654-3110

Ventura Center for Dispute Settlement
4475 Market Street, Suite C
Ventura, CA 93003
805 650-9202

Appendix I
Checklists

The following checklists will help you follow your case and be sure not to miss some important step. Be sure that you have read the parts of this book explaining each step. If there is anything you do not understand, check with the small claims advisor for your county (see appendix F).

Plaintiff's Small Claims Checklist

1. **Decide if you should sue**

   ✓ Did you determine the last day you are permitted to file your case and write it in a calendar?

   ✓ Did you calculate the exact amount of damages which are in dispute? Is there a legal theory which would make the defendant liable?

   ✓ Does the defendant have defenses that would keep you from winning?

   ✓ Did you write the required "demand letter" to the other side?

   ✓ Did you try to negotiate a settlement?

   ✓ Did you attempt mediation?

   ✓ Did you find out if the defendant has money or property to collect if you win?

   ✓ Did you analyze whether the case is worth your time and effort?

2. **Prepare your case**

   ✓ Familiarize yourself with small claims procedures and forms (read this book).

   ✓ Determine which court has venue.

   ✓ If you are unfamiliar with small claims court, attend a session to familiarize yourself with the court procedures and to observe the progress of a hearing.

   ✓ Research the proper parties and their names.

   ✓ Decide when you want to have the hearing. Plan for plenty of time to serve the defendant and return the proof of service to the court.

   ✓ Gather your evidence and contact your witnesses.

   ✓ Prepare the PLAINTIFF'S CLAIM AND ORDER TO DEFENDANT (Form 2 in appendix B).

   ✓ Attempt mediation before you file your case.

   ✓ File your case(and pay filing fee).

   ✓ If you are a business, file fictitious business name statement.

✓ Arrange for service of process on each defendant.

✓ Make sure the proof of service is timely filed with the court.

3. PREPARE FOR THE HEARING

✓ Organize your presentation, either chronologically, or in another order which will be easy for the judge to follow. Prepare an outline that you can follow during your presentation.

✓ Write a summary of your case to give to the judge.

✓ Try to anticipate arguments and facts which the defense will present and have your own arguments and evidence ready.

4. ATTEND THE HEARING

✓ Be prepared to settle if the defendant makes a good offer.

✓ Be prepared to mediate if the defendant agrees.

5. AFTER THE TRIAL

✓ Obtain NOTICE OF ENTRY OF JUDGMENT (Form 18 in appendix B).

✓ If you did not attend the hearing for a good reason, file a NOTICE OF MOTION TO VACATE JUDGMENT AND DECLARATION (Form 23) to request new hearing by small claims court

✓ If you lost on the defendant's counterclaim, decide if you want to appeal. If you decide to appeal, the NOTICE OF APPEAL (Form 20) must be filed within thirty days of the date of the small claims decision or if the clerk mails the NOTICE OF ENTRY OF JUDGMENT (Form 18), within thirty days of the mailing as indicated on the form.

✓ Institute collection procedures (garnishment of wage, levy on bank account, record an abstract of judgment, till tap, keeper, etc.).

✓ File ACKNOWLEDGMENT OF SATISFACTION OF JUDGMENT (Form 36) with the small claims court after the judgment is satisfied.

Defendant's Small Claims Checklist

1. After you are served with the Plaintiff's Claim and Order to Defendant (Form 2)

✓ Analyze whether the case is worth defending.

✓ Consider the possibility of initiating mediation or perhaps negotiating a settlement on your own or through a third party. Keep trying to settle throughout the lawsuit.

✓ Decide if you have defenses that would keep the plaintiff from winning based on improper procedures.

✓ Decide if you have defenses based on principles of law.

✓ Determine whether your homeowners, auto, or business insurance policy covers you.

✓ Determine whether you have a basis for a counterclaim against the Plaintiff arising from the same set of facts.

✓ If you want to pursue your counterclaim file the Defendant's Claim and Order to Plaintiff (Form 11 in appendix B) within the time limits and make sure you get it served.

✓ File your proof of service with the court.

2. Before the hearing

✓ Gather all the evidence and make copies for the other parties and you to refer to while the judge looks at the original.

✓ Subpoena witnesses and documents if necessary (Forms 14, and 15).

✓ Prepare a concise statement of the case so you can explain the case to the judge clearly and quickly.

✓ Make another attempt to resolve the case.

3. Prepare for the hearing

✓ Organize your presentation, either chronologically, or in another order which will be easy for the judge to follow. Prepare an outline that you can follow during your presentation.

✓ Write a summary of your case to give to the judge.

✓ Try to anticipate arguments and facts which the plaintiff will present and have your own arguments and evidence ready.

4. ATTEND THE HEARING

✓ Be prepared to settle if the plaintiff makes a reasonable demand.

✓ Be prepared to mediate if the plaintiff agrees.

5. AFTER THE TRIAL

✓ Obtain NOTICE OF ENTRY OF JUDGMENT (Form 18).

✓ If you did not attend the hearing for a good reason, file a NOTICE OF MOTION TO VACATE JUDGMENT AND DECLARATION (Form 23) to request new hearing by small claims court.

✓ If you lost on the plaintiff's claim, decide if you want to appeal. If you decide to appeal, the NOTICE OF APPEAL (Form 20) must be filed within thirty days of the date of the Small Claims Decision or if the clerk mails the NOTICE OF ENTRY OF JUDGMENT (Form 18), within thirty days of the mailing as indicated on the form.

✓ If you won on your counterclaim, write a letter to the plaintiff asking for payment before you start collection procedures. (You can't start them until the appeal period is over anyway.) Sometimes, the plaintiff will not want his employer to know about the judgment, which will surely happen if you institute garnishment proceedings. Or the plaintiff (now called the *judgment debtor*) does not want to lose another day from work to appear for a judgment debtor exam. On the other hand, if you think the judgment debtor is likely to remove all his money from the only bank account you know about, or is likely to quit his job to avoid garnishment of wages, you may want to lay low until the appeal period is over, so that you can attach the property before the judgment debtor can dispose of it. The steps you take prior to collection require careful analysis of all your options.

✓ Institute collection procedures (garnishment of wage, levy on bank account, record an abstract of judgment, till tap, keeper, etc.)

✓ File ACKNOWLEDGMENT OF SATISFACTION OF JUDGMENT (Form 36) with the small claims court after the judgment is satisfied.

GLOSSARY

The following terms are used in small claims court and should be understood by the parties.

Abstract of Judgment. A document issued by the county clerk when recorded at the county recorder's office places a lien on any real property owned by the debtor in that particular county. *See* **lien**.

Acknowledgment of Satisfaction of Judgment. A form that the judgment creditor must complete, sign, and file when the judgment is fully paid or "satisfied." *See* **judgment**.

advisory arbitration. A procedure, much like a mini, informal trial held in front of a neutral person called an *arbitrator* whose decision is not binding on the parties. Even if the parties decide not to accept the decision, they still have the advantage of an opportunity to reassess their positions based on the analysis and decision of the arbitrator. *See* **neutrals**.

alternative dispute resolution. Also known by the initials ADR, generally refers to mediation and arbitration. These are less formal methods of resolving disputes than having a judge decide the issues in a courtroom setting. In a regular lawsuit, these procedures are generally faster and less expensive than going to court. However, in the small claims setting (which is generally pretty fast and inexpensive anyway,) the main advantages are privacy and a resulting compromise between the parties. This is especially helpful when there are ongoing relationships to preserve. *See* **arbitration**.

appeal. A request to the superior court by the defendant (or by the plaintiff on the claim of the defendant) for a new hearing. The appeal is also called a *trial de novo* which is a fancy way of saying that the superior court hears the entire matter as though there was no small claims action. The parties are permitted to have attorneys represent them in an appeal.

appearance. The act of showing up in court.

Application for Waiver of Court Fees and Costs. A form that permits a plaintiff to apply for a court order waiving fees and costs if the plaintiff's income comes within certain guidelines.

arbitration. A procedure where a neutral party listens to both sides of a dispute, reviews the evidence and makes a decision based on principles of law and evidence.

bad faith. Dishonesty or fraud in a transaction. *See* **fraud**.

bench, the. Refers to the judge while court is in session.

binding arbitration. A procedure, much like a mini, informal trial held in front of a neutral person called an *arbitrator* whose decision is binding on the parties. Some contracts require the parties to submit disputes over the contract to binding arbitration. Some parties choose to have a binding arbitration because it is a final decision. The prevailing party may use the court to enforce the arbitrator's decision. *See* **contract**.

bonded. A bonding company, also known as a *surety* or *guarantor*, issues a bond in the amount of at least $7,500 (in the case of a home improvement contractor) so that a homeowner has another resource besides the contractor to turn to for defective work. After they deny your claim, which they do more often than not, they can be sued for a maximum of $2,500 in small claims court. If you win the case against the contractor and collect, you must refund the money to the bonding company.

breach of contract. The failure to comply with the terms of a contract. *See* **contract**.

burden of proof. The amount of evidence required to prove a fact in court. In small claims court, the burden is called a *preponderance of evidence* which merely means that something was more likely than not. *See* **evidence** *and* **preponderance of evidence**.

calendar year. January 1 through December 31 of a particular year.

case law. The principles of law that come from the written opinions of judges in published cases.

cause of action. The theory of law upon which damages are requested in a lawsuit. *See* **damages**.

claim, defendant's. The defendant's counterclaim against the plaintiff.

Claim of Exemption. The form filed by the judgment debtor that lists the exempt property that cannot be taken to pay the judgment (if approved by the court.)

claim, plaintiff's. A combination of facts, evidence and legal arguments showing why the plaintiff should recover damages.

claim-splitting. When the plaintiff divides one claim and files them as separate claims to stay below the jurisdictional limits.

class action. When several people join their lawsuits against the same defendant because the facts and circumstances are similar. This procedure is not formally established in small claims court but there have been situations where several individual claims have been heard collectively to deal with neighborhood problems such as drug houses.

commissioner. An attorney who is an employee of the court whose job is to take on many of the duties of a judge. Although not a judge, this person is addressed as "your honor" while sitting on the bench.

comparative negligence. A system where a plaintiff sue's the defendant for wrongdoing and the award is then reduced by the percentage of wrongdoing attributable to the plaintiff. Sometimes called *contributory negligence*.

contingency fee. A fee arrangement where the lawyer is paid a percentage of the settlement or award.

contract. An agreement between at least two parties in which an offer is made by one party and accepted by the other for their mutual benefit. Although some contracts are required to be in writing, contracts can be oral, written on a napkin, or sealed by a handshake.

costs. The money actually spent by one of the parties to file, serve, **subpoena,** and otherwise present the case and/or to enforce a judgment against the losing party who does not pay voluntarily. Some costs cannot be recovered such as time taken off from work to go to court, mileage, and postage.

creditor. The person to whom a debtor owes money, goods, or services. *See* **debtor**.

cross-examination. The act of questioning the other party or the party's witness.

damages. The amount of money ordered by the court to be paid as compensation on a claim.

debtor. The person who owes money, goods, or services to a *See* **creditor**.

default. When a party does not attend the small claims action the judge permits the other party to present his case anyway.

default judgment. A judgment entered upon one party proving their case in the absence of the other party. *See* **default**.

defendant. Person or business defending the claim.

defense. A combination of facts, evidence, and legal arguments made by the defendant showing why the plaintiff is not entitled to recover damages.

demand letter. A letter written by the plaintiff to the defendant asking for payment of damages before the lawsuit is filed. A demand letter is required, if possible, before filing a small claims action. (See the sample in appendix C.)

Dismissal, Request for. A document notifying the court that the plaintiff or all the parties have ended the lawsuit on their own.

dismiss without prejudice. The ending of a lawsuit where the plaintiff *can* file the case again.

dismiss with prejudice. The formal ending of a lawsuit where the plaintiff is *not* permitted to file the case again.

evidence. The proof of a fact or facts presented in court to prove a case. Evidence can be written (a contract or receipt) , oral (an eye witness), or circumstantial (fingerprints).

exhibit. Written evidence, photographs, or other tangible evidence shown to the court as evidence.

expert witness. A witness with specialized knowledge of a particular subject who is called to testify about an event even though they were not present when the event occurred.

fraud. Deceitful conduct designed to cause a person to take action, including but not limited to concealment of facts, cheating, and lying.

garnishment. A court-ordered method of collection where a percentage of wages or property are attached to pay a judgment.

good faith. Being honest and without deception.

governmental claim. Claim filed against a government agency within six months of the incident as a prerequisite to filing a lawsuit against the government.

governmental immunity. The exemption given to government entities such as cities, school districts, counties, and their employees for certain acts for which they would otherwise be held liable.

guardian ad litem. The person appointed by the court to look after the best interests of a minor. *See* **minor**.

hearsay. An extremely complicated set of rules of evidence designed to keep certain indirect items of evidence out of the record based on their unreliability. In its most simple form, it is usually a statement or writing based on what someone told the witness about something or someone else.

implied warranty. The protection against defects that comes with a product.

implied warranty of fitness for a particular purpose. Warranty that exists when the buyer is relying upon the promises or statements made by the seller.

implied warranty of habitability. Warranty by landlord that the premises meet certain basic standards of livability.

implied warranty of merchantability. Warranty that guarantees that a product will do what it is intended to do.

joint and several liability. When more than one person or company can be sued, any of them may be held 100% liable for all damages.

judge pro tem. A volunteer attorney who is "judge for the day." You have the right to refuse to have this attorney hear your case.

judgment. A formal decision by the court.

judgment debtor hearing. An examination of the defendant by the plaintiff under court order to discover the amount and location of the defendant's assets.

jurisdiction. Has several meanings but in terms of small claims court it means either the upper limits for which a claim can be made or that the claim is made in the correct geographical location.

keeper. A method of collection where the sheriff or marshal goes to the defendant's business and waits for customers to come in and pay for services and/or goods and then collects the cash, checks, and credit card payments.

latent defect. A defect which is not apparent through reasonable inspection. *See* **patent defect**.

levy. A means of collection where the funds in the defendant's bank account are taken to satisfy a judgment.

liability. Legal responsibility or obligation.

lien. A property right that attaches to a particular piece of personal or real property (such as a car or a house) which is given to a creditor until the property is sold and the creditor can collect the money owed.

minor. A person who is under eighteen years and therefore too young to file a lawsuit in his own name unless the minor is legally emancipated. The suit must be brought by a guardian ad litem. *See* **guardian ad litem**.

mitigation of damages. The act of taking steps to minimize the amount of damages (if a tenant breaks a lease, the landlord has a duty to reasonably attempt to rent to someone else). *See* **damages**.

motion. A request to a judge for an order.

negligence. The failure to act as a reasonable person would under the same or similar circumstances, which causes damages to another person. *Gross* negligence is a more serious level of negligence that specifies that the negligent person acted recklessly and without regard for the rights of others.

neutrals. Individuals or panels who facilitate mediation or negotiation sessions and who do not favor one side or the other.

nuisance. The unreasonable or unlawful use of property causing damages to another.

partnership. An agreement between two or more individuals to share the profits and losses of a business.

patent defect. A defect that is apparent through reasonable inspection. *See* **latent defect**.

plaintiff. Person or business filing the claim.

presumption. A determination that one side has proved the case unless the other side has evidence to refute the facts.

preponderance of evidence. The level of proof needed to prevail in a civil action where the judge is convinced more for the plaintiff than the defendant.

Proof of Service. A document proving that a person or business was served court documents.

punitive damages. Damages meant to make an example of the defendant.

rescind. To cancel a contract, sometimes by agreement of the parties but usually based on fraud, duress, or misrepresentation.

service of process. The act of formally notifying a party that a claim has been filed against the person or business. In the small claims court, this can be accomplished by certified mail by the court, personal service, or *substituted service*.

Statutes of Limitation. The time limit for filing a case calculated from the day of the incident.

stipulation. An agreement between both parties about facts, principles of law, or procedures.

stop payment. When a customer or user of services requests and authorizes the bank to withhold payment on a check. California Civil Code Section 1719 permits additional damages above and beyond the face value of the check and costs.

strict liability. Liability is determined without proof of negligence. *See* **negligence**.

subpoena. The request to the court and the court's act of requiring a person to appear at a hearing or suffer a penalty. Adding the words *duces tecum* means that the subpoenaed person must bring something with him to the hearing.

substituted service. The act of serving a person by leaving the papers at his home with a competent adult, or at a business by leaving the papers at the business address, during business hours with the person in charge of the office and then mailing a copy of the papers to the same address.

till tap. A method of collection where the sheriff or marshal goes to the defendant's business and takes money out of the cash register to pay the judgment.

torts. The set of principles and law that establish a person's right to be compensated by a person who caused injury to him. The *tortfeaser* is the person who causes the injury.

vicarious liability. The act of being held responsible for the acts of someone else, such as an employer being held liable for negligent acts of employees. *See* **negligence**.

waiver. Voluntarily giving up a right such as agreeing to have a small claims action heard by a commissioner or judge pro tem instead of the judge.

Writ of Execution. A form issued by the clerk of the small claims court authorizing the sheriff to use various means to collect the damages ordered by the court.

230

INDEX

Your #1 Source for Real World Legal Information...

SPHINX® PUBLISHING
A Division of Sourcebooks, Inc.®

- Written by lawyers
- Simple English explanation of the law
- Forms and instructions included

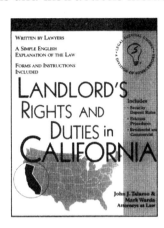

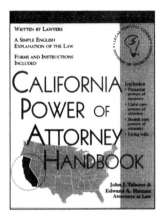

HOW TO FILE FOR DIVORCE IN CALIFORNIA

This book provides a step-by-step guide for obtaining a divorce in California without a lawyer. Learn about alimony; child support, custody and visitation; property division; simplified procedures; emergency procedures and more.

208 pages; $19.95;
ISBN 1-57071-355-3

LANDLORDS' RIGHTS & DUTIES IN CALIFORNIA

Covering the law for residential and commercial landlords, from tenant applications to evictions, this book will help California landlords avoid legal problems. Includes California statutes; flowcharts; sample and blank forms.

240 pages; $19.95;
ISBN 1-57071-359-6

CALIFORNIA POWER OF ATTORNEY HANDBOOK

Now it is easier than ever to authorize someone to act on your behalf for your convenience or necessity. With forms and instructions, this book allows you to draft your own power of attorney for financial matters, health care, real estate and child care.

128 pages; $12.95;
ISBN 1-57071-360-X

OTHER CALIFORNIA LEGAL SURVIVAL GUIDES

How to Make a CA Will	$12.95
How to Probate an Estate in CA	$19.95
How to Start a Business in CA	$16.95

SEE OUR ORDER FORM FOR BOOKS WRITTEN FOR OTHER STATES. COMING SOON: OHIO!

WHAT OUR CUSTOMERS SAY ABOUT OUR BOOKS:

"Your real estate contracts book has saved me nearly $12,000.00 in closing costs over the past year." —A.B.

"...many of the legal questions that I have had over the years were answered clearly and concisely through your plain English interpretation of the law." —C.E.H.

"If there weren't people out there like you I'd be lost. You have the best books of this type out there." —S.B

Legal Survival Guides are directly available from Sourcebooks, Inc., or from your local bookstores.

For credit card orders call 1–800–43–BRIGHT, write P.O. Box 372, Naperville, IL 60566,
or fax 630-961-2168

SPHINX® PUBLISHING'S NATIONAL TITLES

Valid in All 50 States

LEGAL SURVIVAL IN BUSINESS

How to Form Your Own Corporation (2E)	$19.95
How to Form Your Own Partnership	$19.95
How to Register Your Own Copyright (2E)	$19.95
How to Register Your Own Trademark (2E)	$19.95
Most Valuable Business Legal Forms You'll Ever Need (2E)	$19.95
Most Valuable Corporate Forms You'll Ever Need (2E)	$24.95
Software Law (with diskette)	$29.95

LEGAL SURVIVAL IN COURT

Crime Victim's Guide to Justice	$19.95
Debtors' Rights (3E)	$12.95
Defend Yourself Against Criminal Charges	$19.95
Grandparents' Rights	$19.95
Help Your Lawyer Win Your Case	$12.95
Jurors' Rights (2E)	$9.95
Legal Malpractice and Other Claims Against Your Lawyer	$18.95
Legal Research Made Easy (2E)	$14.95
Simple Ways to Protect Yourself From Lawsuits	$24.95
Victims' Rights	$12.95
Winning Your Personal Injury Claim	$19.95

LEGAL SURVIVAL IN REAL ESTATE

How to Buy a Condominium or Townhome	$16.95
How to Negotiate Real Estate Contracts (3E)	$16.95
How to Negotiate Real Estate Leases (3E)	$16.95
Successful Real Estate Brokerage Management	$19.95

LEGAL SURVIVAL IN PERSONAL AFFAIRS

How to File Your Own Bankruptcy (4E)	$19.95
How to File Your Own Divorce (3E)	$19.95
How to Make Your Own Will	$12.95
How to Write Your Own Living Will	$9.95
How to Write Your Own Premarital Agreement (2E)	$19.95
How to Win Your Unemployment Compensation Claim	$19.95
Living Trusts and Simple Ways to Avoid Probate (2E)	$19.95
Most Valuable Personal Legal Forms You'll Ever Need	$14.95
Neighbor vs. Neighbor	$12.95
The Power of Attorney Handbook (3E)	$19.95
Simple Ways to Protect Yourself from Lawsuits	$24.95
Social Security Benefits Handbook (2E)	$14.95
Unmarried Parents' Rights	$19.95
U.S.A. Immigration Guide (3E)	$19.95
Guia de Inmigracion a Estados Unidos	$19.95

Legal Survival Guides are directly available from Sourcebooks, Inc., or from your local bookstores.

For credit card orders call 1–800–43–BRIGHT, write P.O. Box 372, Naperville, IL 60566,
or fax 630-961-2168

SPHINX® PUBLISHING ORDER FORM

BILL TO:		SHIP TO:	
Phone #	Terms	F.O.B. Chicago, IL	Ship Date

Charge my: ☐ VISA ☐ MasterCard ☐ American Express

☐ **Money Order or Personal Check**

Credit Card Number   Expiration Date

Qty	ISBN	Title	Retail	Ext.
		SPHINX PUBLISHING NATIONAL TITLES		
	1-57071-166-6	Crime Victim's Guide to Justice	$19.95	
	1-57071-342-1	Debtors' Rights (3E)	$12.95	
	1-57071-162-3	Defend Yourself Against Criminal Charges	$19.95	
	1-57248-001-7	Grandparents' Rights	$19.95	
	0-913825-99-9	Guia de Inmigracion a Estados Unidos	$19.95	
	1-57248-021-1	Help Your Lawyer Win Your Case	$12.95	
	1-57071-164-X	How to Buy a Condominium or Townhome	$16.95	
	1-57071-223-9	How to File Your Own Bankruptcy (4E)	$19.95	
	1-57071-224-7	How to File Your Own Divorce (3E)	$19.95	
	1-57071-227-1	How to Form Your Own Corporation (2E)	$19.95	
	1-57071-343-X	How to Form Your Own Partnership	$19.95	
	1-57071-228-X	How to Make Your Own Will	$12.95	
	1-57071-331-6	How to Negotiate Real Estate Contracts (3E)	$16.95	
	1-57071-332-4	How to Negotiate Real Estate Leases (3E)	$16.95	
	1-57071-225-5	How to Register Your Own Copyright (2E)	$19.95	
	1-57071-226-3	How to Register Your Own Trademark (2E)	$19.95	
	1-57071-349-9	How to Win Your Unemployment Compensation Claim	$19.95	
	1-57071-167-4	How to Write Your Own Living Will	$9.95	
	1-57071-344-8	How to Write Your Own Premarital Agreement (2E)	$19.95	
	1-57071-333-2	Jurors' Rights (2E)	$9.95	
	1-57248-032-7	Legal Malpractice and Other Claims Against...	$18.95	
	1-57071-400-2	Legal Research Made Easy (2E)	$14.95	
	1-57071-336-7	Living Trusts and Simple Ways to Avoid Probate (2E)	$19.95	
	1-57071-345-6	Most Valuable Bus. Legal Forms You'll Ever Need (2E)	$19.95	
	1-57071-346-4	Most Valuable Corporate Forms You'll Ever Need (2E)	$24.95	
	1-57071-347-2	Most Valuable Personal Legal Forms You'll Ever Need	$14.95	

Qty	ISBN	Title	Retail	Ext.
	0-913825-41-7	Neighbor vs. Neighbor	$12.95	
	1-57071-348-0	The Power of Attorney Handbook (3E)	$19.95	
	1-57248-020-3	Simple Ways to Protect Yourself from Lawsuits	$24.95	
	1-57071-337-5	Social Security Benefits Handbook (2E)	$14.95	
	1-57071-163-1	Software Law (w/diskette)	$29.95	
	0-913825-86-7	Successful Real Estate Brokerage Mgmt.	$19.95	
	1-57071-399-5	Unmarried Parents' Rights	$19.95	
	1-57071-354-5	U.S.A. Immigration Guide (3E)	$19.95	
	0-913825-82-4	Victims' Rights	$12.95	
	1-57071-165-8	Winning Your Personal Injury Claim	$19.95	
		CALIFORNIA TITLES		
	1-57071-360-X	CA Power of Attorney Handbook	$12.95	
	1-57071-355-3	How to File for Divorce in CA	$19.95	
	1-57071-356-1	How to Make a CA Will	$12.95	
	1-57071-408-8	How to Probate an Estate in CA	$19.95	
	1-57071-357-X	How to Start a Business in CA	$16.95	
	1-57071-358-8	How to Win in Small Claims Court in CA	$14.95	
	1-57071-359-6	Landlords' Rights and Duties in CA	$19.95	
		FLORIDA TITLES		
	1-57071-363-4	Florida Power of Attorney Handbook (2E)	$9.95	
	1-57071-403-7	How to File for Divorce in FL (5E)	$21.95	
	1-57071-401-0	How to Form a Partnership in FL	$19.95	
	1-57248-004-1	How to Form a Nonprofit Corp. in FL (3E)	$19.95	
	1-57071-380-4	How to Form a Corporation in FL (4E)	$19.95	
	1-57071-361-8	How to Make a FL Will (5E)	$12.95	
		Form Continued on Following Page	**SUBTOTAL**	

To order, call Sourcebooks at 1-800-43-BRIGHT or FAX (630)961-2168 (Bookstores, libraries, wholesalers—please call for discount)

SPHINX® PUBLISHING ORDER FORM

Qty	ISBN	Title	Retail	Ext.
		FLORIDA TITLES (CONT'D)		
_____	1-57248-056-4	How to Modify Your FL Divorce Judgement (3E)	$22.95	_____
_____	1-57071-364-2	How to Probate an Estate in FL (3E)	$24.95	_____
_____	1-57248-005-X	How to Start a Business in FL (4E)	$16.95	_____
_____	1-57071-362-6	How to Win in Small Claims Court in FL (6E)	$14.95	_____
_____	1-57071-335-9	Landlords' Rights and Duties in FL (7E)	$19.95	_____
_____	1-57071-334-0	Land Trusts in FL (5E)	$24.95	_____
_____	0-913825-73-5	Women's Legal Rights in FL	$19.95	_____
		GEORGIA TITLES		
_____	1-57071-387-1	How to File for Divorce in GA (3E)	$19.95	_____
_____	1-57248-047-5	How to Make a GA Will (2E)	$9.95	_____
_____	1-57248-026-2	How to Start and Run a GA Business (2E)	$18.95	_____
		ILLINOIS TITLES		
_____	1-57071-405-3	How to File for Divorce in IL (2E)	$19.95	_____
_____	1-57071-415-0	How to Make an IL Will (2E)	$12.95	_____
_____	1-57071-416-9	How to Start a Business in IL (2E)	$16.95	_____
		MASSACHUSETTS TITLES		
_____	1-57071-329-4	How to File for Divorce in MA (2E)	$19.95	_____
_____	1-57248-050-5	How to Make a MA Will	$9.95	_____
_____	1-57248-053-X	How to Probate an Estate in MA	$19.95	_____
_____	1-57248-054-8	How to Start a Business in MA	$16.95	_____
_____	1-57248-055-6	Landlords' Rights and Duties in MA	$19.95	_____
		MICHIGAN TITLES		
_____	1-57071-409-6	How to File for Divorce in MI (2E)	$19.95	_____
_____	1-57248-015-7	How to Make a MI Will	$9.95	_____
_____	1-57071-407-X	How to Start a Business in MI (2E)	$16.95	_____
		MINNESOTA TITLES		
_____	1-57248-039-4	How to File for Divorce in MN	$19.95	_____
_____	1-57248-040-8	How to Form a Simple Corporation in MN	$19.95	_____
_____	1-57248-037-8	How to Make a MN Will	$9.95	_____
_____	1-57248-038-6	How to Start a Business in MN	$16.95	_____

Qty	ISBN	Title	Retail	Ext.
		NEW YORK TITLES		
_____	1-57071-184-4	How to File for Divorce in NY	$19.95	_____
_____	1-57071-183-6	How to Make a NY Will	$12.95	_____
_____	1-57071-185-2	How to Start a Business in NY	$16.95	_____
_____	1-57071-187-9	How to Win in Small Claims Court in NY	$14.95	_____
_____	1-57071-186-0	Landlords' Rights and Duties in NY	$19.95	_____
_____	1-57071-188-7	New York Power of Attorney Handbook	$19.95	_____
		NORTH CAROLINA TITLES		
_____	1-57071-326-X	How to File for Divorce in NC (2E)	$19.95	_____
_____	1-57071-327-8	How to Make a NC Will (2E)	$12.95	_____
_____	0-913825-93-X	How to Start a Business in NC	$16.95	_____
		PENNSYLVANIA TITLES		
_____	1-57071-177-1	How to File for Divorce in PA	$19.95	_____
_____	1-57071-176-3	How to Make a PA Will	$12.95	_____
_____	1-57071-178-X	How to Start a Business in PA	$16.95	_____
_____	1-57071-179-8	Landlords' Rights and Duties in PA	$19.95	_____
		TEXAS TITLES		
_____	1-57071-330-8	How to File for Divorce in TX (2E)	$19.95	_____
_____	1-57248-009-2	How to Form a Simple Corporation in TX	$19.95	_____
_____	1-57071-417-7	How to Make a TX Will (2E)	$12.95	_____
_____	1-57071-418-5	How to Probate an Estate in TX (2E)	$19.95	_____
_____	1-57071-365-0	How to Start a Business in TX (2E)	$16.95	_____
_____	1-57248-012-2	How to Win in Small Claims Court in TX	$14.95	_____
_____	1-57248-011-4	Landlords' Rights and Duties in TX	$19.95	_____

SUBTOTAL THIS PAGE _____

SUBTOTAL PREVIOUS PAGE _____

Illinois residents add 6.75% sales tax

Florida residents add 6% state sales tax plus applicable discretionary surtax _____

Shipping— $4.00 for 1st book, $1.00 each additional _____

TOTAL _____

Projects for Blocks and Borders

by Marsha McCloskey

Dedicated to my children, Amanda and Matthew

Acknowledgments

My thanks to:

Sharon Yenter for permission to use two applique patterns — Tulips and Ribbons and the Washington Monument Album Block — from her pattern-of-the-month series on Easy Historic Applique in 1982 for In the Beginning-Quilts.

Glendora Hutson and Nancy Dice whose work for Wall Quilts is, in part, reproduced here.

Pam Boag, Rose Burkette and Gretchen Eagle for help making the sample projects for photography.

Nancy Martin for use of her Washington Monument Album Wall Quilt for photography.

Sharon Yenter for use of her Tulips and Ribbons Pillow for photography.

The Northwest School for the Arts, Humanities and Environment for the opportunity to make for them the Star Set Tall Pine Tree raffle quilt, and in the process to get to know so many kind and wonderful people.

Nancy Martin and her staff at That Patchwork Place.

Suzanne Wall for use of her "Hearts and Tulips" quilt for photography.

Credits:

Photography . . . . *Carl Murray*
Illustration and Graphics . . . . *Stephanie Benson*
Marsha McCloskey
Editor . . . . *Roberta Fuehrer*

All quilts and patchwork projects made by the author unless otherwise noted.

Projects for Blocks and Borders©

©Marsha Reynolds McCloskey, 1984

0-943574-28-5

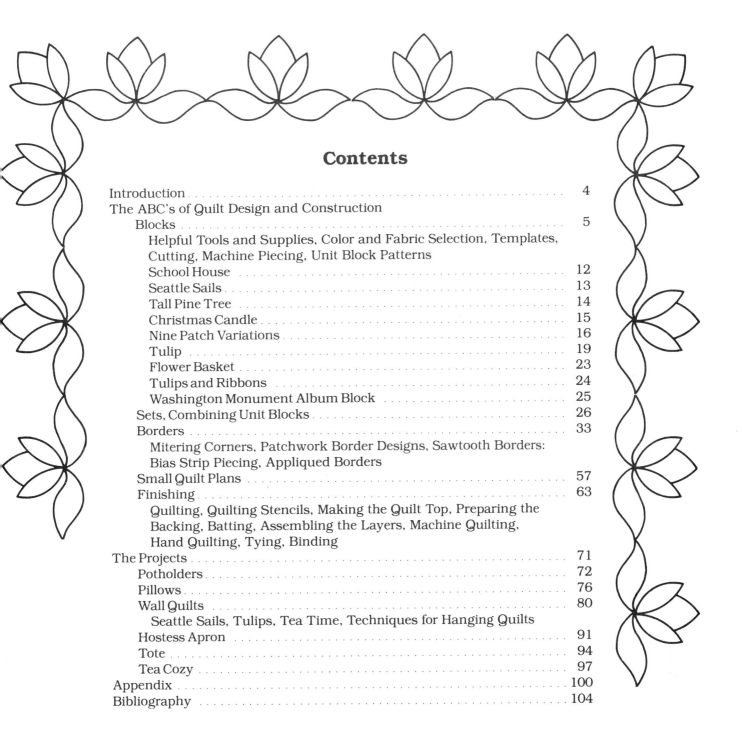

Contents

Introduction

Projects for Blocks and Borders is a patchwork design book for the novice quilter who enjoys personalizing quilts and projects. No quilt or project is as satisfying as one you have designed yourself.

This book presents logical thinking about patchwork unit block and border designs and their many uses in quilts and patchwork projects. It contains a collection of simple 8" blocks and 2" and 4" repeat borders, along with templates to use in construction. These blocks and borders can be combined in many ways to create exciting quilts and projects. The novice quilt designer will enjoy using the concepts and patterns presented here to create unique patchwork items.

The book is divided into two major sections. First, the ABC's of Quilt Design and Construction includes unit block motifs, quilt and border design tips, sample quilt plans and advice on color and fabric selection. Here also are the basic sewing techniques needed to successfully complete the quilts and projects. These are simply descriptions of my own sewing methods. Experienced stitchers may feel more comfortable with other techniques. Feel free to adapt whatever you find here.

The second section of **Projects for Blocks and Borders** contains detailed instructions for the construction of six basic patchwork projects. They are designs I used when I was selling my patchwork at craft fairs and to shops. The construction of these projects is fairly simple. Most are offered in several patchwork styles to accommodate the various block and border designs in this book.

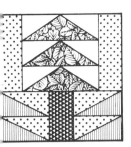
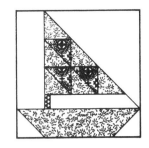
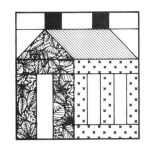
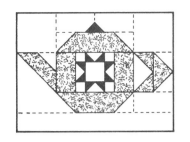

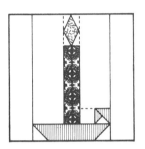

The ABC's of Quilt Design and Construction

Blocks

Most traditional American quilt designs are based on repeated small designs called unit blocks. There are thousands of pieced and appliqued unit block designs. Some are pictorial, such as the School House and Tulip blocks; others are purely geometric, such as the Nine Patch Variations that begin on page 16.

Although names for the traditional blocks vary through time and geography, learning the names for the different motifs can be a good introduction to that special jargon I call the "language of quilt." Sawtooth, Sherman's March, Shoo Fly, Variable Star and Nonsense are all names that cause certain designs to flash across a quilter's mind. It is a kind of descriptive shorthand that can save many long explanations.

Not all of the designs in this book are traditional blocks. The Tulip, Teapot, Cup and Saucer, Seattle Sails and Christmas Candle are all products of my busy fingers sketching on graph paper. Other people probably have come up with the same or similar designs in the past. It is a lot of fun to play with these pieced pictures. Try some yourself. I have seen patchwork angels, camels, geese, cars, trucks — all manner of things. These images could, of course, be done in applique, but piecing them, especially on the machine, is much quicker.

There are many unit block designs in this book. With a few exceptions (the 7" potholder blocks and the Tea Time blocks) all measure 8" square and can be used interchangeably in the projects and quilts described. The opportunity to use these blocks in different ways gives you a chance to design your own patchwork projects without risks. For instance, you can choose to use the 8" School House block in Quilt Plan A or B or as the design block for Pillows, page 76; Hostess Apron, page 91; Tote, page 94; or Wall Quilts, page 80.

These choices might even inspire you to use the design block for other things as well. You are the designer of your own project. You choose motif, color and form. Use this book as a guide, a place to start.

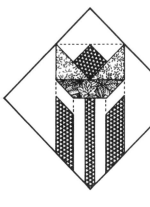

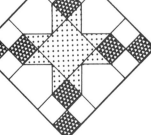

Helpful Tools and Supplies

You will need the following tools and supplies to complete the processes described in this section.

Drawing Supplies: Graph paper in a 1/8" grid and colored pencils for drawing quilt plans and sketching design ideas.

Rulers: I use two rulers; both are clear plastic with a red grid of 1/8" squares. A short ruler is for drawing quilt designs on graph paper; a longer one, 2" wide and 18" long, is for drafting designs full size, making templates, measuring and making borders and quilting lines. If your local quilt shop doesn't carry them, try a stationery store or any place that carries drafting or art supplies. Another useful tool is a 12" plastic 45°/90° right angle.

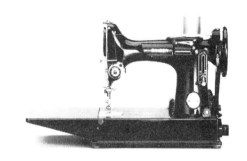

Scissors: You will need scissors for paper, a good sharp pair for cutting fabric only, and possibly a little pair for snipping threads. If your fabric scissors are dull, have them sharpened. If they are close to "dead," invest in a new pair. It's worth it.

Template Material: To make templates, you will need graph paper or tracing paper, lightweight posterboard (manila file folders are good) or plastic, and a glue stick.

Markers: Most marking can be done with a regular #2 lead pencil and a white dressmaker's pencil. Keep them sharp. There is a blue felt tip marking pen available that is water erasable; it works especially well for marking quilting designs. (When you no longer need the lines for guides, spray them with cool water and the blue marks will disappear.) Ask the salespeople at a local fabric or quilt shop about the different kinds of marking pens available.

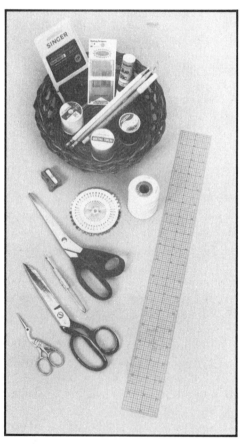

Sewing Machine: It needn't be fancy. All you need is an evenly locking straight stitch. Whatever kind of sewing machine you have, get to know it and how it runs. If it needs servicing, have it done, or get out the manual and do it yourself. Replace the old needle with a new one. Often, if your machine has a zigzag stitch, it will have a throat plate with an oblong hole for the needle to pass through. You might want to replace this plate with one that has a little round hole for straight stitching. This will help eliminate problems you might have with the edges of fabrics being fed into the hole by the action of the feed dogs.

Needles: A supply of new sewing machine needles for light to medium weight cottons is necessary. You'll also need an assortment of Sharps for handwork and quilting needles (Betweens #8, #9 or #10) if you plan to hand quilt. A sharp needle with an eye large enough for sport-weight yarn is necessary if you plan to tie.

Pins: Multi-colored glass or plastic headed pins are generally longer, stronger and easier to see and hold than regular dressmaker's pins.

Iron and Ironing Board: A shot of steam is useful.

Seam Ripper: I always keep one handy.

Color and Fabric Selection

The fabrics chosen for the patchwork designs in this book should be lightweight, closely woven cottons or cotton blends. They should be uniform in weight and have a high cotton content. For patchwork, 100% cotton is best; high polyester content makes small patchwork pieces difficult to cut and sew.

Cotton should be preshrunk before use. Wash light and dark fabrics separately with regular laundry detergent and warm water. Test dark fabrics for running before you wash them by rinsing them separately in warm water. Keep rinsing until the rinse water stays clear. A half cup of white vinegar added to rinse water for dark fabrics may help set dyes and may prevent running or fading later.

The first step in color and fabric selection is to choose a project. What are you making and what is the occasion? A quilt for the new baby will have different colors than a lap quilt for Uncle Harry. The function of an item will very often suggest a color theme. A Christmas quilt might be red and green. A throw for the couch should have colors that complement the couch and the room. A tea cozy could match the colors of the teapot or table linens. A color theme tells you which colors to look for, and a quilt or project *plan* will tell you how many fabrics to choose and the yardage to buy. Examples of plans for Small Quilts are found on page 57.

With a plan and color theme in mind, pull out all the fabrics in your home collection that might work. Then play with them, arranging the fabrics in different orders: from light to medium to dark and back again. Try to imagine what they will look like in your patchwork design. Squint at the fabrics; light, medium and dark values become obvious this way. Choose one fabric that fits your color theme, that you particularly like and definitely want to use.

This main fabric or "idea print" will give you color clues as to what other fabrics will go with it. Think in terms of related colors and contrasts. If your "idea print" is dark, choose something light in a related color to go with it. When two fabrics are side by side, there should be a definite line where one stops and the other begins. This shows contrast.

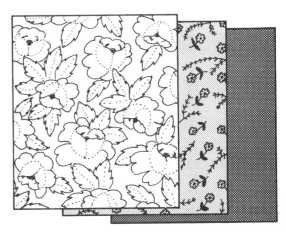

Good fabric selections for three-color quilt designs. Note contrast in color and visual texture.

Good background prints

The contrast should be not only in light and dark, but also in color, the size of the prints and their visual texture. Visual texture is the way a print looks — is it spotty, smooth, plain, dappled, linear, rhythmical or swirly? Are the figures far apart or close together, large or small? Mix large prints with small prints, flowery allover designs with little dots or checks. Use solids to add even more variety to the visual texture. Too many similar prints create a dull and uninteresting surface.

Plain, dark solid-looking colors are usually more dominant than lighter, more busy prints and should be placed in the part of the design that you want to stand out. Step back and squint at the fabrics and you should be able to tell which fabrics come forward visually and which recede.

Choose a background fabric carefully. Many quilt patterns have relatively large unpieced areas as background to pieced designs. These areas are generally light in color while the design motif is dark. Good background prints for such designs have subtle allover texture, fine detail and movement without being spotty or linear. Light solids are too plain for large unbroken areas unless a fair amount of quilting is planned and are better used in small amounts than as main background fabrics.

7

Keep in mind that some prints are too large, or have motifs spaced too far apart, to be used in small pieces for patchwork. The test is this: Make a "window" of your fingers the approximate size and shape of the templates you will be using. Move this "window" over the fabric. If the pattern is coherent within the size and shape, then use it. If all you see are blank spaces and parts of flowers, try another fabric with a smaller print. Don't despair, though, if you really like the fabric; some widely spaced design motifs can be centered in a piece to achieve a very special effect. Also, large prints can always be used on the backs of quilts.

Another fabric option is to use scraps. Several similar scrap pieces can be substituted for a fabric in a pattern provided they equal roughly the same amount. It is important when using scraps to maintain good contrast of lights and darks and of visual texture.

After playing with your own fabrics for a while, you may find you don't have enough for the project. Take the usable pieces with you to the fabric store and continue working with fabric combinations until a satisfactory effect is achieved.

Sometimes it is better not to proceed with a block design or color combination. Upon completion, you will either like a unit block or you won't. A sample block that makes you happy, that gives you a lift when you look at it, is worth repeating for a quilt. But if a block brings a scowl to your face, it is probably not worth proceeding. Trust your reactions and don't spend hours and hours working on a quilt that never pleased you in the first place. Keep making sample blocks until you get one that "sings." The other blocks, not destined for quilts, can be used for small projects, sampler quilts or just put aside.

Using large or widely spaced prints

I never throw a block away, but I definitely do not like every block and design I construct. One of my favorite quilts, called False Starts and Rejects (see page 51), is a sampler quilt made entirely of discarded blocks and unfinished project starts. These bits of patchwork were sewn together to make a bright, cheerful quilt that holds a lot of memories and makes me smile when I see it.

Making a stiffened template

Templates

To make each unit block, you will need a set of pattern pieces or templates. Carefully trace the templates from the book onto graph paper or tracing paper. Trace accurately and transfer to the paper all information printed on the templates in the book.

There are two ways to use these templates: Use them as paper patterns to cut around, or use them stiffened to trace around before you cut. Paper templates are simply cut out and used. To make stiffened templates, roughly cut out the pattern pieces (outside the cutting line). Glue each one to a thin piece of plastic (x-ray film is good) or lightweight posterboard. Cut out the paper pattern and its stiffening together. Be precise. Make a template for each shape in the design.

Cutting

Study the design and templates. Determine the number of pieces to cut of each shape and each fabric. Trim the selvage from the fabric before you begin cutting. When one fabric is to be used both for borders and in the unit block designs, cut the borders first and the smaller pieces from what is left over (see Borders on page 33).

At the ironing board, press and fold the fabric so that one, two or four layers can be cut at one time (except for linear prints such as stripes and checks that should be cut one at a time). Fold the fabric so that each piece will be cut on the straight grain.

When using a stiffened template, position it on the fabric so the arrows match the straight grain of the fabric. With a sharp pencil (white for dark fabrics, lead for light ones), trace around the template on the fabric. This is the cutting line. Cut just inside this line to most accurately duplicate the template.

For a paper template, line it up with the straight grain of fabric. Hold it in place on the fabric and cut around it. Be precise. Compare cut pieces with the template to be sure they are true.

In machine piecing, there are no drawn lines to guide your sewing. The seamline is 1/4" from the cut edge of the fabric, so this outside edge must be precisely cut to ensure accurate sewing.

Always make one sample block of a design before embarking on a large project. After cutting the necessary number of pieces of each color and shape for one unit block, arrange the pieces on a flat surface in the desired design. This will help you determine which pieces to sew together first and evaluate your fabric choices and arrangement.

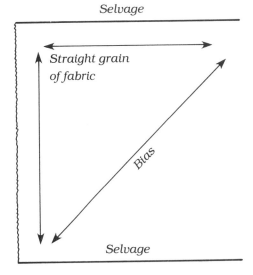

Bias

Using a paper template

Machine Piecing

For machine piecing, use white or neutral thread as light in color as the lightest fabric in the project. Use a dark neutral thread for piecing dark solids. It is easier to work with 100% cotton thread on some machines. Check your needle. If it is dull, burred or bent, replace it with a fresh one.

Sew exact 1/4" seams. To determine the 1/4" seam allowance on your machine, place a template under the presser foot and gently lower the needle onto the seamline. The distance from the needle to the edge of the template is 1/4". Lay a piece of masking tape at the edge of the template to act as the 1/4" mark; use the edge as a guide. Stitch length should be set at 10-12 stitches per inch. For most of the sewing in this book, sew from cut edge to cut edge (exceptions will be noted). Backtack if you wish, although it is really not necessary as each seam will be crossed and held by another.

Use chain piecing whenever possible to save time and thread. To chain piece, sew one seam, but do not lift the presser foot. Do not take the piece out of the sewing machine and do not cut the thread. Instead, set up the next seam to be sewn and stitch as you did the first. There will be a little twist of thread between the two pieces. Sew all the seams you can at one time in this way, then remove the "chain." Clip the threads.

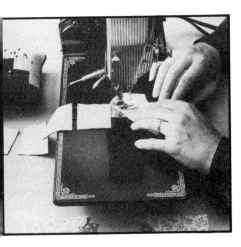

Chain piecing

Press the seam allowances to one side, toward the darker fabric when possible. Avoid too much ironing as you sew because it tends to stretch biases and distort fabric shapes.

To piece a unit block, sew the smallest pieces together first to form units. Join smaller units to form larger ones until the block is complete. The Single Irish Chain block is a simple example. First make the four corner square units by sewing the smaller squares together as shown. Then sew these units together with the larger squares in rows. Sew the long seams last. Pay close attention to the design drawing and sewing instructions given with the patterns.

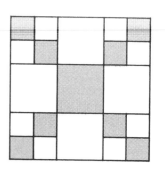

Piecing sequence of Single Irish Chain

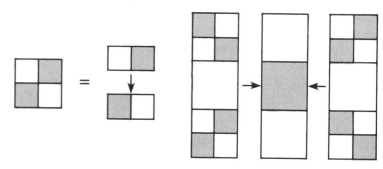

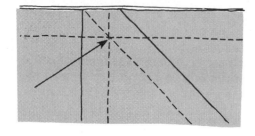

Opposing seams

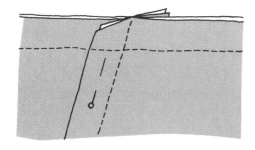

Positioning pin

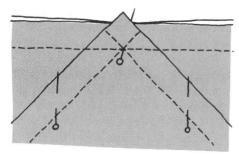

The "X"

Short seams need not be pinned unless matching is involved, or the seam is longer than 4". Keep pins away from the seamline. Sewing over pins tends to burr the needle and makes it hard to be accurate in tight places.

Ideally, if pieces are cut and sewn precisely, patchwork designs will come out flat and smooth with crisply matched corners and points. In practice, it doesn't always happen that way. Here are four matching techniques that can be helpful in many different piecing situations.

1. Opposing Seams: When stitching one seamed unit to another, press seam allowances on the seams that need to match in opposite directions. The two "opposing" seams will hold each other in place and evenly distribute the bulk. Plan pressing to take advantage of opposing seams.

2. Positioning Pin: A pin, carefully pushed straight through two points that need to match and pulled tight, will establish the proper point of matching. Pin the seam normally and remove the positioning pin before stitching.

3. The "X": When triangles are pieced, stitches will form an "X" at the next seamline. Stitch through the center of the "X" to make sure the points on the sewn triangles will not be chopped off.

4. Easing: When two pieces to be sewn together are supposed to match but instead are slightly different lengths, pin the points of matching and stitch with the shorter piece on top. The feed dogs will ease the fullness of the bottom piece.

You can do beautiful and accurate piecing on the sewing machine. Try to correct mistakes when they happen (keep a seam ripper handy), but don't spend too much time ripping out and resewing. Some sewing inaccuracies are correctable, some are not. Sometimes the best thing is to move on and make the next block better. The quality of your piecing will improve as you go along.

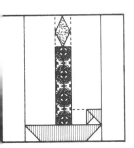
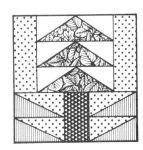
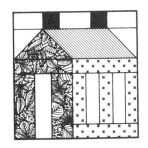
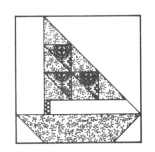

Unit Block Patterns

On this and the next few pages are unit block designs and their templates. These blocks are grouped together because they require only the machine piecing techniques just described. They are all 8" unit blocks and can be used interchangeably in the quilts and patchwork projects described later in the book.

Each template for the unit blocks is labeled with a number, the design name, the finished block size, and the number to cut for one block. A notation such as Cut 4 + 4 indicates the same template is used for two colors in the design. An "R" in a cutting notation means "reverse." The pieces are mirror images: Cut the first number of pieces with the template face up and then flip it over face down to cut the remainder. Where it is needed, shapes are marked with a grain line (see page 16). All templates, except those for applique, include 1/4" seam allowances.

Where specific fabric placement is important to the design, templates are marked with a fabric suggestion. I have tried not to be too specific about fabric placement for most of the blocks because there are many ways the colors could be arranged, and I don't want to rule out any possibilities.

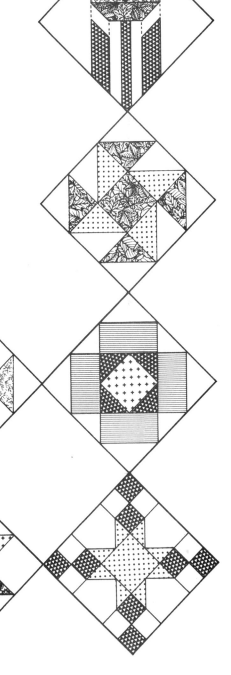

11

School House

Use this design for Pillows, page 76; Hostess Apron bib, page 91; Tote, page 94; Small Quilts, page 57; or Wall Quilts, page 80.

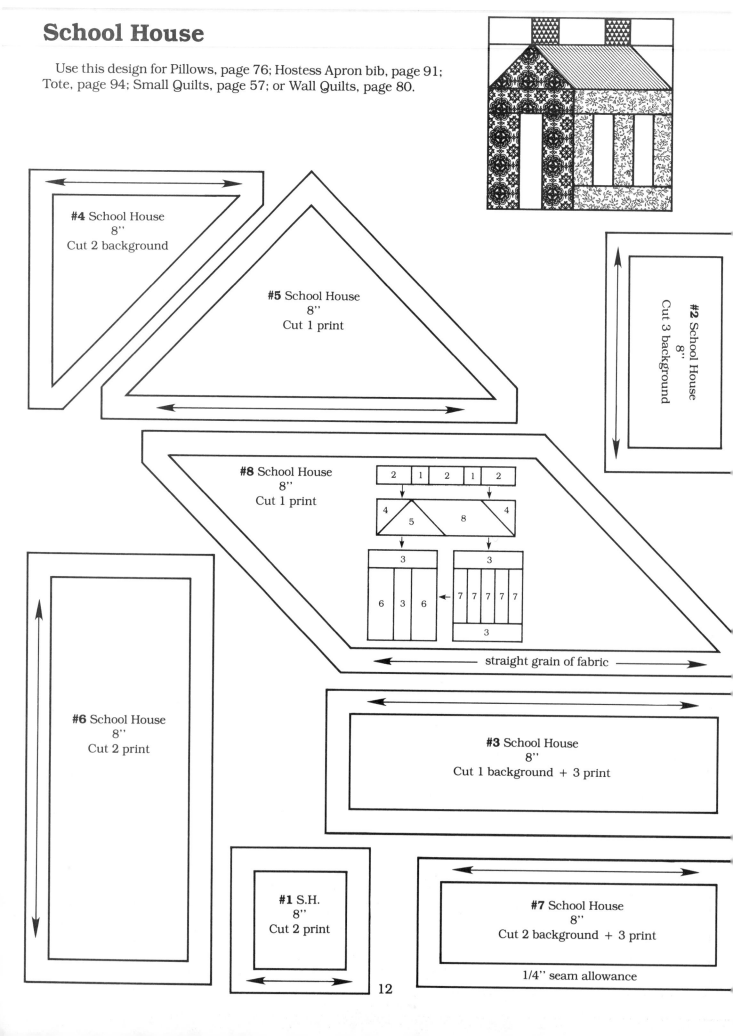

#4 School House
8"
Cut 2 background

#5 School House
8"
Cut 1 print

#2 School House
8"
Cut 3 background

#8 School House
8"
Cut 1 print

| 2 | 1 | 2 | 1 | 2 |

| 4 | 5 | 8 | 4 |

3		3
6 3 6		7 7 7 7 7
		3

straight grain of fabric

#6 School House
8"
Cut 2 print

#3 School House
8"
Cut 1 background + 3 print

#1 S.H.
8"
Cut 2 print

#7 School House
8"
Cut 2 background + 3 print

1/4" seam allowance

12

Seattle Sails

Use this design for Pillows, page 76; Hostess Apron bib, page 91;
Tote, page 94; Small Quilts, page 57; or Wall Quilts, page 80.

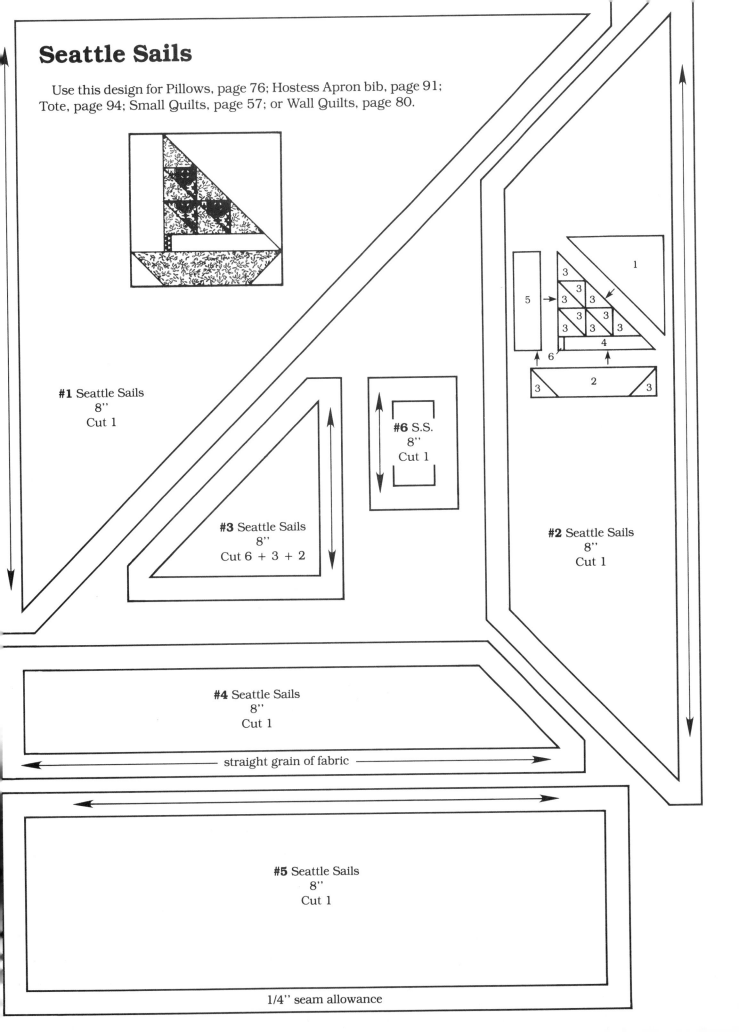

#1 Seattle Sails
8''
Cut 1

#3 Seattle Sails
8''
Cut 6 + 3 + 2

#6 S.S.
8''
Cut 1

#2 Seattle Sails
8''
Cut 1

#4 Seattle Sails
8''
Cut 1

straight grain of fabric

#5 Seattle Sails
8''
Cut 1

1/4'' seam allowance

Tall Pine Tree

This block can be used for Pillows, page 76; Hostess Apron bib, page 91; Tote, page 94; Small Quilts, page 57; and Wall Quilts, page 80.

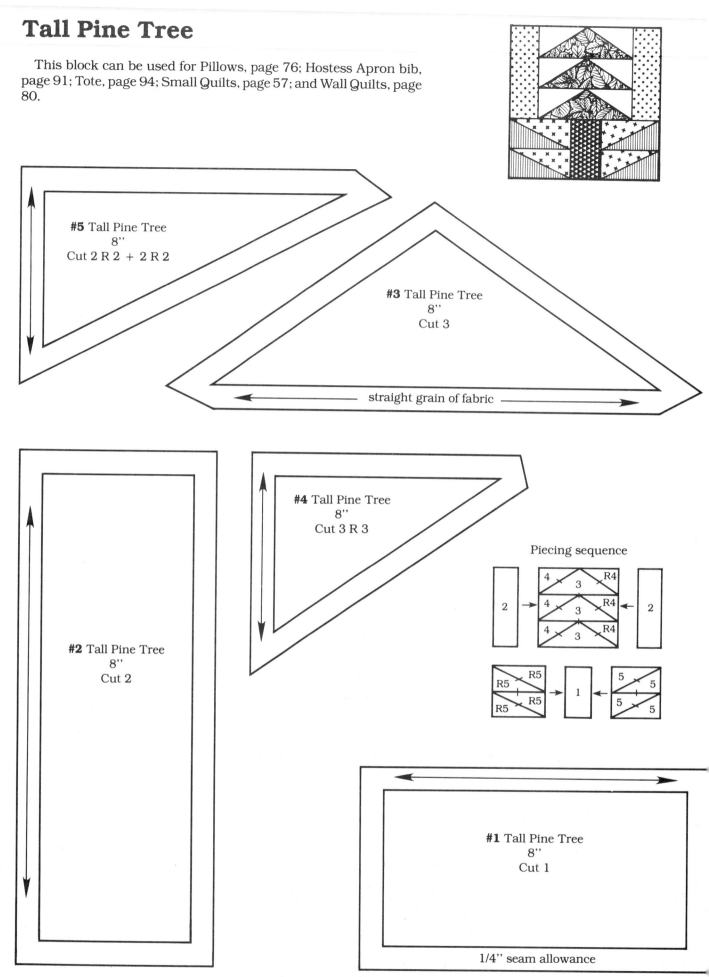

#5 Tall Pine Tree
8''
Cut 2 R 2 + 2 R 2

#3 Tall Pine Tree
8''
Cut 3

straight grain of fabric

#4 Tall Pine Tree
8''
Cut 3 R 3

#2 Tall Pine Tree
8''
Cut 2

Piecing sequence

#1 Tall Pine Tree
8''
Cut 1

1/4'' seam allowance

14

Christmas Candle

Use this design for Pillows, page 76; Hostess Apron bib, page 91; ote, page 94; Small Quilts, page 57; and Wall Quilts, page 80.

#10 Christmas Candle
8"
Cut 2

#9 C.C.
8"
Cut 1

#8 C.C.
8"
Cut 2 R 2

#5 Christmas Candle
8"
Cut 1

#3 C.C.
8"
Cut 1

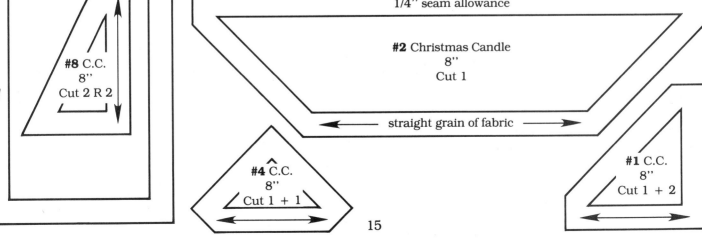

Piecing sequence

		8 8		
10	7	9	6	10
		8 8		
		5		
			4	
		3	1	
			4	
1	2		1	

#6 Christmas Candle
8"
Cut 1

#7 Christmas Candle
8"
Cut 1

1/4" seam allowance

#2 Christmas Candle
8"
Cut 1

straight grain of fabric

#4 C.C.
8"
Cut 1 + 1

#1 C.C.
8"
Cut 1 + 2

15

Nine Patch Variations

Many unit block designs are very similar. The blocks presented in this group are all based on the same nine-square grid. Because they are also all drafted in the same size, they share templates. To make a change in a unit block design, add or subtract lines to make new shapes or simply alter the coloring, adding colors or reversing the lights and the darks.

The templates given on the next few pages are for 8" blocks. Some of these designs are offered again on page 75 in a 7" size as the motifs for potholders. Be careful not to mix the templates.

Because these templates will be used differently in the various blocks, the triangles have no grain line drawn on them. The basic rule for positioning the straight grain of the fabric is that on the edge pieces of the unit block, straight grain should run parallel to the outside of the block. Unfinished bias edges in these positions can stretch with handling and ironing and distort block dimensions.

Use these designs for Pillows, page 76; Hostess Apron bib, page 91; Tote, page 94; Small Quilts, page 57; or Wall Quilts, page 80.

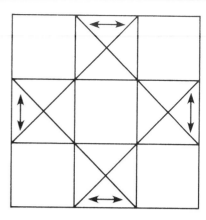

Straight grain on triangles can be on either the long or short side, depending which edge is on the outside of the block.

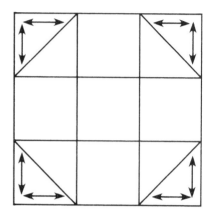

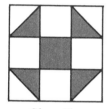
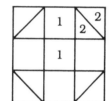

Shoo Fly

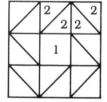

Perpetual Motion

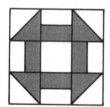
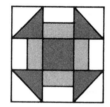
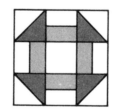
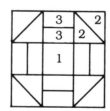

Hole in the Barn Door   Sherman's March I   Sherman's March II

16

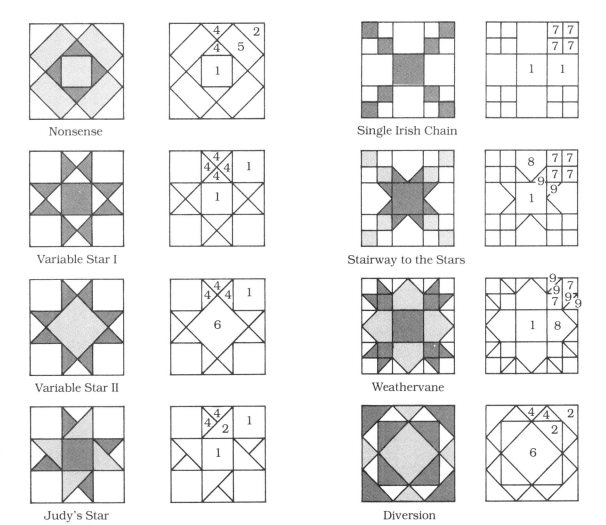

Nonsense

Variable Star I

Variable Star II

Judy's Star

Single Irish Chain

Stairway to the Stars

Weathervane

Diversion

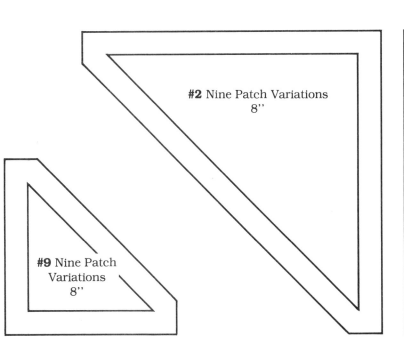

#2 Nine Patch Variations
8"

#9 Nine Patch Variations
8"

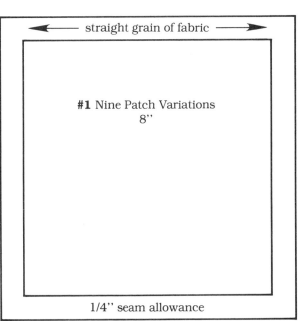

← straight grain of fabric →

#1 Nine Patch Variations
8"

1/4" seam allowance

#3 Nine Patch Variations
8"

#4 Nine Patch Variations
8"

#7 Nine Patch
Variations
8"

#8 Nine Patch Variations
8"

1/4" seam allowance

#6 Nine Patch Variations
8"

#5 Nine Patch Variations
8"

straight grain of fabric

Tulip

Use this block for Pillows, page 76; Tote, page 94; Small Quilts, page 57; or Wall Quilts, page 80.

The Tulip block requires two set-in seams. The piecing is pictured below.

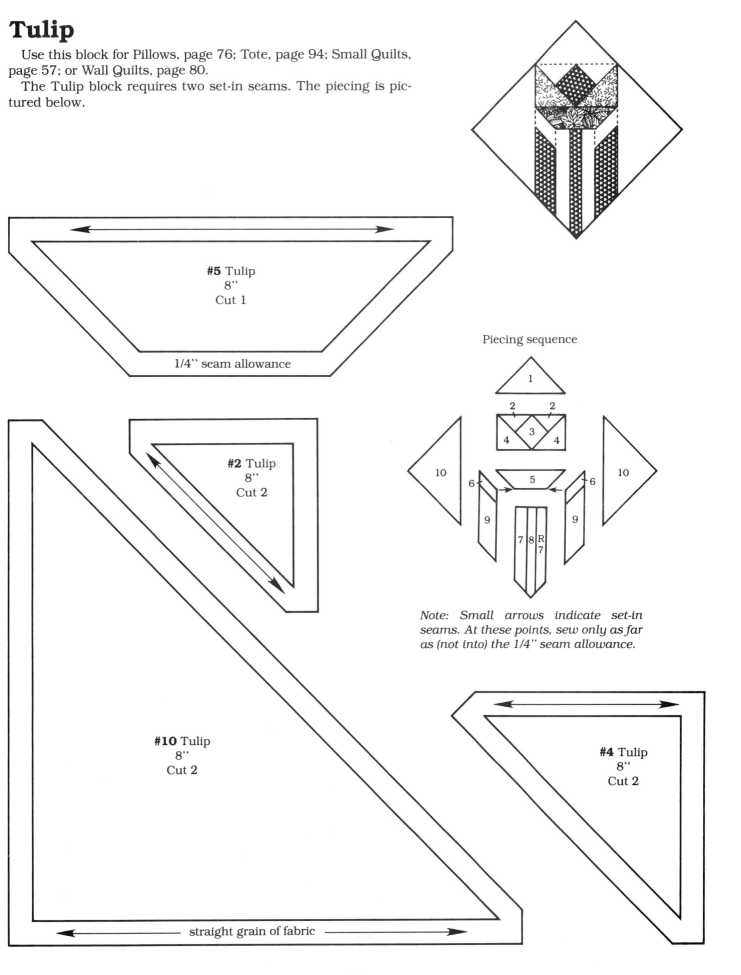

#5 Tulip
8''
Cut 1

1/4'' seam allowance

#2 Tulip
8''
Cut 2

#10 Tulip
8''
Cut 2

#4 Tulip
8''
Cut 2

straight grain of fabric

Piecing sequence

Note: Small arrows indicate set-in seams. At these points, sew only as far as (not into) the 1/4'' seam allowance.

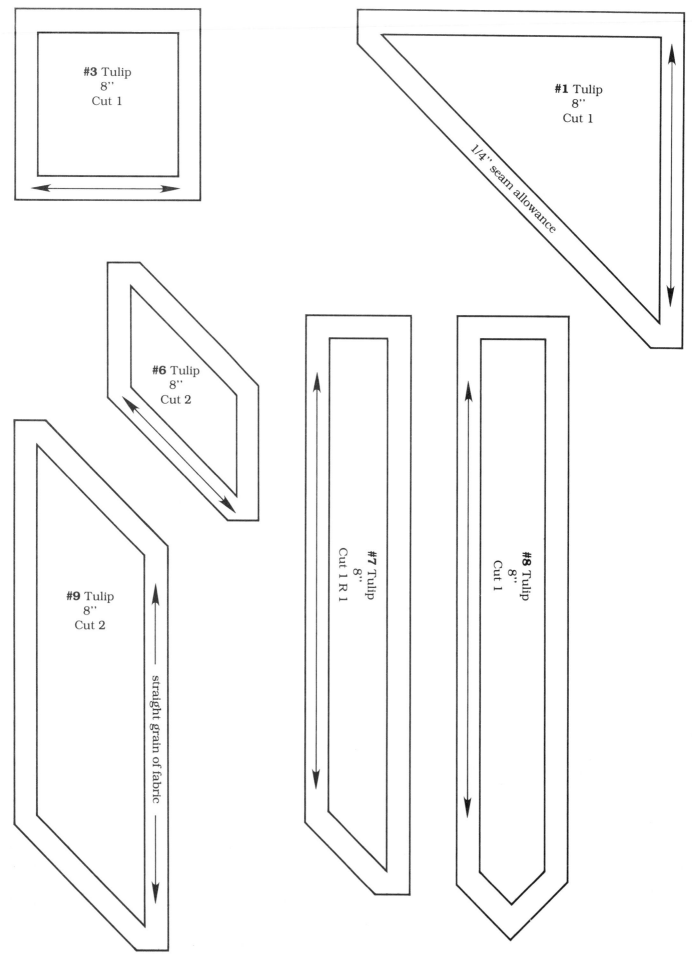

#3 Tulip
8"
Cut 1

#1 Tulip
8"
Cut 1

1/4" seam allowance

#6 Tulip
8"
Cut 2

#9 Tulip
8"
Cut 2

straight grain of fabric

#7 Tulip
8"
Cut 1 R 1

#8 Tulip
8"
Cut 1

Paper-Patch Applique

Being a "piecer," and a "machine piecer" at that, I carefully avoided applique for many years. I tried it a few times when I needed a basket handle or stem and leaves to complete a pieced design, but was never pleased with the results. Curves were choppy and points were blunt and bumpy. My perfectionist soul rebelled. If I couldn't do it well, I just wouldn't do it at all. Then I learned about paper-patch applique and began to use this technique for my applique projects. With this method, I could make crisp points and smooth curves, and that makes me quite happy.

In applique, small fabric shapes are sewn or applied to a larger background fabric to create a design. This background fabric is called the base fabric and deserves some attention before we go on to discuss design shapes. Choose a subtle allover print or solid for the background. Applique stitches are less noticeable on a print, making it a good choice for first time applique. Most applique is done on light fabrics, but if you choose a dark base, make sure the fabrics to be sewn over it are heavy enough to keep the darker fabric from showing through.

The applique blocks in this book are sized to be sewn to an 8 1/2" (cut size) background block. However, the many stitches on a complicated applique can draw up the background block and make it smaller. Therefore, it is best to cut it to size after the applique is finished. Cut your blocks 9" or even 10" to start with and trim them to size later.

If you must applique to a triangular background piece, as for the Flower Basket on page 23, staystitch 1/8" from the raw edge along the bias edge to keep it from stretching as you work.

Apply border motifs to plain border strips either before or after sewing the borders to the quilt center, whichever seems easier and allows the best design placement.

For proper placement of the applique pieces, lightly trace the design outline on the background fabric. This will help guide your sewing. Use a light pencil line or a water erasable marking pen.

Directions:

Read these instructions carefully before you begin. Illustrations show the handle on the Flower Basket block on page 23.

1. Make a stiffened template of each shape in the applique design. Do not add seam allowances to the templates.
2. On paper, trace around the stiffened templates to make a paper patch for each shape in the applique. Experiment a bit with different weights of paper for the paper patches. Newsprint is too light and file folders are too heavy.
3. Baste or pin each paper patch to the wrong side of the fabric.
4. Cut out fabric shapes, adding 1/4" seam allowance around each paper shape.

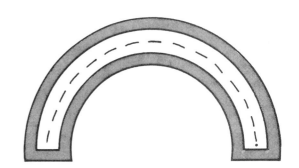

Paper template is basted or pinned to wrong side of fabric. Add 1/4" seam allowances as the pieces are cut.

5. With your fingers, turn the seam allowance over the edge of the paper and baste to paper. Baste inside curves first (a little clipping may be necessary to help the fabric stretch). On outside curves, take small running stitches through fabric only to ease in fullness. Take an occasional stitch through the paper to hold fabric in place. This basting order (inside curves first, outside curves last) is also followed in stitching and allows fullness and bias stretch to be eased outward.

6. When all the seam allowances are turned and basted, press the applique pieces, then position and pin the pieces in place on the background material.

7. Using a small, blind hemming stitch and a single matching thread (i.e., green thread for a green leaf), applique the shapes to the background.

8. Before the stitching on each piece is completed, the paper patch must be removed. To take the paper out, leave a small opening unstitched. Remove all the basting threads. Pull the paper out through the opening and finish stitching.

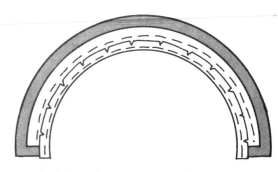

Baste inside curve over edge of paper. Clip where necessary.

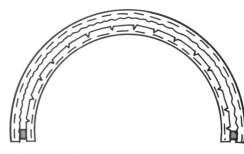

On outside curves, gather the edge of the fabric to ease in fullness, taking an occasional stitch through the paper to hold the fabric in place. The ends of the basket handle will be sewn into a seam and therefore need not be turned under.

Leave a section of the applique unstitched. Remove all the basting stitches and the paper, then finish the stitching.

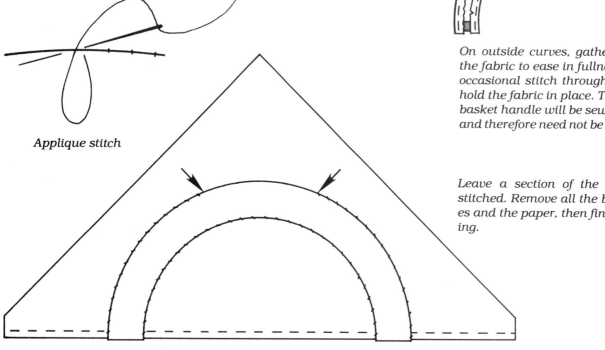

Applique stitch

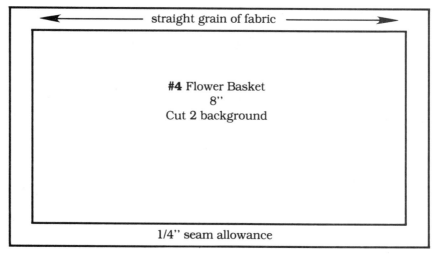

#4 Flower Basket
8"
Cut 2 background

straight grain of fabric

1/4" seam allowance

Flower Basket

A diagonally set block, the Flower Basket can be used for Pillows, page 76; Tote, page 94; Small Quilts, page 57; or Wall Quilts, page 80. The block has an appliqued handle and can be varied by using the small triangular template (#2) to make a more complicated pieced body for the basket.

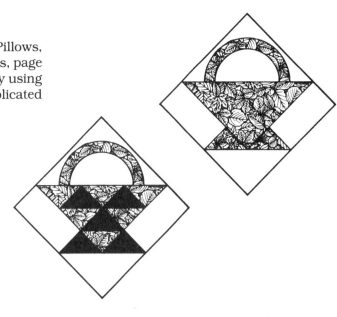

Note: The basket handle template does not include seam allowance. Refer to page 21 on Paper-Patch Applique. Applique the handle to the #1 background triangle before piecing the block. Stay-stitch 1/8'' from the long bias edge of the background triangle to keep it from distorting as you work.

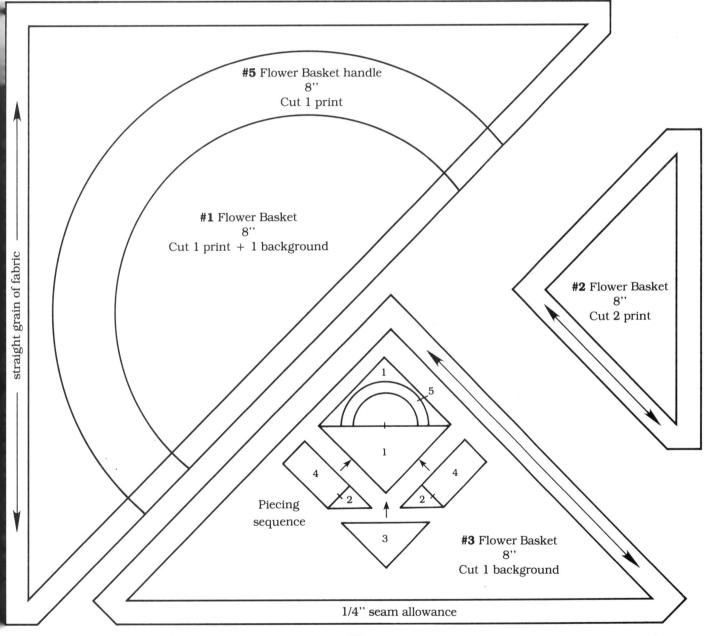

#5 Flower Basket handle
8''
Cut 1 print

#1 Flower Basket
8''
Cut 1 print + 1 background

straight grain of fabric

#2 Flower Basket
8''
Cut 2 print

Piecing sequence

#3 Flower Basket
8''
Cut 1 background

1/4'' seam allowance

23

Applique Blocks

These two applique blocks can be set straight-on or on the diagonal and can be used for Pillows, page 76; Hostess Apron bib, page 91; Tote, page 94; Small Quilts, page 57; or Wall Quilts, page 80.

Elements of the appliqued designs can be isolated and used for border repeats for the Hostess Apron skirt, Tea Cozy, and quilt borders. The outlines of these appliques can be used for a quilting motif in 8" set blocks or on plain borders. Refer to Paper-Patch Applique, page 21; Borders, page 33; and Quilting, page 63.

Tulips and Ribbons[1]

This block is adapted from a quilt in the collection of the American Museum in Britain. The quilt is from Pennsylvania, circa 1840-1850.

Note: Make a template for each numbered shape. Add 1/4" seam allowances as the pieces are cut.

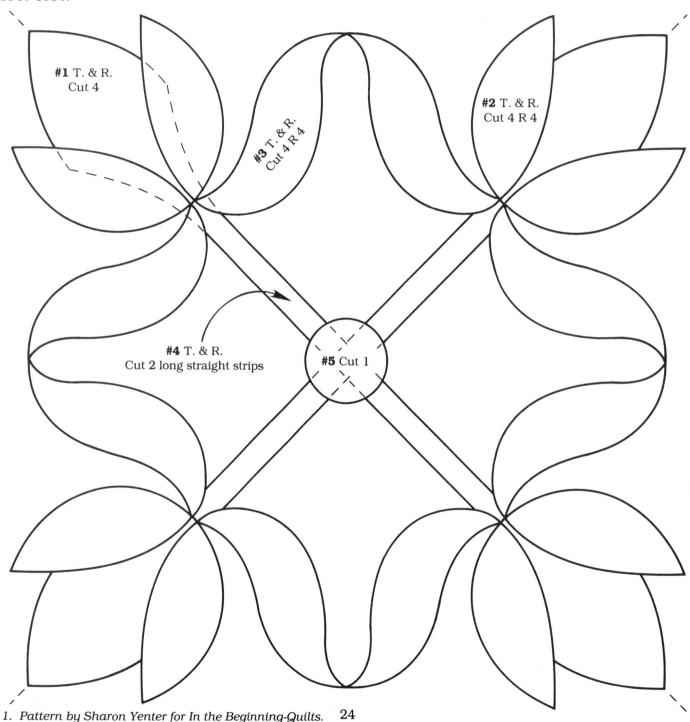

#1 T. & R. Cut 4

#2 T. & R. Cut 4 R 4

#3 T. & R. Cut 4 R 4

#4 T. & R. Cut 2 long straight strips

#5 Cut 1

1. *Pattern by Sharon Yenter for In the Beginning-Quilts.* 24

Washington Monument Album Block[2]

This 8" applique was adapted from a block in the "Washington Monument Album Quilt," by Miss Mary Everist, dated 1849-1850 and now in the Baltimore Museum of Art.

Note: Make a template for each numbered shape. Add 1/4" seam allowances as the pieces are cut.

#1 W.M.A.B.
8"
Cut 4

#2 W.M.A.B.
Cut 8

#4 Cut 1

#3 W.M.A.B.
8"
Cut 1

2. Pattern by Sharon Yenter for In the Beginning-Quilts.

Sets, Combining Unit Blocks

When unit blocks are sewn together to make a quilt top, it is called the "set." Though there are literally thousands of unit block designs, there are relatively few basic ways to put them together. Yet, an amazing number of quilt top designs can be achieved by using and combining these few basic variations.

First, a square unit block can be set straight-on or on the diagonal.

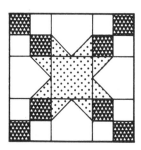

Straight-on

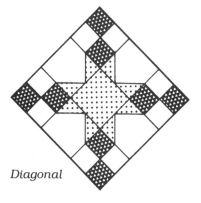

Diagonal

Blocks can be sewn together side by side or separated by un-pieced blocks or lattice strips which are called "set pieces." Alternate blocks are pieced or unpieced squares the same size as the unit blocks and are placed between them in a checkerboard fashion. Diagonal sets using alternate blocks require side triangles to complete the set.

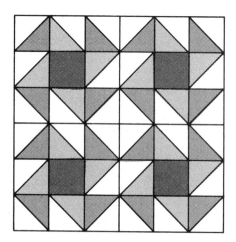

Blocks sewn side by side

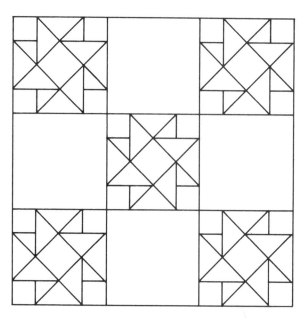

Straight set blocks with alternate un-pieced blocks.

26

Diagonal set with alternate unpieced squares and triangles to fill in the sides and corners.

Strips of fabric called lattices can also be used to separate the unit blocks.

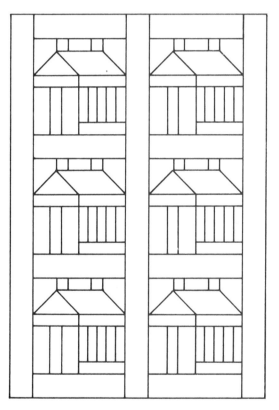

Blocks set straight-on with lattices

Diagonal set with pieced lattices

The coloring of the set pieces in a quilt design is a very important part of the quilt's look. Set pieces that are the same color as the background of the unit blocks will "float" the design motifs. Set pieces cut from contrasting fabrics will outline each block and make it look square.

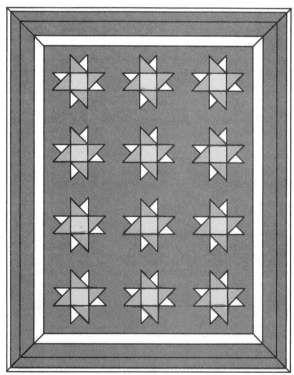

Changing the coloring of set pieces to vary quilt designs.

Set pieces need not be plain squares or lattice strips. They can be pieced in different ways to add to the overall quilt design. In Diversion, pieced alternate blocks are set with the pieced design blocks to create a coherent overall effect.

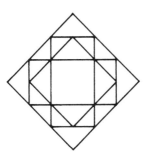

Diversion unit block

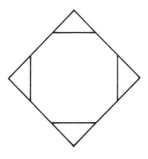

Pieced set square

Diversion

Lattices can also be pieced by using simple squares at the block corners or by using more extensive piecing within the strips. The **Star Set** shown here has lattices that are pieced to create stars where the blocks and lattices meet. Templates for the Star Set lattices are on page 102.

Units of pieced lattices

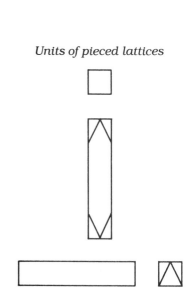

Note: These pieces are needed to complete the stars around the outside edge.

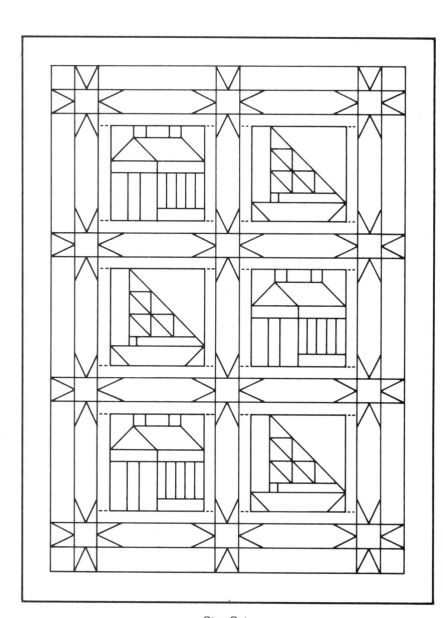

Star Set

Zigzag set

Instead of using square alternate blocks for set pieces, consider half blocks. In the Seattle Sails Wall Quilt, the set pieces are half squares (4" x 8") with some piecing. The arrangement of the three unit blocks is offset and asymmetrical.

Another interesting way to vary a set is to offset the blocks by one-half to create stair-stepped or zigzag sets. The set pieces on a zigzag set are all triangles. Use set pieces B and C on page 101.

Another set option is to make a Strippy quilt. In this set, the unit blocks are arranged in rows that are separated by long lattice strips or pieced borders.

Strippy set sampler quilt

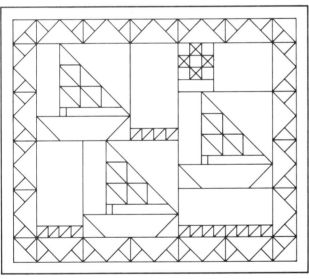

Seattle Sails Wall Quilt

Note: See Chain of Squares border on page 37.

Unit blocks are set together in sequence to complete the pieced section of the quilt top.

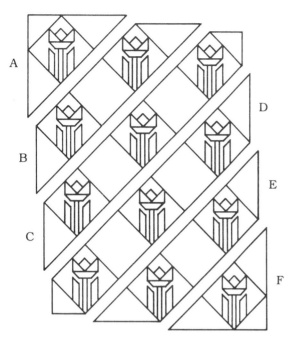

Assembly sequence for diagonally set quilt with alternate unpieced squares

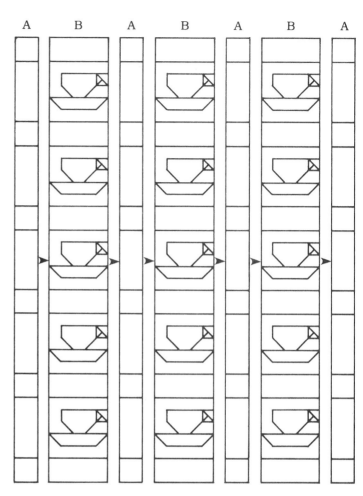

Assembly sequence for straight set quilt with lattice strips and square set pieces

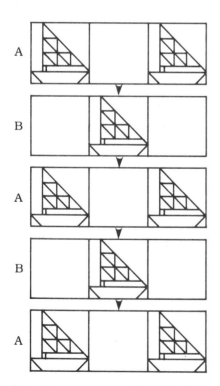

Assembly sequence for blocks set straight-on with alternate unpieced squares

Feel free to experiment with different sets. Remain open to new possibilities. Although I usually have a quilt plan in mind when I make a group of unit blocks, when they are finished, I like to play a bit to see how they look in various arrangements. Allow time for this important part of the quilt design process. Discovering a better quilt plan to suit the blocks as they really are is an exciting part of quiltmaking. Often the blocks appear quite different made up in fabric from the way they looked drawn on paper, and the original quilt design will need adjustments. Lay the blocks out on the floor or bed. Try diagonal and straight-on sets. Vary spatial arrangements and try to think ahead to appropriate border treatments.

It may be wise to put off buying fabric for alternate blocks or lattices until part or all of the unit blocks are finished. To find the best fabric for the set pieces, lay the blocks out on a few different lengths of uncut fabric that you are considering. When these fabric possibilities are real in front of you, the best choice often becomes obvious.

Borders

Borders are a very important part of a good quilt plan and function to frame a quilt design. They visually contain it and keep it from running off the edge. Borders emphasize and enhance the central quilt design if they relate to it properly in scale, motif and color. Scale is size. Motif is the shape of the pieces. So the sizes and shapes of border pieces should echo or be similar to those present in the quilt. The color of an outside border will bring out that color in the quilt design. For instance, if a quilt is rust, cream and blue in about equal amounts, adding a blue border will emphasize the blue.

Borders can also be used to bring a quilt out to size without making more unit blocks. Be careful, though, not to make the borders so wide that they outweigh the quilt design in visual importance.

Borders can be:
A. Plain with straight sewn corners
B. Striped fabric with mitered corners
C. Multiple plain strips with mitered corners (see Mitering Corners on page 34)
D. Patchwork (pieced or appliqued)
E. Any combination of the above

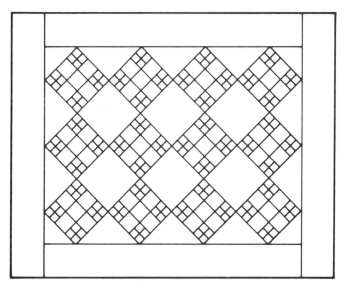

Single Irish Chain Small Quilt with plain borders and straight sewn corners.

If you choose plain borders with straight sewn corners, first sew borders to the long sides of the quilt, then to the width. Striped fabrics make lovely quilt borders, but the corners must be mitered to make the design turn the corner gracefully. Mitering corners is not difficult and worth the effort in many design situations. It is especially important to miter corners when using stripes or multiple plain borders.

Most border strips for projects in this book can be cut from the 45" width of yardage, then sewn together to get the proper length. Seams should be pressed open and placed in the center of the quilt side for minimum visibility. Yardage for most borders in this book will be given for border strips cut and pieced in this manner. If you are using a stripe for a border, it is best not to piece it. You will need to buy fabric the length of the longest outside border plus about 4" to allow for shrinkage. It is often wise when cutting border strips to leave them 3" or 4" longer than the length given in the pattern. When the actual dimensions of the quilt top are known, the border strips can be trimmed to fit.

Wall Quilt with multiple plain borders and mitered corners.

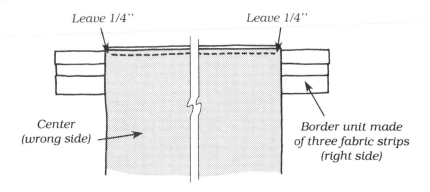

Leave 1/4"   *Leave 1/4"*

*Center
(wrong side)*

*Border unit made
of three fabric strips
(right side)*

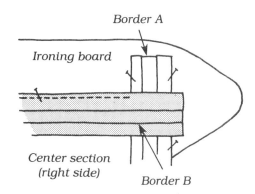

Border A

Ironing board

*Center section
(right side)*

Border B

Mitering Corners

1. Prepare the borders. Determine the finished outside dimensions of your quilt. Cut the borders this length plus 1/2" for seam allowances. When using a striped fabric for the borders, make sure the design on all four borders is cut the same way. Multiple borders should be sewn together and the resulting "striped" units treated as a single border for mitering.

2. To attach the border to the pieced section of the quilt, center each border on a side so the ends extend equally on either side of the center section. Using a 1/4" seam allowance, sew the border to the center leaving 1/4" unsewn at the beginning and end of the stitching line. Press the seam allowances toward the border.

3. Arrange the first corner to be mitered on the ironing board as illustrated. Press the corner flat and straight. To prevent it from slipping, pin the quilt to the ironing board. Following the illustration, turn border "B" right side up, folding the corner to be mitered under at a 45° angle. Match the raw edges underneath with those of border "A". Fuss with it until it looks good. The stripes and border designs should meet. Check the squareness of the corner with a right angle. Press the fold. This will be the sewing line. Pin the borders together to prevent shifting and unpin the piece from the board. Turn wrong side out and pin along the fold line, readjusting if necessary to match the designs.

4. Machine baste from the inside to the outside corner on the fold line, leaving 1/4" at the beginning unsewn. Check for accuracy. If it is right, sew again with a regular stitch. Backtack at the beginning and end of the stitching line. (After you have mitered several times, the basting step ceases to be necessary.) Trim the excess fabric to 1/4" along the mitered seam. Press this seam open. Press the other seams to the outside.

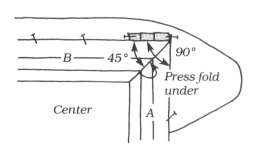

B — *45°*   *90°*

*Press fold
under*

Center   *A*

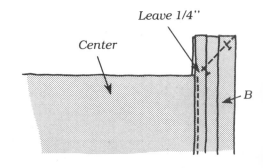

Leave 1/4"

Center

B

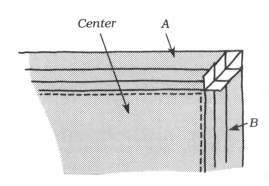

Center   *A*

B

Patchwork Border Designs

It is fun to work with patchwork border designs. They can be used as decoration for projects and clothing as well as for quilt borders.

Patchwork border designs are basically unit blocks or parts of unit blocks strung together in rows. Each design unit within a border design is called a repeat. A repeat can be simple or complex, square or oblong, pieced or appliqued. It can be set straight-on or on the diagonal.

For a pieced border to fit, the finished dimensions of a central patchwork design need to be equally divisible by the border repeat measurement. To use 2" repeats, for instance, it is necessary that the space the border is to fit have a finished dimension divisible by 2. A 4" border repeat fits only measurements evenly divisible by 4 and so on.

To bring the size of a quilt center out to a measurement that is divisible by a border repeat, consider using a spacer strip. This is a plain inner border strip added to the central quilt design before the patchwork border. It makes the math simple and can also function as a visual resting space between busy design areas. A spacer strip the same color as the background of the central patchwork section makes the design appear to "float." A contrasting spacer strip will have visual impact in itself.

The patchwork border designs offered here are fairly simple to complement the nature of the unit block designs. They have either 2" or 4" repeats which make them mathematically compatible with 8" unit blocks. Eight is equally divisible by 8, 4, 2 and 1. Using only these measurements, especially 2" and 4", as border repeats, it is quite simple to design borders that fit the blocks.

This principle of using mathematically compatible dimensions for plain and pieced borders carries over to other sized blocks as well. Twelve inch blocks, for instance, fit easily with 1", 1 1/2", 2", 3", 4" and 6" border widths and repeats because 12 is divisible by those numbers. Ten is divisible by 1, 2, 2 1/2 and 5, so repeats of those dimensions would work with 10" unit blocks and so on.

A A
RM M
L

35

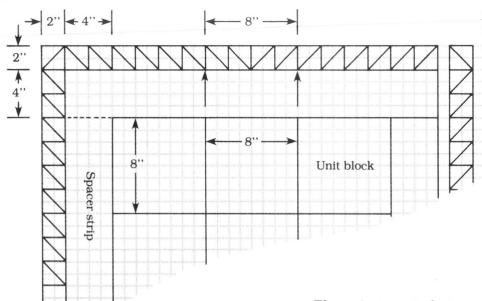

Plan 1: Sawtooth border with 2" repeat. There are four 2" repeats to each 8" unit block in this drawing.

The easiest way to design patchwork borders for a quilt or project is to make a scale drawing of the design on 1/8" graph paper. Don't hesitate to try this yourself. Sketch the unit block or blocks and set pieces to scale, using one graph paper square to equal 1". The planning of four different pieced borders is shown here as it would appear on 1/8" graph paper. The lines provide a great guide, showing pattern scale and relationships quite clearly.

If the dimensions of the lattices and interior borders are kept mathematically compatible with the blocks, borders will be easy to design.

Border Plans 1 and 2 are for pieced borders to fit with straight set 8" unit blocks. Note the relationship of the border repeats to the block dimensions.

Plan 2: Pinwheel border with 4" repeat. There are two 4" repeats to each 8" unit block here.

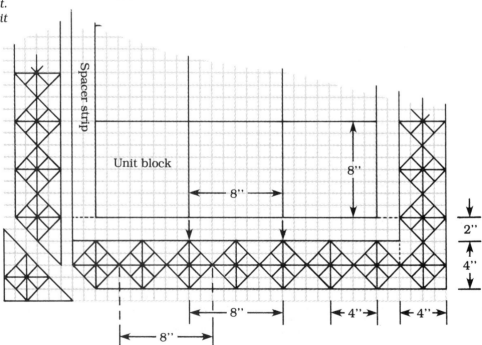

Corner piecing sequence

Note: Dimensions given are finished: for actual construction, add 1/4" seam allowances.

36

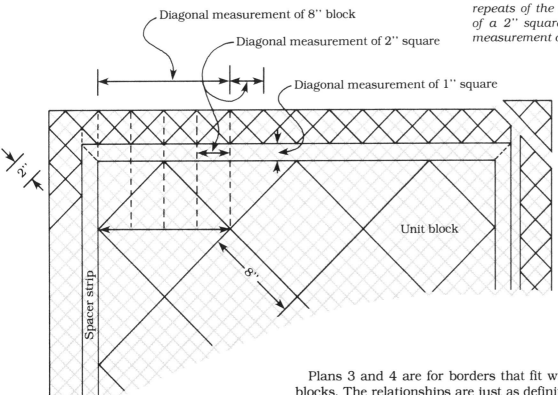

Diagonal measurement of 8" block

Diagonal measurement of 2" square

Diagonal measurement of 1" square

Plan 3: Chain of Squares border. Four repeats of the diagonal measurement of a 2" square fit with the diagonal measurement of the 8" unit block.

2"

Spacer strip

8"

Unit block

Plans 3 and 4 are for borders that fit with diagonally set unit blocks. The relationships are just as definite, but the dimensions are all on the diagonal. To plan a project with a diagonal set, draw the unit blocks and borders straight according to the lines on the graph paper, then turn the paper to achieve the diagonal effect.

Note: To figure the diagonal measurement of any square, multiply the side of the square by the square root of 2 ($\sqrt{2}$), also known as 1.414. Usually 1.4 is precise enough for these sewing calculations.

Plan 4: Unnamed Border I. Four border repeats fit with the diagonal measurement of the 8" unit block.

Spacer strips

8"

Unit block

4"

Diagonal of 1" square

Diagonal of 8" unit block

Diagonal of 2" square

Note: Dimensions given are finished: for actual construction, add 1/4" seam allowances.

37

Equally important to fitting a border design into a given space is how well it turns corners. You obviously don't need to worry about the corners on a Hostess Apron skirt or Tea Cozy, because there aren't any corners to turn. But quilt borders do turn corners. Some designs turn gracefully and naturally with just another repeat at the corner; others require special design solutions. For each border design offered here, a corner solution and piecing diagram are included.

Use these patchwork border patterns for Small Quilt and Wall Quilt borders, the Hostess Apron skirt, Tea Cozy and Tote projects. Because the border repeats are 2" or 4" and all the unit blocks are 8", theoretically any border design in this book will fit with any block. Play with the borders, though, and pay attention to straight and diagonal sets; some blocks and borders combine better than others, due to similarity in scale or shapes.

Keep in mind when cutting triangular pieces for pieced borders that the straight grain should be on the long side of triangles used along the outside edges of a border section.

Slight variances in seam allowances and cutting can alter the finished dimensions of the most carefully planned borders. So, when piecing borders, strive for accuracy and check your work. Make needed adjustments as you sew to assure that the border sections will be accurate. It is sometimes wise to wait to cut spacer strips until borders are pieced. The plain interior borders can then be cut either narrower or wider than planned to accommodate the actual dimensions of the pieced sections.

Like unit blocks, border designs can be altered in different ways to create new designs. One way is to take a basic drafting such as the Chain of Squares border and add lines or drop them out to create new shapes within the same repeats. This process is illustrated in the border designs presented in this section.

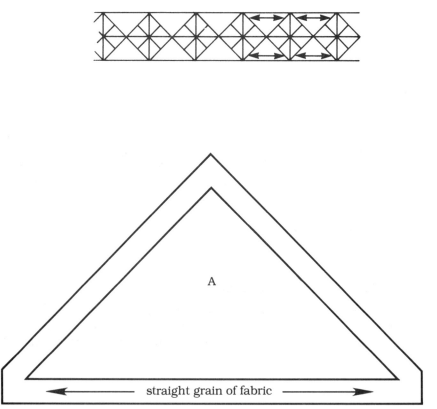

A

straight grain of fabric

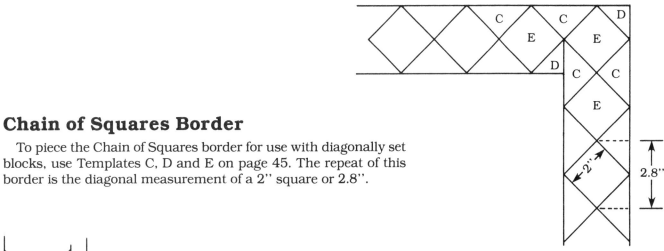

Chain of Squares Border

To piece the Chain of Squares border for use with diagonally set blocks, use Templates C, D and E on page 45. The repeat of this border is the diagonal measurement of a 2" square or 2.8".

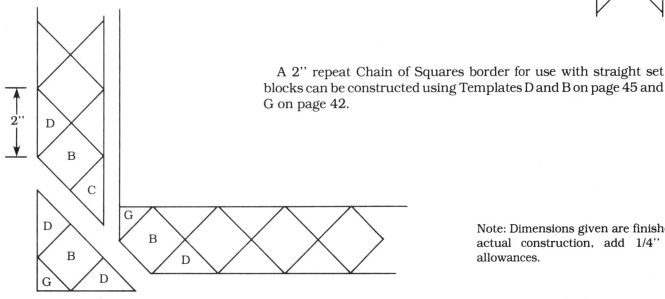

A 2" repeat Chain of Squares border for use with straight set blocks can be constructed using Templates D and B on page 45 and G on page 42.

Piecing sequence for corner section

Note: Dimensions given are finished: for actual construction, add 1/4" seam allowances.

Piecing sequence for corner section

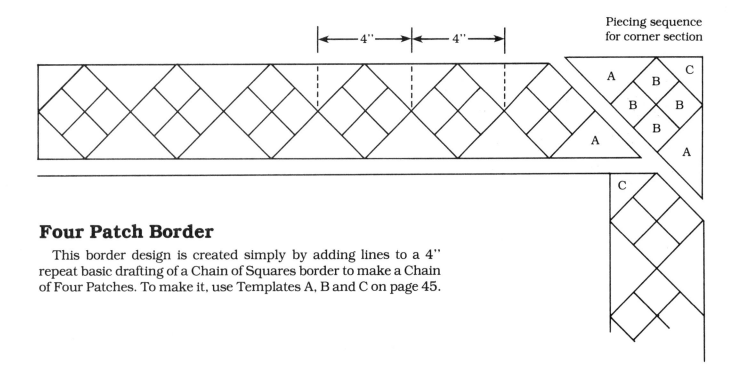

Four Patch Border

This border design is created simply by adding lines to a 4" repeat basic drafting of a Chain of Squares border to make a Chain of Four Patches. To make it, use Templates A, B and C on page 45.

Pinwheel Border

The Pinwheel border is closely related to the Four Patch border. The only difference is in the repeating design unit where adding lines creates eight triangles to replace four squares. The repeats and basic piecing order are the same. To make this border design, use Templates A, C and D on page 45.

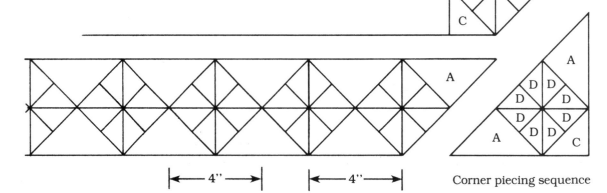

Corner piecing sequence

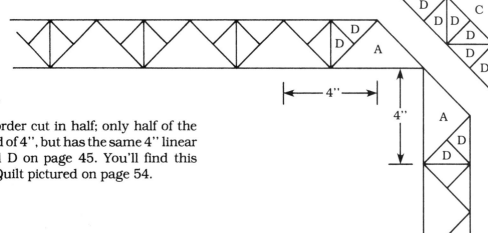

Half-Pinwheel Border

This design is the Pinwheel border cut in half; only half of the design is used. It is 2" deep instead of 4", but has the same 4" linear repeat. Use Templates A, C and D on page 45. You'll find this border on the Seattle Sails Wall Quilt pictured on page 54.

Note: Dimensions given are finished: for actual construction, add 1/4" seam allowances.

Tulip Border

The Tulip border is a variation of the Half-Pinwheel. Some lines are added, others are omitted. It was designed to go with the Tulip block on page 19 and is used in the Tulip Wall Quilt pictured on page 54. Use Templates B, C, D and F on page 45.

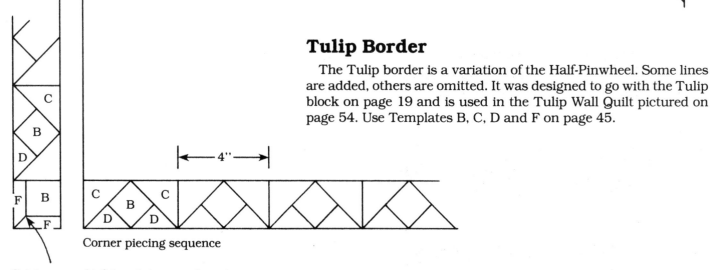

Corner piecing sequence

Set-in seam: At this point, sew only up to 1/4" seamline and backtack.

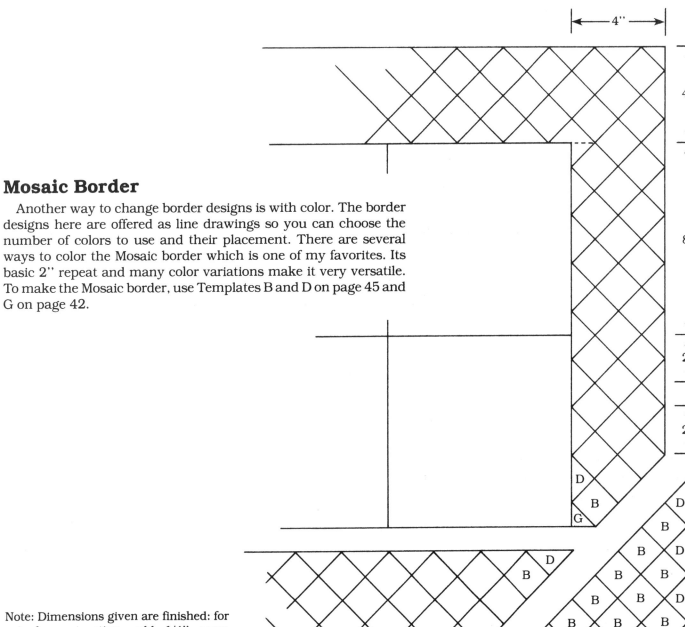

Mosaic Border

Another way to change border designs is with color. The border designs here are offered as line drawings so you can choose the number of colors to use and their placement. There are several ways to color the Mosaic border which is one of my favorites. Its basic 2" repeat and many color variations make it very versatile. To make the Mosaic border, use Templates B and D on page 45 and G on page 42.

Note: Dimensions given are finished: for actual construction, add 1/4" seam allowances.

Corner piecing sequence

Changing the Mosaic border with coloring

41

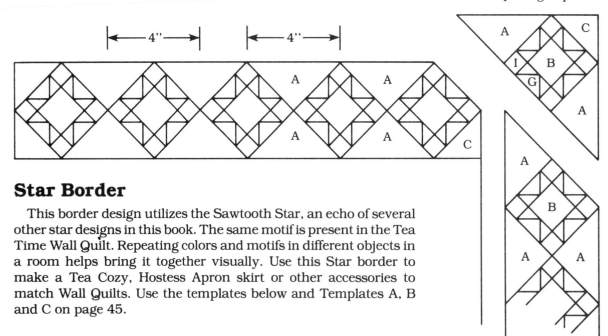

Star Border

This border design utilizes the Sawtooth Star, an echo of several other star designs in this book. The same motif is present in the Tea Time Wall Quilt. Repeating colors and motifs in different objects in a room helps bring it together visually. Use this Star border to make a Tea Cozy, Hostess Apron skirt or other accessories to match Wall Quilts. Use the templates below and Templates A, B and C on page 45.

Note: Dimensions given are finished: for actual construction, add 1/4" seam allowances.

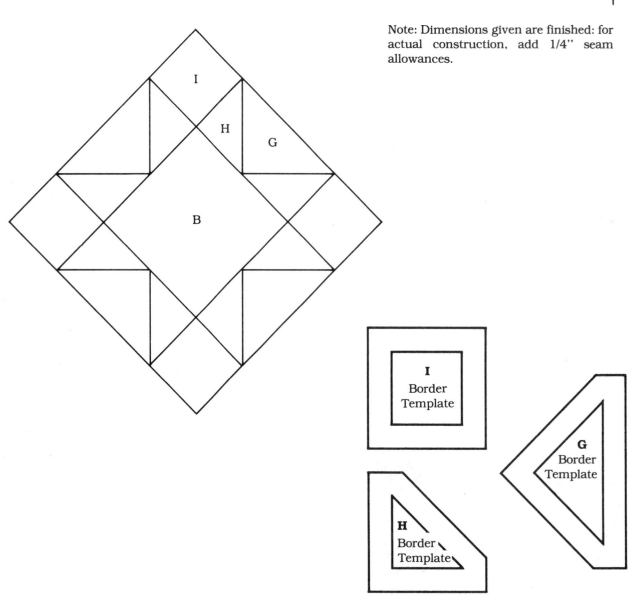

I Border Template

H Border Template

G Border Template

Corner piecing sequence

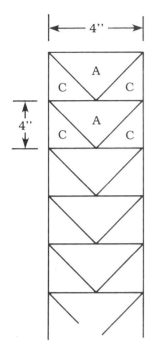

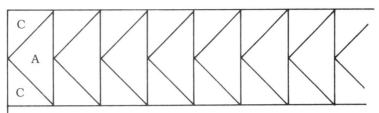

Flying Geese Border

This border repeats every 2" and is 4" deep. Use Templates A and C on page 45.

Unnamed Border I

This border was designed to go with blocks set on the diagonal. The repeat is 2.8" or the diagonal measurement of a 2" square. To make it, use Templates A and C on page 45.

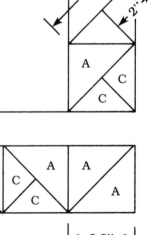

Corner piecing sequence

Note: Dimensions given are finished: for actual construction, add 1/4" seam allowances.

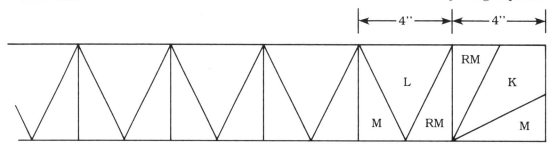

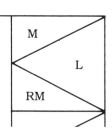

Unnamed Border II

This border was designed for the Blocks and Borders Sampler shown on page 61. To make it, use Templates K, L and M below.

Note: Dimensions given are finished: for actual construction, add 1/4" seam allowances.

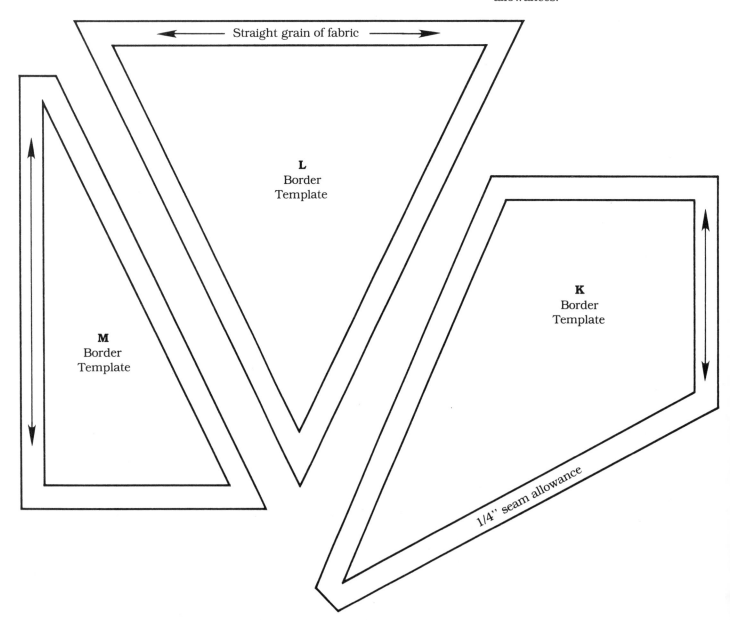

Straight grain of fabric

L
Border
Template

M
Border
Template

K
Border
Template

1/4" seam allowance

Templates for Border Designs

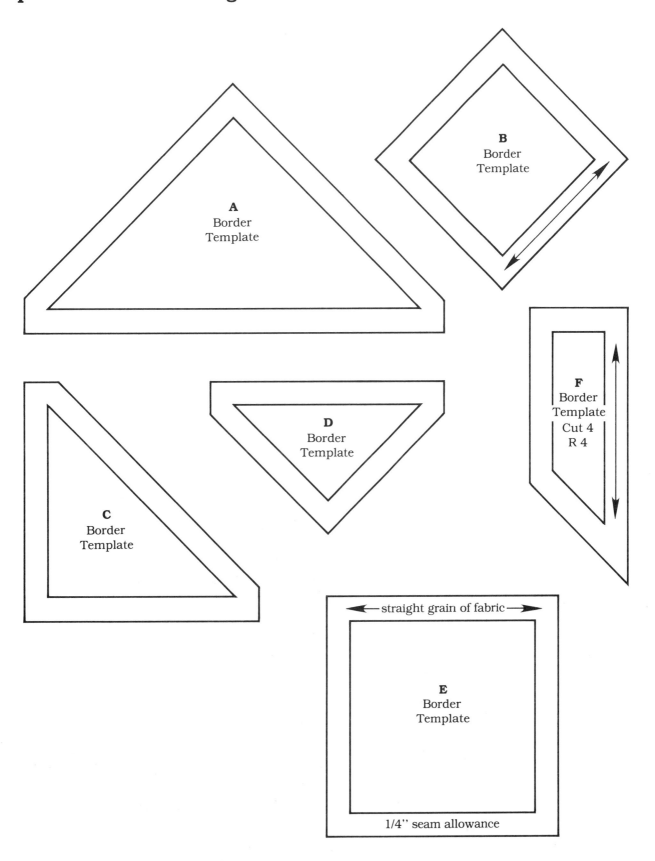

A
Border
Template

B
Border
Template

C
Border
Template

D
Border
Template

E
Border
Template

← straight grain of fabric →

1/4'' seam allowance

F
Border
Template
Cut 4
R 4

Sawtooth Borders: Bias Strip Piecing

Bias strip piecing, described below, is a technique I use often. It is a super machine piecing technique for accurately making square units consisting of two equal triangles. I use the method to make the small repeating units in the Sawtooth border.

Cut two bias strips: one of light and one of dark fabric. Layer the two fabrics, mark the top layer as shown, and cut two strips at a time. To determine the width of the bias strips, measure the square template to be used from corner to corner (including seam allowances) on the diagonal. Add 3'' and divide by 2.

$$\frac{X'' + 3''}{2} = \text{Width of each bias strip}$$

Sew the strips together on the long bias edge, using 1/4'' seam allowance. Press seams open or toward the dark fabric. Place a stiffened square template on the right side of the bias strip unit with opposite corners lined up with the seamline. Trace around the template. Start at one end and make a string of squares the length of the seamline. Carefully cut out the fabric squares, cutting only on the drawn lines (actually right inside the drawn lines). This will yield several squares made of two triangles with outside edges on the straight grain of the fabric. There will be two funny shaped pieces left over. Seam the long straight edges of these together, press, and make another set of squares.

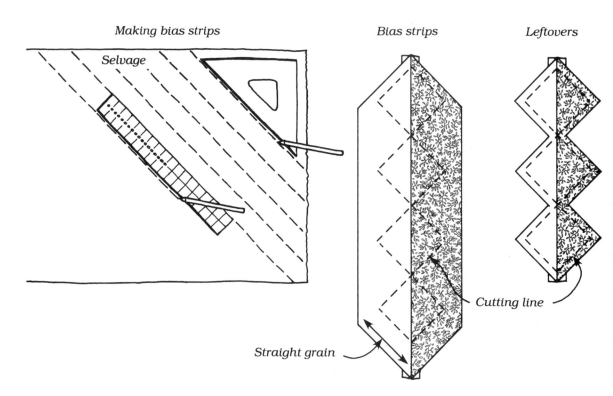

Making bias strips   *Bias strips*   *Leftovers*

Selvage

Cutting line

Straight grain

46

Patterns for Bias Strip Piecing

The Sawtooth border on the School House quilt is based on a 2"
square. The small Sawtooth section in Seattle Sails is based on a 1"
finished square.

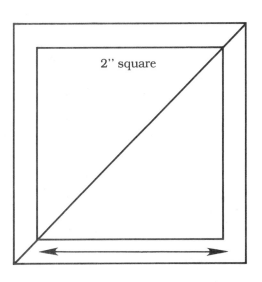

2" square

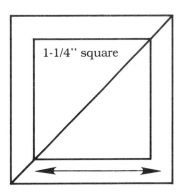

1-1/4" square

Use this template in Tea Time
Wall Quilt on page 83.

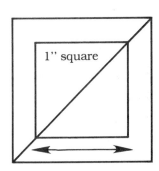

1" square

Use this template in Seattle
Sails Wall Quilt on page 80.

Appliqued Borders

The same principles of design apply to appliqued borders as to pieced borders. Most importantly, there must be a regular repeat of the pattern that fits the quilt, and the corners should turn gracefully.

Sections of the applique blocks on pages 24 and 25 have been adapted here to create border designs. The repeats are also 4". Turn to page 21 for further information on applique.

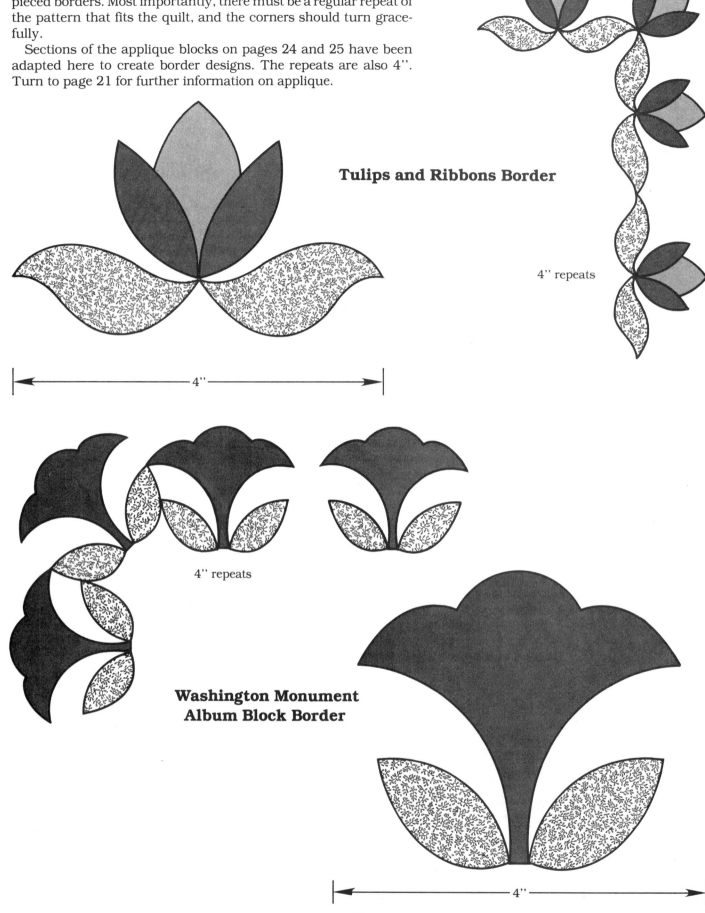

Tulips and Ribbons Border

4" repeats

4"

4" repeats

**Washington Monument
Album Block Border**

4"

Upper left: Multiple mitered borders frame the Washington Monument Album Block Wall Quilt, 26'' x 26'', made by Nancy Martin. The appliqued Tea Cozy border was adapted from the same block. A Tulips and Ribbons Pillow, made by Sharon Yenter, is framed by a Sawtooth border. Upper right: A pieced Christmas Candle block is a versatile motif to use on holiday decorations and gift items. Right: Fashioned in color-coordinated blues by Pam Boag, each of these three Pillows features a unit block: Tulip, Flower Basket variation and School House.

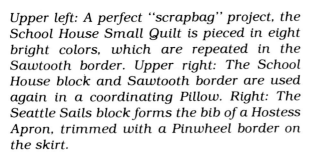

Upper left: A perfect "scrapbag" project, the School House Small Quilt is pieced in eight bright colors, which are repeated in the Sawtooth border. Upper right: The School House block and Sawtooth border are used again in a coordinating Pillow. Right: The Seattle Sails block forms the bib of a Hostess Apron, trimmed with a Pinwheel border on the skirt.

Vibrant in color and exciting in visual movement, the unique False Starts and Rejects Quilt is an imaginative combination of discarded blocks and unfinished projects.

Upper left: Pinks and blues are highlighted against a muslin background in the Tulips Wall Quilt, which is mounted on a wooden stretcher bar frame and hung diagonally. A Tulips and Ribbons block and a Chain of Squares border decorate a Hostess Apron. Upper right: Flower Basket blocks in muted blues are set together in a Small Quilt; the popular motif is repeated in an accompanying Pillow.

Lower left: Attractive table accessories include a padded Tea Cozy embellished with a Chain of Stars border and Potholders made in coordinating fabrics. Right: Geometric shapes in bold colors create a beautiful accent Pillow, using a Tall Pine Tree block and a Chain of Squares border.

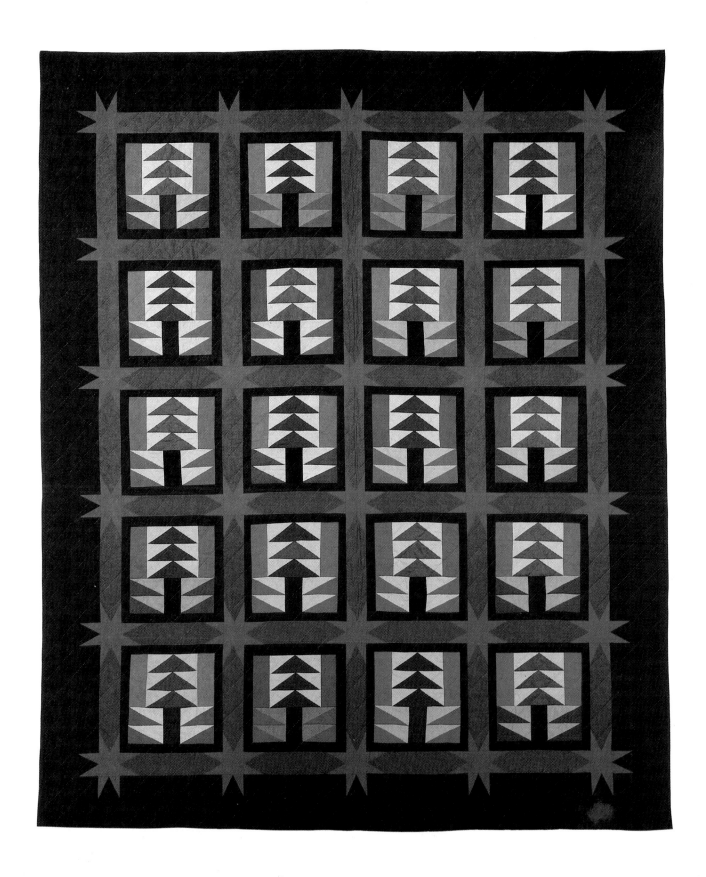

The Star Set Tall Pine Tree Quilt, 76" x 88", was designed by the author. The quilt was completed in 1984 by parents, teachers and friends of the Northwest School of the Arts, Humanities and Environment in Seattle as a raffle quilt to benefit the scholarship fund.

53

Original designs for Wall Quilts were inspired by familiar scenes in the author's life. Upper left: Springtime blossoms are stylized in the Tulips Wall Quilt, 28" x 28". Upper right: The Tea Time Wall Quilt, 20" x 27", expresses the restful companionship of sharing tea with friends. Right: Sailboats on Northwest waters are pictured in the Seattle Sails Wall Quilt, 22' x 26".

Left: In Suzanne Wall's "Hearts and Tulips" Quilt, 53" x 47", the Washington Monument Album Block is skillfully combined with other applique motifs. Lower left: A Stairway to the Stars block decorates the bib of this Hostess Apron and the colors are repeated in a Four Patch skirt border. Lower right: Handy patchwork Totes incorporate the Flying Geese border and the Tulip block.

Top: Set blocks in the background color "float" the block motif and emphasize the diagonal quality of the design in the Stairway to the Stars Small Quilt, 56" x 56". Above: A portion of the Tulips and Ribbons applique block is adapted to decorate a Tea Cozy. The vivid colors are repeated in the Sherman's March Potholder block. Right: An African violet inspired the colors for the Single Irish Chain Small Quilt. The diagonally set blocks, alternate unpieced squares and side triangles are the same color as the unit block background and emphasize the rows of contrasting squares.

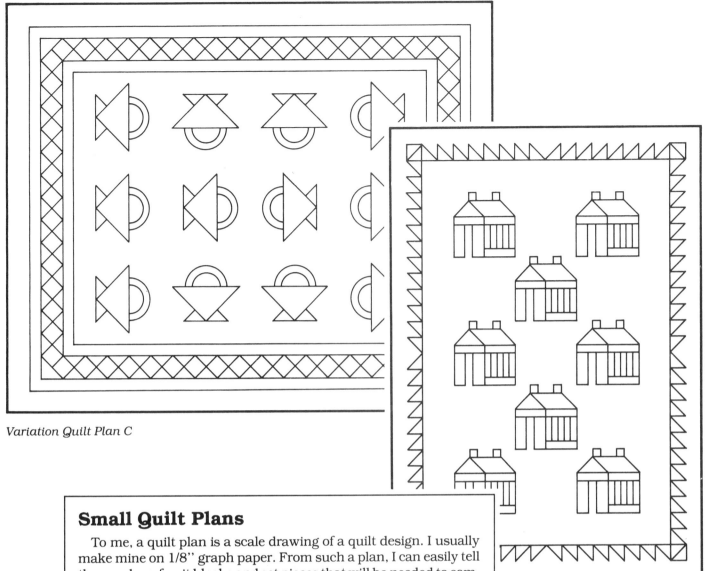

Variation Quilt Plan C

Variation Quilt Plan A

Small Quilt Plans

To me, a quilt plan is a scale drawing of a quilt design. I usually make mine on 1/8" graph paper. From such a plan, I can easily tell the number of unit blocks and set pieces that will be needed to complete a given quilt, as well as finished dimensions of plain borders and number of repeats in patchwork borders.

Here are some quilt plans to get you started planning your own quilts, using 8" unit blocks and border designs. Perhaps one of the quilt plans will fit your design objectives.

Some of the unit block designs in this book look best set straight-on. These blocks are pictorial in nature and have a definite top and bottom, such as the School House, Seattle Sails, Teapot, Christmas Candle and the Tall Pine Tree.

For the same reason, the Flower Basket and Tulip blocks are usually set on the diagonal. The other blocks have no specific orientation and can be set either way.

There are three basic quilt plans offered here, although there are many more possible plans. These plans are intended as a place to start and inspiration to get your creativity working. Feel free to interchange blocks, sets and borders, make small quilts or large ones, or otherwise depart from or adapt these plans.

Quilt Plan A

Dimensions: 40" x 56"

This plan makes a crib or wall quilt, using eight 8" unit blocks set straight-on with seven alternate unpieced squares, and plain and pieced borders. These unit block designs can be used for this quilt plan: School House, Seattle Sails, Tall Pine Tree, Tulips and Ribbons, Washington Monument Album Block and variations on the Nine Patch.

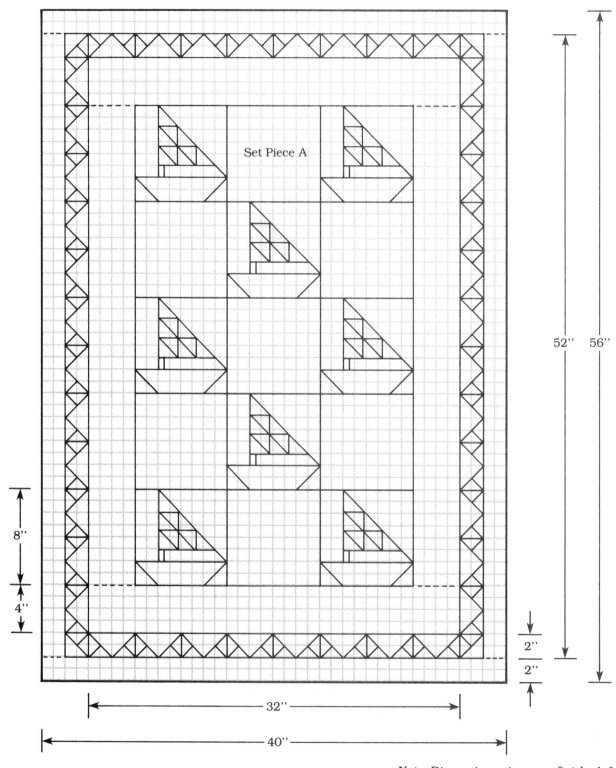

Set Piece A

8"

4"

52"   56"

2"

2"

32"

40"

Note: Dimensions given are finished: for actual construction, add 1/4" seam allowances.

Quilt Plan B: The Star Set

Dimensions: 34" x 46"

The Star Set quilt plan makes a Wall Quilt with six 8" unit blocks and pieced lattices that form stars at the corners of the blocks. There is one pieced border to complete the stars and a plain outside border 2 1/2" wide.

In the Star Set, each 8" unit block is bordered out to measure 10" finished size. This involves adding 1" borders to 8" blocks. (These are all finished dimensions; add 1/4" seam allowances when cutting border strips.) This quilt plan, like others presented, can easily be expanded by adding more rows of blocks and the necessary set pieces.

Templates for the Star Set latticework are on page 102. These unit blocks can be used with the Star Set: School House, Seattle Sails, Tall Pine Tree, and variations on the Nine Patch.

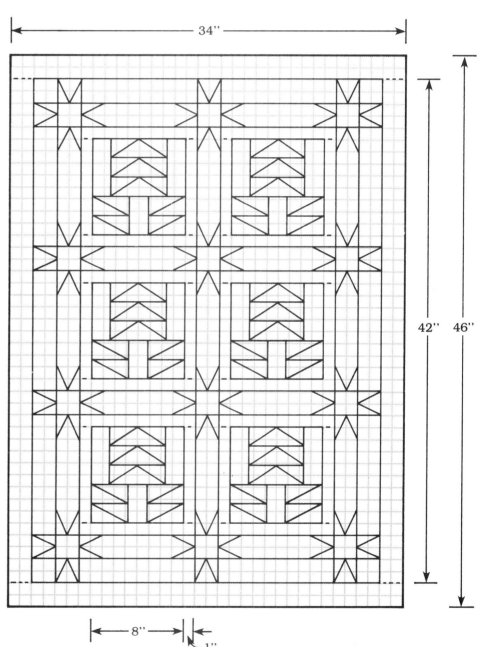

Note: Dimensions given are finished: for actual construction, add 1/4" seam allowances.

Quilt Plan C

Dimensions: 45.2" x 56.5"

This plan makes a crib or wall quilt, using twelve 8" unit blocks set on the diagonal with six alternate unpieced squares (Set Piece A), 10 of Set Piece B, four of Set Piece C, and plain and pieced borders. These unit block designs can be used for this quilt plan: Flower Basket, Tulip, Tulips and Ribbons, Washington Monument Album Block and variations on the Nine Patch.

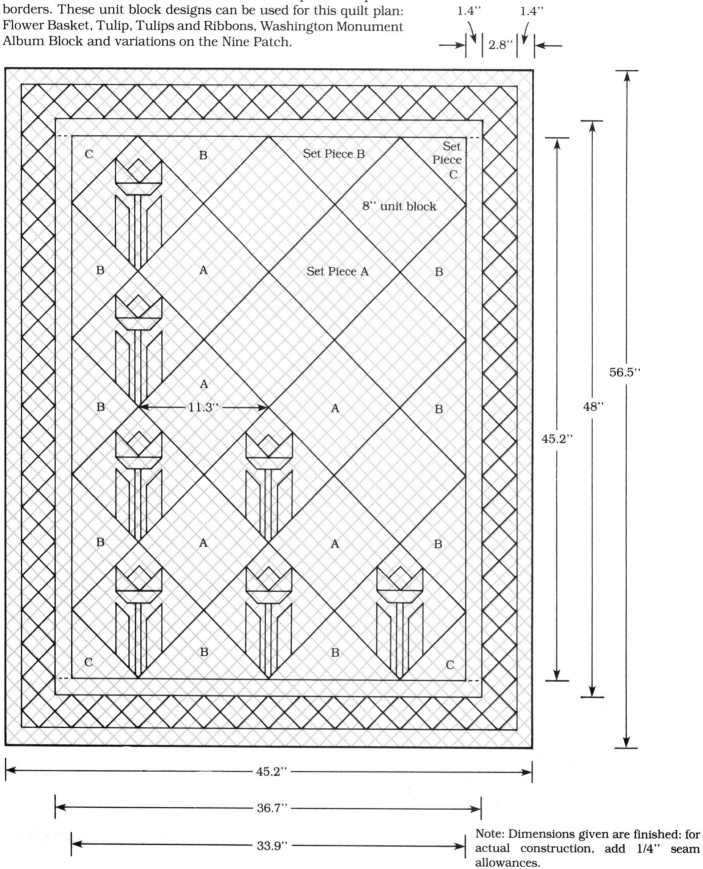

Note: Dimensions given are finished: for actual construction, add 1/4" seam allowances.

60

Blocks and Borders Sampler

Scale drawing 1/8" = 1"

Dimensions: 52" x 68"

Figuring Yardage for Quilt Tops

To get a "ball park" figure or rough estimate of the fabric needed for a quilt, first figure the yardage for the quilt back. For example, a finished quilt 80" x 104" would require six yards of fabric for the backing: two three-yard lengths (108") of 45"-wide fabric, seamed down the middle to get the 80" width. Then multiply the amount of fabric needed for the backing (six yards in this case) by 1.5.

6 yards x 1.5 = 9 yards

Nine yards is a conservative rough estimate of fabric needed for the quilt top. Use it for reference. The amount of fabric you actually need will probably be a bit more. Figure the yardage as outlined below, then look at the total. Is it close to your rough estimate? If your calculations total 3 1/2 yards (nowhere near nine yards!), you'll know there is something wrong. Likewise, a 40 yard total is unreasonable. Ten yards or 11 1/2 yards, however, is in the "ball park."

To figure specific yardage requirements, you will need a quilt plan. This is generally a scale drawing on graph paper that shows unit block design and size; type of set and number of set pieces; and indicates border treatment and dimensions. Sample quilt plans are given on pages 57-60.

Base yardage requirements on a good quilt plan and follow these steps.

1. Identify and make templates for all the shapes in the quilt design, i.e., pieces in the patterned blocks and the set pieces (lattices or alternate blocks). You don't have to make templates for large border pieces; knowing their dimensions is enough.
2. For each template, write the number of pieces to be cut from each fabric in your design.
3. Armed with shapes, sizes and numbers, proceed to figure out how many of each template will fit on the usable width of the fabric. With fabric that is 45" on the bolt, you can really count on a usable width of only 42". Selvages should be cut off and you must allow for some shrinkage. For example, twelve 8 1/2" squares are needed as set pieces in the quilt plan. Divide 42" by 8.5" and find that four complete squares can be cut from the width of the fabric. Each set of four squares requires 8.5 linear inches of fabric. To get 12 squares, 3 x 8.5" or 25.5 linear inches of fabric are needed. This is nearly 3/4 yard (27"), but to buy only 3/4 yard would be cutting it pretty close. I would go on to the next highest eighth of a yard and buy 7/8 yard. It is a good idea to buy at least four extra inches of a fabric to allow for shrinkage, straightening and cutting mistakes.

Complete this process for each shape and fabric in the quilt plan. Total the amounts and compare with your ball park figure. If it seems reasonable, you are ready to buy.

Finishing

Quilting

In most cases, before you quilt, the quilt top, pillow front or design block must be marked with lines to guide stitching. Where you place the quilting lines will depend on the patchwork design, the type of batting used, and how much quilting you want to do. You can mark an allover, straight-line pattern, such as a grid of squares or parallel diagonal lines. Or, you can outline quilt the design either "in the ditch" (close to but not on the seamlines) or 1/4" away on each side of every seamline, for which no marking is required. Try to avoid quilting too close to the seamlines where the bulk of seam allowances might slow you down or make the stitches uneven. Keep in mind also that the purpose of quilting, besides its esthetic value, is to securely hold the three layers together. Don't leave large areas unquilted.

There are many pretty, traditional quilting motifs that fit nicely in plain areas, such as unpieced blocks and borders. For this book, I have adapted two 8" applique designs for use as quilting motifs (see pages 64 and 65). If the fabric is light enough to see through, center a fabric square over the motif page in the book and trace the lines for quilting. If the fabric is quite dark, you will probably need to make a stencil to transfer the design.

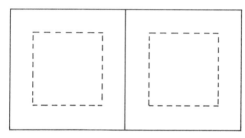

Outline quilting, 1/4" away from seamlines

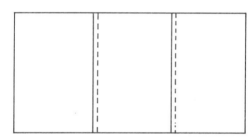

"In the ditch"

Quilting Stencils

To make quilting stencils, you will need a sharp pencil, tracing paper, carbon paper, lightweight cardboard (manila file folders are good), sharp pointed scissors, curved fingernail scissors and perhaps a razor blade or other fine sharp cutting tool.

1. With a sharp pencil, trace the quilting motif from the book onto tracing paper, including positioning lines. Notice that the shaded areas are meant to be cut out. The dotted lines will be drawn freehand on the fabric, with a ruler or with the aid of a small template of a repeated shape (for example, a leaf), after part of the quilting lines and the basic shapes have been established with the stencil.

2. To transfer the design from the tracing paper to the cardboard, place carbon paper between the two and carefully trace over the lines.

3. With the cutting tools, cut out the design areas marked "cut out." Cut just outside the lines to be sure the inside shape is large enough to allow for the width of the pencil line.

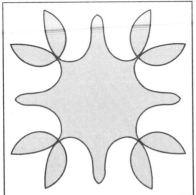

Tulips and Ribbons Stencil

Make templates to trace

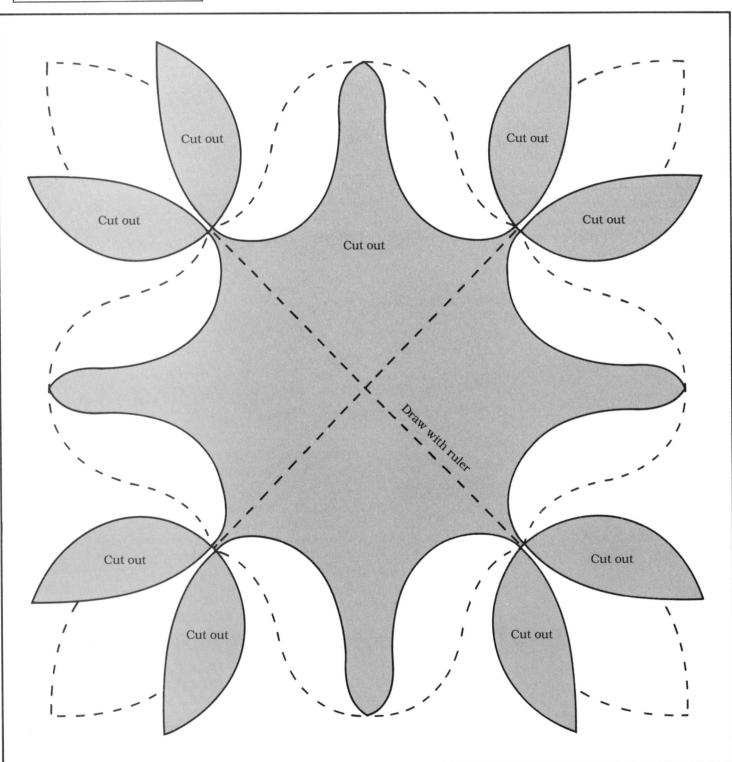

Washington Monument Album Block Stencil

Make templates to trace

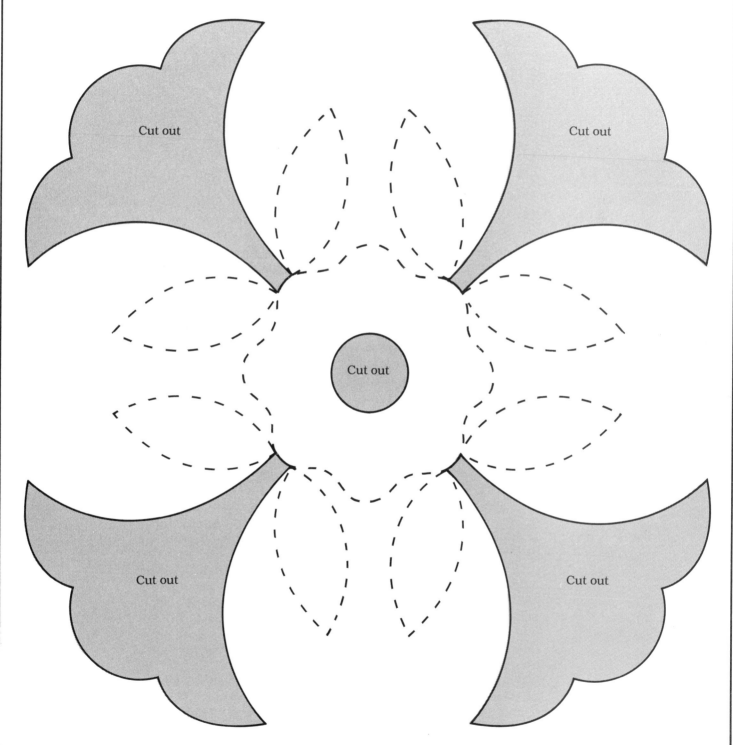

Cut out

Cut out

Cut out

Cut out

Cut out

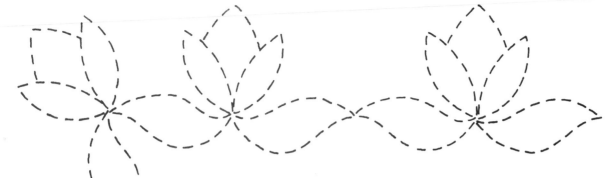

Marking the Quilt Top

Thoroughly press the quilt top and mark it before it is assembled with the batting and backing. You will need marking pencils, a long ruler or yardstick, stencils or templates for quilting motifs, and a smooth, clean hard surface on which to work. Use a sharp marking pencil and lightly mark the quilting lines on the fabric. No matter what kind of marking tool is used, light lines will be easier to remove than heavy ones. If you are using the quilting patterns provided here, position the stencils on the quilt top according to the illustrations given, and trace the cut-out shapes onto the fabric. Remember that not all the quilting lines will be drawn using the stencil. The dotted lines on the stencil patterns in the book need to be drawn freehand on the fabric or with the aid of a ruler or small template.

Preparing the Backing

A single length of 45"-wide fabric can often be used for backing small quilts. To be safe, plan on a usable width of only 42" after shrinkage and cutting off selvages. For larger quilts, two lengths of fabric will have to be sewn together to get one large enough.

Cut the backing an inch larger all the way around than the quilt top. Press thoroughly with seams open. Lay the backing face down on a large, clean, flat surface. With masking tape, tape the backing down (without stretching) to keep it smooth and flat while you are working with the other layers.

Batting

Batting is the filler in a quilt or comforter. Thick batting is used in comforters that are tied. If you plan to quilt, use thin batting and quilt by hand or, on some projects, with the machine.

Thin batting comes in 100% polyester, 100% cotton and a cotton-polyester (80%-20%) combination. All-cotton batting requires close quilting to prevent shifting and separating in the wash. Most old quilts have cotton batting and are rather flat. Cotton is a good natural fiber that lasts well and is compatible with cotton and cotton-blend fabrics. Less quilting is required on 100% polyester batting. If polyester batting is glazed or bonded, it is easy to work with, won't pull apart and has more loft than cotton. Some polyester batting, however, has a tendency to "beard." This "fiber migration" (the small white polyester fibers creep to the quilt's surface between the threads in the fabric) happens mostly when polyester blends are used instead of 100% cotton fabrics. The cotton-polyester combination batting is supposed to combine the best features of the two fibers. A single layer of preshrunk cotton flannel can be used for filler instead of batting. The quilt will be very flat, and the quilting stitches highly visible.

Assembling the Layers

If the quilt is to be finished with a binding, cut the batting the same size as the backing and lay it on top. Smooth it out as well as you can. Batting for wall quilts to be mounted on wooden stretcher bar frames should extend 1" beyond the edge of the wooden frame, not all the way to the edge of the fabric borders.

Center the freshly ironed and marked quilt top face up on top of the batting. Starting in the middle, pin baste the three layers together while gently smoothing out fullness to the sides and corners. Take care not to distort the straight lines of the quilt design and the borders.

After pinning, baste the layers together with needle and light colored thread. Start in the middle and make a line of large stitches to each corner to form a large X. Continue basting in a grid of parallel lines 6" to 8" apart. Finish with a row of basting around the outside edges. Quilts to be quilted with a hoop or on your lap will be handled more than those quilted on a frame; therefore, they will require more basting.

After basting, remove the pins. Now you are ready to quilt.

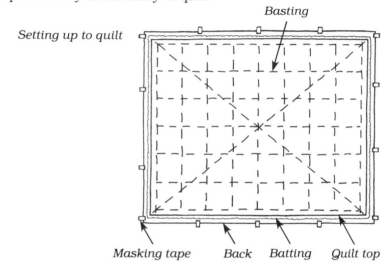

Setting up to quilt

Basting

Masking tape   *Back*   *Batting*   *Quilt top*

Machine Quilting

Machine quilt patchwork projects that will get a lot of wear — potholders and totes especially. Other projects can be quilted either by hand or on the machine. Hand quilting is a lovely finish to patchwork, of course, but sometimes machine quilting is just more practical.

Prepare a project to be machine quilted just as you would for hand quilting (the exception is potholders, see page 72). Mark the top and baste the layers together. Plan simple straight-line quilting lines that extend across the piece from edge to edge. Use regular thread that won't show too much.

Many machines have special attachments for sewing through several layers. Check with a sewing machine dealer to see what is available for your machine. A regular sewing presser foot pushes the top layer of fabric along faster than the ones beneath and tends to pucker and pleat the piece as you sew. An "even-feed" or walking foot feeds all three layers smoothly and evenly, making the whole process a joy rather than a struggle.

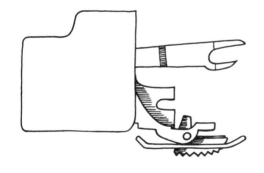

In general, begin machine quilting lines with the one in the middle of the piece and work toward the edges. If the part not being worked on is bulky and gets in the way, roll it neatly so it will fit under the sewing machine arm. Carefully stitch on the marked quilting lines until the whole piece is quilted. Go slowly and you will be finished before you know it.

Hand Quilting

To quilt by hand, you will need quilting thread, quilting needles, small scissors, a thimble and perhaps a balloon or large rubber band to help grasp the needle if it gets stuck. Quilt on a frame, a large hoop, or just on your lap or a table. Use a single strand of quilting thread no longer than 18". Make a small single knot in the end of the thread. The quilting stitch is a small running stitch that goes through all three layers of the quilt. Take two, three or even four stitches at a time if you can keep them even. When crossing seams, you might find it necessary to "hunt and peck" one stitch at a time.

To begin, insert the needle in the top layer about 3/4" from the point you want to start stitching. Pull the needle out at the starting point and gently tug at the knot until it pops through the fabric and is buried in the batting. Make a backstitch and begin quilting. Stitches should be tiny (8 to 10 per inch is good), even and straight. At first, concentrate on even and straight; tiny will come with practice.

Several factors will influence how well you do: the size of the needle (a #9 is good, #10 is better), the thickness of the quilt (weight of the fabrics, batting and whether you are going over seams), and the tension of the piece. If the tension is too tight, stitches tend to get too large and far apart; if the tension is too loose, the lines get crooked. Make some test stitches until you find the proper tension. If you quilt on your lap, you can keep the tension right by holding the piece down between your sewing hand and knee or table while you stitch.

When you come almost to the end of the thread, make a single knot fairly close to the fabric. Make a backstitch to bury the knot in the batting. Run the thread off through the batting and out the quilt top. Snip it off. The first and last stitches look different from the running stitches between. To make them less noticeable, start and stop where quilting lines cross each other or at seam joints.[3]

Hand quilting stitch

Tying

There are several ways to go about preparing a quilt or comforter to be tied. Two methods are described here. The first is preferable when using thick batting and is by far the quickest finishing method I know. The edges are sewn as side seams before the batting is added and no binding is required. The second method is better for thin batting. It requires binding and, therefore, takes a little longer.

To tie a comforter with a thick batting, press the pieced top and prepare the backing as you would before quilting. No marking is necessary. Pin the backing and the pieced top together with right sides together. Trim the backing to match the top. On the sewing machine, sew top and backing together on three sides, using a 1/2" seam allowance. On the fourth unsewn side, press the raw edges under 1/2".

Lay the quilt on a flat surface, pieced side up. Lay the batting on top and baste it to the seam allowance with needle and thread. Trim excess batting. Turn the whole thing right side out as you would a pillowcase. Smooth it and pin baste the three layers along the side seams. This will help keep the comforter flat and the side seams from rolling to the front or back. Pin the unsewn end closed, using the pressed creases as a guide. Then, place pins at every point you want to locate a tie (see diagram). Don't leave more than 5-7 square inches unsecured.

3. *Bits of quilting wisdom from Nancy Dice.*

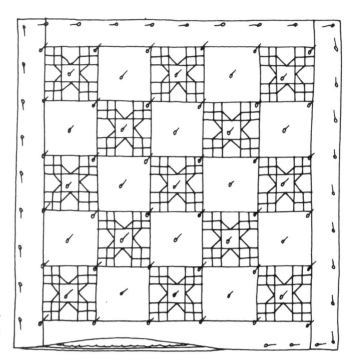

Place pins along edges first to stabilize side seams. Then put a pin in each place you want to put a tie.

Pinning in preparation for tying

Ties can be placed at the corners and center of each unit block and along the middle of each border. Tie to the front or back of the comforter. Ties on the back don't interfere with the pieced design on the front.

To tie, use a large sharp needle and sportweight yarn or pearl cotton. Cut a long (2-3 foot) piece of yarn. Double it if the thread is very thin. Make a stitch where the first tie is to be. Don't cut the yarn yet, but skip over and make a stitch at the next location and so on, until you run out of yarn in the needle. Snip the yarn between the stitches and make the ties. Tie square knots (right over left and left over right). Trim ties to about 1'' or 1 1/2'' long if they are too straggly. After tying, close the open end of the comforter by hand, using a blind stitch.

Another way to approach tying is to put the quilt "sandwich" together as for quilting, but instead of basting, place pins at each point you want a tie. Tie the comforter as described above. Trim excess batting and backing, and bind the edges. This method works better with thin batting than with thick ones.

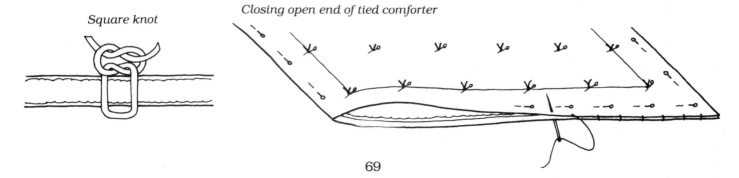

Tying stitches

Square knot

Closing open end of tied comforter

69

Binding

After quilting or tying, trim excess batting and backing to the edge of the quilt front. Finish the raw edges with bias binding. Bias binding can be purchased by the package or by the yard, or you can make your own.

To make bias binding from yardage, press a single layer of fabric. Use a 12" right angle to establish the bias (45° angle) of the fabric by aligning one of the angle's short sides with the selvage. Draw a line on the fabric along the 45° angle. Using this first marked line as a guide, draw several more parallel lines, each 2" apart. You'll find the 2"-wide plastic ruler very handy for this procedure. Cut the strips and seam them together where necessary to get a bias strip long enough for each side of the quilt (the length of the side plus 2").

Using the "even-feed" presser foot and a 1/2" seam allowance, sew the binding strips to the front of the quilt. Be careful not to stretch the bias or the quilt edge as you sew. If your machine doesn't have an "even-feed" foot, sometimes it is best to put the binding on entirely by hand. Overlap the corners. Fold under the raw edge of the binding on the back side of the quilt. Pin it in place. Enclose the raw edges at the corners. Using thread to match the binding, hand sew the binding in place with a hemming stitch.

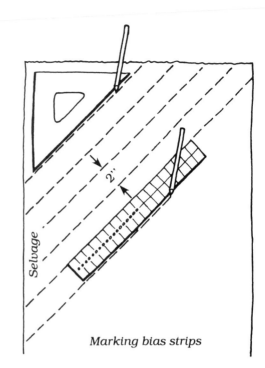

Marking bias strips

Joining bias strips

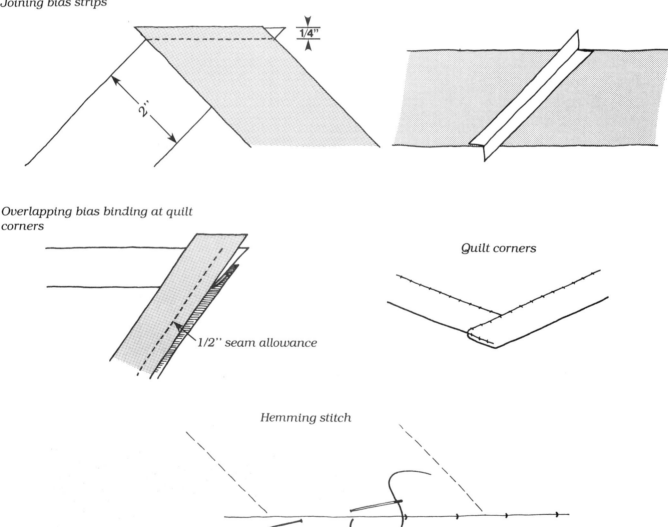

Overlapping bias binding at quilt corners

1/2" seam allowance

Quilt corners

Hemming stitch

The Projects

Potholders
Pillows
Wall Quilts
Hostess Apron
Tote
Tea Cozy

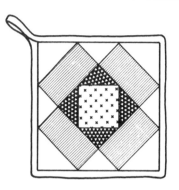

Introduction

The projects in this book have been part of me for a long time. I came to quiltmaking as a craftsperson, selling my wares at craft fairs and through gift shops. From the beginning, I learned that craft buyers loved to look at my quilts, but they bought my patchwork potholders that sold for less than $5.00.

So, I made potholders — more than 2,000 before I quit counting. When I was making potholders to sell, I would sometimes have orders for many dozen at a time. The prospect of making 60 to 100 potholders was not always a pleasant one, and I would often lapse into a pattern of behavior known to my family and friends as "potholder avoidance." I would clean house, cut the grass, cook complicated meals, rearrange furniture — in essence, do *any* useful task that would justify *not* making potholders!

Between bouts of "potholder avoidance," I did sew. As I made all those potholders, I learned to mix and match colors and prints, and to cut and sew the pieces quickly and accurately. I also made pillows, tea cozies, book covers, aprons and eyeglass cases — all to sell. And once in a while, when I had time, I would make a small quilt and hang it on the wall so I could look at it for a few weeks before it, too, would be sold.

I don't "do" craft fairs anymore. There is a time for everything, and now I write pattern books, teach others to mix and match colors and prints, and to cut and sew the pieces quickly and accurately. For a long time, I have wanted to put my patchwork projects together in a book. I always enjoyed making them. I hope you do too.

Yardage for Patchwork Projects

The main yardage requirements for each project are given in this book, but because I don't know which unit block or number of fabrics you will choose for the patchwork, specific fabric requirements cannot be given. For one pieced or appliqued block for a Pillow or Tote, or the pieced border section on a Tea Cozy, use scraps of fabric or pieces from your fabric collection. Or, buy a small amount (1/8 yard, 1/4 yard or a "quilter's quarter") of each fabric needed for the patchwork. Study the design and templates to make sure there is enough fabric for each set of shapes.

Potholders

The smallest quilt I know how to make is a potholder. It has all the parts and processes of a bed quilt: a pieced top, filler, backing, quilting and binding. It takes me 45 minutes to make one, and I consider it a very good way for a beginner to learn piecing and color combination. Make your first project a potholder, just for the practice. Use up scraps; try new block designs and different fabric combinations. Make as many potholders as you can stand; make a drawer full. Your piecing will improve and you will like your work better as you go along. Besides having potholders to use and to give as gifts, you will have gained valuable practice in cutting, piecing and combining fabrics.

Finished Size: 7" x 7"

Materials:

1/3 yd. main color fabric for backing, binding and part of patchwork

1/8 yd. or scrapbag pieces of two coordinating fabrics for the rest of the patchwork

8" x 8" square filling (can be old towels, blankets, flannel or cotton batting; try two thicknesses)

8" x 8" square unbleached muslin for lining pieced block

Directions:

1. Cut and piece a 7" unit block. Choose from the designs on page 74. Turn to page 9 for general cutting and piecing instructions.
2. For the back of the potholder, cut an 8" square of the main fabric. For the binding, cut two strips 2" x 8 1/2" and one 2" x 20".
3. At the ironing board, assemble the parts of the potholder. Place backing square face down. Press. On top of that, put the filler and then the muslin lining square. Press. Last, add the 7" pieced unit block, face up. Press. Do not pin.
4. Machine quilt the layers together. Quilt vertical and horizontal lines first, diagonal lines last. Sew edge to edge across the potholder 1/8" to one side of the long seams in the pieced design. After each line of quilting, smooth out the layers before beginning the next row. After quilting, trim excess filler and backing to the edge of the pieced block.
5. Study the binding diagrams, steps 1-4. Sew binding strip A to the potholder edge as shown, using a 1/4" seam allowance. Fold the A strip back, overlap the end of the B strip 1" and sew as shown in step 2. The remaining long binding strip C will bind the other two sides and form the corner loop. Overlap the end of strip C over B, as shown, and stitch, ending the line of stitching 1/4" from the edge of the potholder. Backtack. Leaving a 4" to 5" loop at the corner, stitch the remaining portion of strip C to the fourth side of the potholder. Begin the line of stitching 1/4" from the edge, backtack and sew to the outside edge at the end of the stitching line.

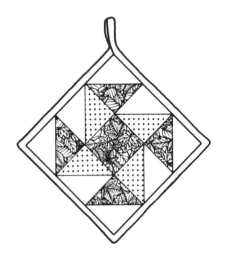

Binding a potholder

1.
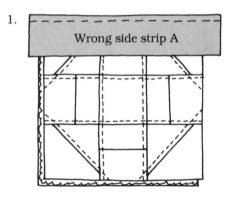

2.
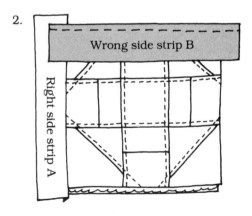

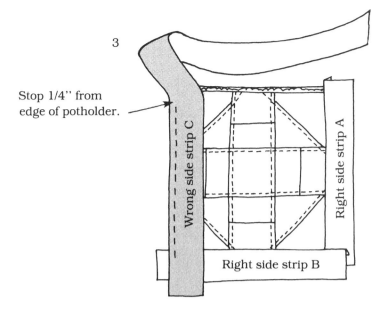

3

Stop 1/4'' from
edge of potholder.

Wrong side strip C

Right side strip A

Right side strip B

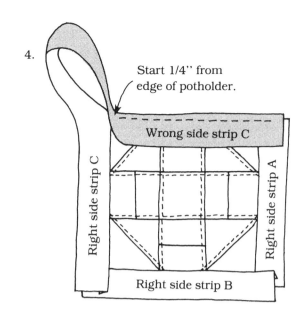

4.

Start 1/4'' from
edge of potholder.

Wrong side strip C

Right side strip C

Right side strip A

Right side strip B

6. Turn the potholder over, fold the raw edges of the binding under and pin in place. Hem stitch the four edges (the corners will need a few extra stitches), stopping just before coming to the loop. To enclose the raw edges of the loop, place your finger through it and pull it away from the potholder. Holding it thus, fold the raw edges under so they meet in the center. Fold once more, matching the folded edges. Pin and whipstitch closed.

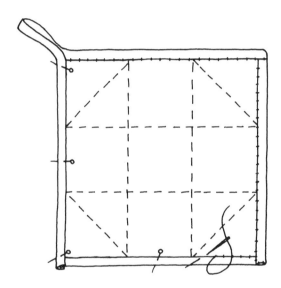

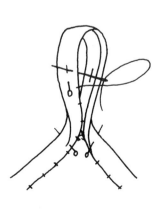

Making the loop

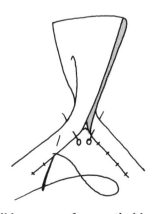

1. Pull loop away from potholder.

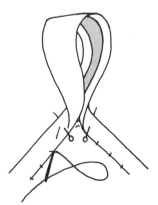

2. Fold raw edges to center.

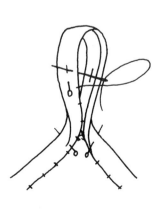

3. Fold again, matching folded edges. Pin and whipstitch closed.

Potholder Patterns

Nine Patch Variations

To make these designs, use Templates 1 through 6 on page 75.

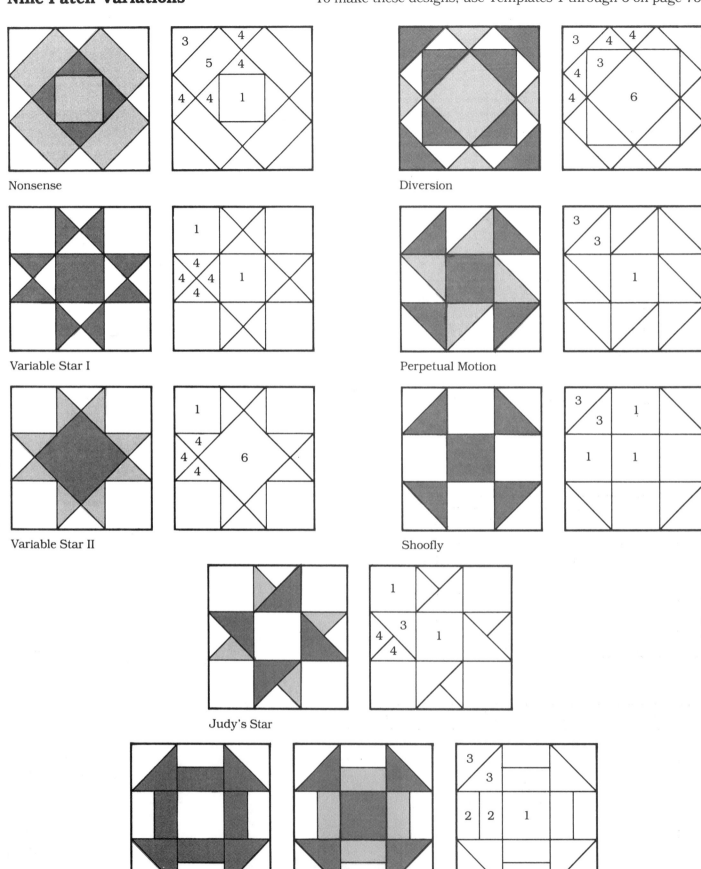

Nonsense

Diversion

Variable Star I

Perpetual Motion

Variable Star II

Shoofly

Judy's Star

Hole in the Barn Door

Sherman's March

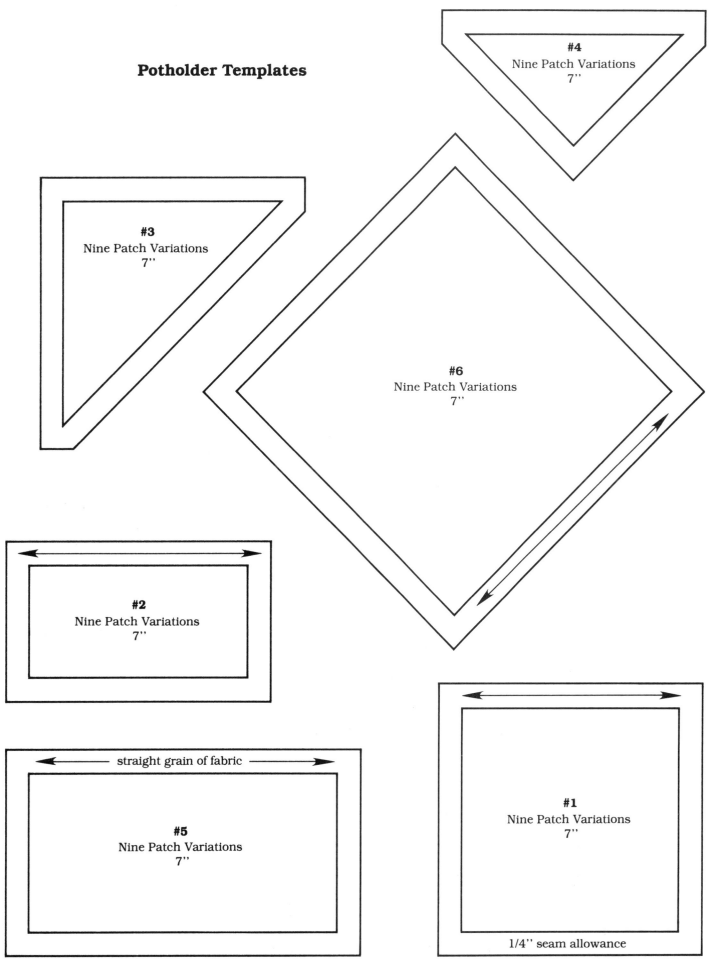

Potholder Templates

#4
Nine Patch Variations
7''

#3
Nine Patch Variations
7''

#6
Nine Patch Variations
7''

#2
Nine Patch Variations
7''

straight grain of fabric

#5
Nine Patch Variations
7''

#1
Nine Patch Variations
7''

1/4'' seam allowance

Pillows

A patchwork pillow is another good project on which to practice your quilting skills. With carefully chosen colors and designs, you can make them cute, country or very sophisticated. They will add warmth, depth and color to your home decor, and they are always welcome gifts for family and friends.

The pillow construction method outlined below is for a knife-edged pillow with a piped edge and hand sewn closing. The technique was shown to me by Glendora Hutson, a well-known designer and quilting teacher in Berkeley, California. Her method is surprisingly simple and gives such a finished, professional look that it is well worth the effort. For other pillow treatments (ruffles, boxing, zippers, etc.), I have found the Sunset book *How to Make Pillows* very helpful.

Finished Size: 14" x 14" or 16" x 16"

Materials:

    Patchwork design block
    1/2 yd. fabric for pillow back and front borders
    1/2 yd. unbleached muslin for lining
    2 yds. covered upholstery piping
    Thread to match piping
    14" or 16" square pillow form
    Zipper foot for sewing machine

Pillow Design Suggestions

Here are three possible pillow designs using 8" unit blocks. Style A is a 14" pillow; it has three simple borders with straight sewn corners and is suitable for straight-set blocks (School House, Seattle Sails, Tall Pine Tree, etc.). Style B is also for straight-set blocks and measures 14", but incorporates a Sawtooth border in the pillow design. See Bias Strip Piecing on page 46; use 1" square template. Style C measures 16" finished and is suitable for blocks set on the diagonal (Tulip, Flower Basket, etc.). The borders on this pillow can be straight sewn or mitered. Miter if you use a striped fabric for the outer border (see Mitering Corners, page 34).

A.

(14"; 1 1/2"; 1"; 1/2"; 8")

B.

(14"; 8"; 1" 1" 1")

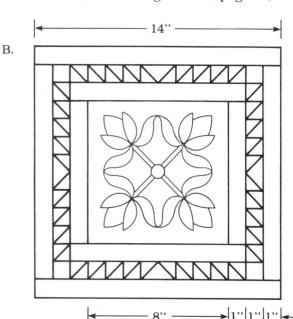

C.

(11.2"; 1/2"; (1.9") 2"; 16")

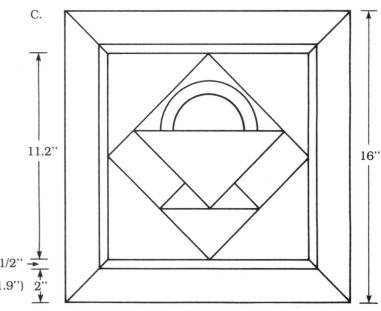

Note: Dimensions given are finished; for actual construction, add 1/4" seam allowances.

76

Directions:

1. Make an 8" unit block for pillow front. Press.
2. Add appropriate borders. Borders function as a frame to the pieced design, keep the shapes from distorting over the curved edges of the pillow, and provide unpieced edges on which to sew the piping. Choose a border treatment for the pillow. Do you want single or multiple borders? Plain fabrics or prints? How about stripes or pieced borders? Corners can be mitered or straight sewn. See Borders on page 33. Consider piping in a contrasting color to be a visual border as well.

   To figure border widths, subtract the finished dimension of the patchwork from the finished size of the pillow.

   Example: 16" (finished pillow size) - 12"
   (finished patchwork = 4" left for borders
   4" ÷ 2 sides = 2"-wide borders on each side

   Remember to add 1/4" seam allowances to all finished border dimensions. Cut border strips on the straight grain of the fabric.

3. Cut pillow backing. Back and borders can be of the same or different fabrics. For texture and good durability, consider using brushed denim, corduroy or other pants-weight fabric for the pillow back. Cut the pillow back 3/4" to 1" larger all the way around than the pillow front.

4. From unbleached muslin, cut a lining for both the pillow front and back. The lining for the front should extend about an inch beyond the edge of the borders. The lining for the back is cut the same size as the pillow back. Press and pin baste the linings to the wrong sides of the front and the back. If you wish to quilt the pillow front or back, place a thin batting between the outside layer and the lining and follow the quilting instructions that begin on page 63.

5. Fabric-covered upholstery piping is available in many colors. It usually can be found in stores that carry upholstery and drapery fabric. Lightweight, packaged piping is fine for pincushions and clothing. The thicker upholstery weight makes a better edge for pillows. Follow the five steps (A-E) to make a piped edge for the pillow. Read the directions before you begin and refer to the diagrams for further help.

A. Sew the right side of the piping to the right side of the pillow front. The wrong side of the piping is sewn with a commercial chain stitch. The right side of the piping exposes a regular straight stitch. Work with the chain-stitched side up. Use a zipper foot, a regular stitch length (8 to 10 per inch), and a 1/4" seam allowance. Place one end of the piping in the middle of one side of the pillow front, matching raw edges. Begin stitching 1" from the end of the piping. Backtack. Sew right on top of the chain stitches. At the corners, clip the seam

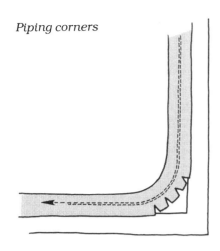

Piping corners

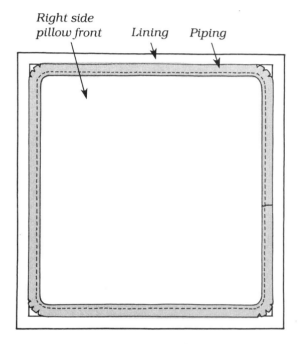

Right side pillow front   *Lining*   *Piping*

Step A: Sew the piping to the pillow front.

Joining piping

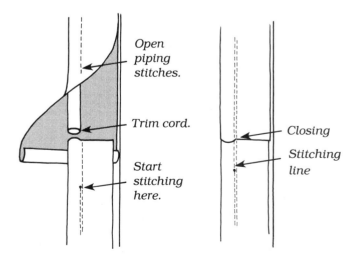

Open piping stitches.

Trim cord.

Start stitching here.

Closing

Stitching line

allowance on the piping to help make a graceful freehand curve, as illustrated. Continue stitching around the corner. Stop stitching (with the needle down) about 2" before the point where the two ends of the piping will meet. The ends should overlap 1". Trim away excess length. Open the stitches on the top piping end for 1 1/2". Trim the exposed cord so the two cord ends abut. Fold under the raw edge of the top piping cover and tuck it neatly around the bit of piping that was left unstitched. Continue the line of machine stitching to close.

B. Choose one side of the pillow to leave open for stuffing. On the side that is to remain open and on the wrong side of the pillow front, stitch as close to the piping as possible.

Step B: On back of pillow front, stitch close to piping on the one side that is to remain open for stuffing.

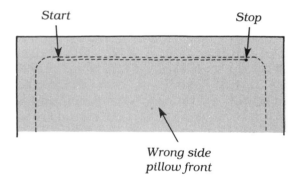

Start   Stop

*Wrong side
pillow front*

C. With right sides together, pin baste the pillow front to the pillow back. Using the existing stitching line as a guide, sew the front and back together. Work with the wrong side of the pillow front toward you — the back side has no stitching line to follow. Remember to leave an opening for stuffing.

D. Turn the pillow over. On the wrong side of the back, stitch as close to the piping as possible without sewing through it. Use the existing stitching as a guide. Leave an opening for stuffing. This third line of sewing may seem superfluous to you, but it is this extra step that will give the pillow a professionally finished look.

E. Trim the excess fabric along the edges to match the raw edge of the piping. Turn the pillow right side out. Check for unwanted stitches showing along the piping. If you can see stitches on the piping, especially at the corners, turn the pillow wrong side out again and sew closer to the piping where necessary.

Step C: Stitch pillow front to pillow back. Stitch closer to piping than previous row of stitches. Leave one side open.

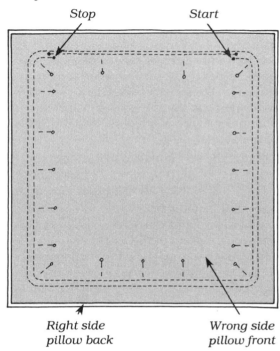

Stop   Start

*Right side   Wrong side
pillow back   pillow front*

Step D: Stitch close to piping on pillow back.

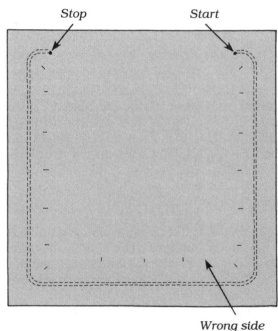

Stop   Start

*Wrong side
pillow back*

6. Turn the pillow right side out. Insert the pillow form and hand stitch the opening closed with a blind stitch.

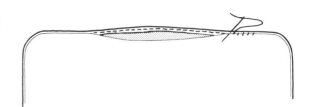

Pillow Forms

I usually buy ready-made polyester pillow forms for my pillows. A good form will measure 1" larger from side seam to side seam than the pillow for which it is intended. Thus a 16" pillow form should actually measure 17". I try to plan pillows to fit available form sizes (mostly 12", 14", 16" or 18" squares). If a pillow is an odd size (15") or a shape that is not square, the construction of a pillow form becomes necessary. It is not hard, and if you have batting scraps to use, can be a lot cheaper than buying manufactured forms.

Materials:

Thick bonded polyester batting (available by the yard
   from quilt and fabric stores)
Loose polyester stuffing or batting scraps
Needle and thread

Directions:

1. Cut two pieces of bonded batting to measure 1" larger than the finished pillow. Whipstitch the edges together, leaving an 8" to 10" opening on one side for stuffing.
2. Insert the unfinished pillow form in the pillow casing, matching corners and opening left for stuffing.
3. Evenly stuff loose polyester between the two layers of thick batting. The smooth surface of the bonded batting will help keep the pillow from feeling lumpy. Fill it as full as you like, then whipstitch the bonded batting closed. Close the pillow as described above.

Making your own pillow form

Whipstitching   *Opening left for stuffing*

Wall Quilts

I have quilts on the walls in my house. I like looking at them and I change the show often. There are quilt plans in this section for three Wall Quilts. They all seem to depict everyday scenes in my life. You will probably enjoy them for the same reasons I do.

These Wall Quilts require so little of many of the fabrics used that I hesitate to give yardage for these pieces. They were created mostly from my scrapbag. Study the photographs of the projects on pages 52 and 54. See if there are materials in your collection that can be used. Also feel free to change coloration. The Tulip Wall Quilt, for instance, would look smashing with red tulips and border instead of pink.

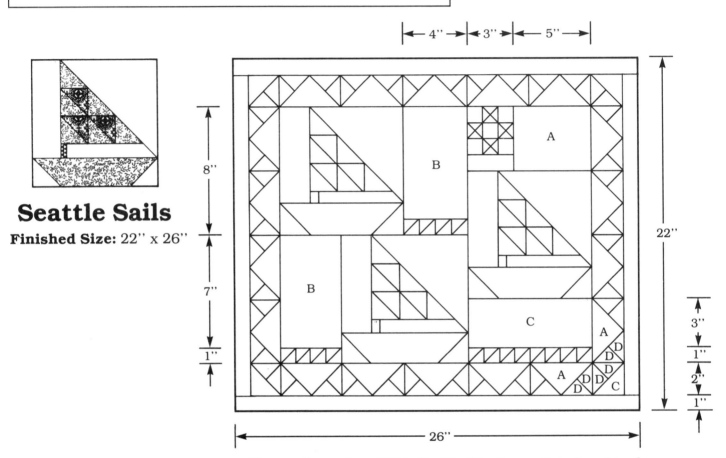

Seattle Sails

Finished Size: 22" x 26"

I live on Queen Anne Hill in Seattle. We often walk to the edge of the hill to look out over Elliott Bay and Puget Sound to the Olympic Mountains. On nice days, sail boats dot the water far below. Random in their placement, they create a pattern with repeated white sails against the gray, green and blue that are the colors of the Northwest.

Materials:

- 1/4 yd. or scrapbag pieces of three different dark green prints and one light blue print
- 1/8 yd. or scrapbag pieces of a light green, a gray-on-white and a medium gray print
- 1/2 yd. medium blue print for background
- 3/4 yd. backing fabric
- 3/4 yd. thin batting

80

Directions:

1. Cut and piece three 8" Seattle Sails unit blocks. Make them all the same or choose different fabrics for each one as shown on page 54. Templates and piecing diagram for Seattle Sails are on page 13.

2. Set pieces. This Wall Quilt has four pieced half blocks to join the unit blocks. Piece them as follows:

    Set Block A: Cut and piece one 3" Variable Star unit block. Use Templates 1 and 2 on this page. From the medium blue background fabric, cut one of Template 3 and sew it to the bottom edge of the small Variable Star. Also from the background fabric, cut a 4 1/2" x 5 1/2" rectangle and sew it on the right side of the previous unit.

    Set Blocks B and C: There are two of set block B and one of C. All three contain 1" scale Sawtooth borders. Use the Bias Strip Piecing method described on page 46 and the 1" square template to make 16 of the two-triangle units. With these units, make two border strips of four repeats each and one of eight repeats. Cut two rectangles that measure 4 1/2" x 7 1/2" (includes seam allowance) and sew a 4" Sawtooth border to the bottom of each one, as pictured, to make two of set block B. Cut one 3 1/2" x 8 1/2" rectangle and to it sew the 8" Sawtooth border to make set block C.

3. Set the four half blocks and the three Seattle Sails blocks together as shown.

4. Pieced Border: For the Half-Pinwheel border on this Wall Quilt, turn to page 40. Use Templates A, D and C on page 45.

    Template A: cut 18 light blue print

    Template D: cut 22 medium gray print, 22 white-on-gray print, and 36 green print

    Template C: cut 4 green print

    Piece border and sew to central pieced section as shown.

5. Read the section on wooden stretcher bar frames and rod pockets, beginning on page 88. Choose the best way to finish the piece. The example pictured on page 54 was quilted, bound and hung with a rod pocket and dowel.

6. Cut border strips and sew them to the pieced section with straight sewn corners. For a Wall Quilt mounted on a wooden stretcher bar frame, cut two 4 1/2" x 20 1/2" strips and two 4 1/2" x 31 1/2" strips. (If you choose this border treatment, add 1/2 yard more to the green print yardage requirement.) For a Wall Quilt to be quilted, bound and hung with a rod pocket and dowel, cut two 1 1/2" x 20 1/2" strips and two 1 1/2" x 26 1/2" strips.

7. Finish by one of the methods outlined on page 88.

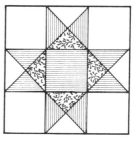

3" Variable Star

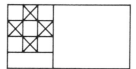

Set Block A

Set Block B (make two)

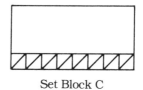

Set Block C

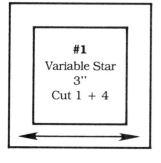

#1
Variable Star
3"
Cut 1 + 4

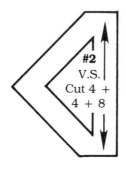

#2
V.S.
Cut 4 +
4 + 8

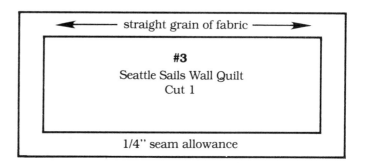

straight grain of fabric

#3
Seattle Sails Wall Quilt
Cut 1

1/4" seam allowance

Tulips

Finished Size: 28" x 28"

The Northwest has a long, slow gentle spring. Tulips come up in my garden in February and bloom in March when other parts of the country still have snow.

Make twenty 4" repeats.

Set-in seam

Make four corner sections.

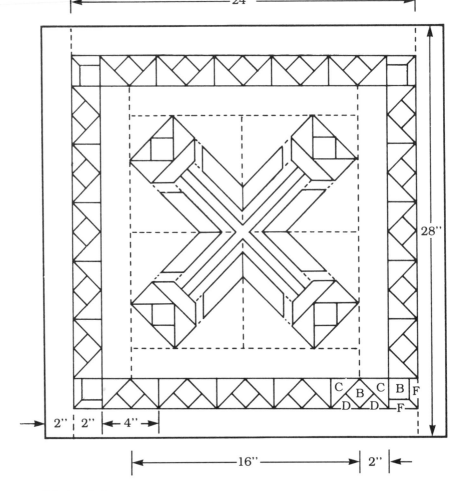

Materials:

1 yd. unbleached muslin or delicate background print

1/8 yd. or scrapbag pieces of two green prints for stems and leaves

Scrapbag pieces of pink, lavender and blue prints and solids for flowers

1/8 yd. or scrapbag pieces of two pink prints, one light blue print and one light pink solid

1 yd. backing fabric

1 yd. thin batting

Directions:

1. Cut and piece four 8" Tulip blocks, as shown on page 19. Set them together as shown here.

2. Cut four spacer strips: two that measure 2 1/2" x 16 1/2" and two that measure 2 1/2" x 20 1/2" (seam allowances included). Sew these strips to the center piece section as shown.

3. Pieced border. Study the Tulip border on page 40. Use Templates B, C, D and F on page 45.
   Template B: cut 24 solid pink
   Template C: cut 20 first pink print
                cut 20 second pink print
   Template D: cut 40 light blue print
   Template F: cut 4; reverse and cut 4 light blue print

   Piece twenty 4" repeats and four square corner units. Note set-in seam in corner unit. Join the 4" repeats in four sections of five each. Join to center section with square corner units as shown.

82

4. Read the sections on Stretcher Bar Frames and Rod Pockets and Dowels, beginning on page 88. Choose the best way to finish the piece. The example shown on page 54 was hand quilted and mounted on a wooden stretcher bar frame.

5. Cut border strips from the background fabric and sew them to the central pieced section with straight sewn corners. For a Wall Quilt mounted on a stretcher bar frame, cut two 5" x 24 1/2" strips and two 5" x 33 1/2" strips. For a Wall Quilt to be quilted, bound and hung with a rod pocket and dowel, cut two strips 2 1/2" x 24 1/2" and two 2 1/2" x 28 1/2" strips.

6. Finish by one of the methods outlined on page 88.

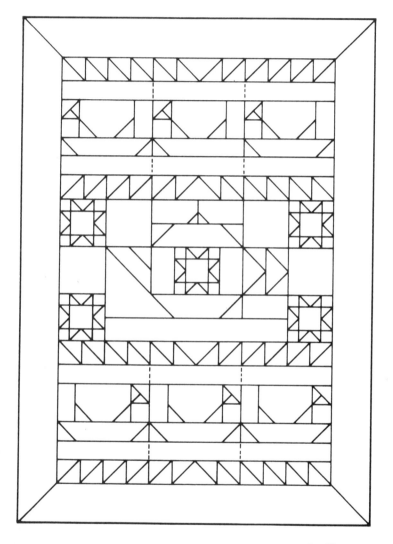

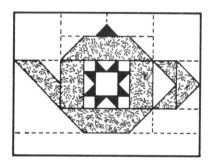

Tea Time

Finished Size: 20" x 27"

At Christmastime this year, I served tea and cookies to guests so frequently that I gave up trying to keep the tea things put away. The teapot and cups and saucers were on a tray ready for instant service when I sat down at the table to design the January pattern of the month for the store where I teach. I just drew what I saw within the confines of the lines on the graph paper, and Tea Time is the result.

The Teapot block is 7 1/2" x 10" and the Cup and Saucer block is 5" square. These two are obviously not 8" blocks like the others in this book, but they are sized to fit together in a Wall Quilt I call Tea Time. Both blocks can be bordered out to sizes that will fit in other projects as well. The Sawtooth Star on the Teapot is also given on page 42 as part of a border design for a Tea Cozy.

Materials:

- 1/3 yd. light background print
- 1/4 yd. unbleached muslin
- 1/8 yd. or scrapbag pieces of four or five prints of equal value but varying visual textures
- 7/8 yd. dark striped fabric for outside border (1/2 yd. of non-stripe)
- 3/4 yd. backing fabric
- 3/4 yd. thin batting

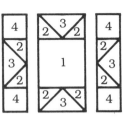

2 1/2" Sawtooth Star

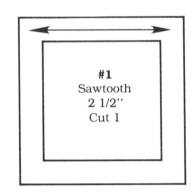

Piecing sequence

Directions:

1. Cut and piece five 2 1/2" Sawtooth Stars. Use Templates 1, 2, 3 and 4.
2. Put four stars aside and piece the Teapot block with one star in the middle. Use Templates 2 and 5-13.

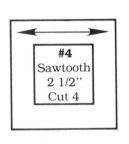

#4 Sawtooth 2 1/2" Cut 4

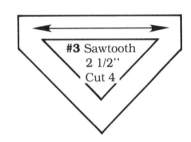

#3 Sawtooth 2 1/2" Cut 4

#2 Sawtooth 2 1/2" Cut 8

#1 Sawtooth 2 1/2" Cut 1

Teapot

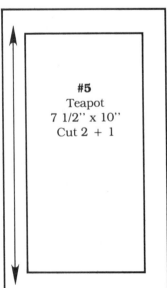

Piecing sequence

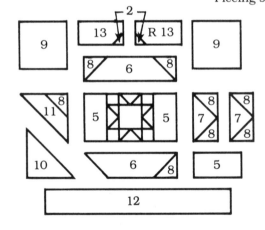

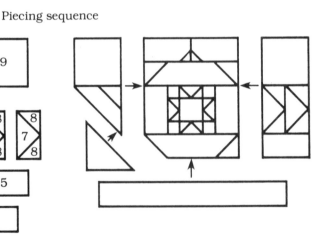

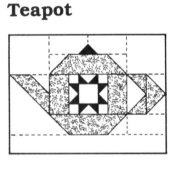

#5 Teapot 7 1/2" x 10" Cut 2 + 1

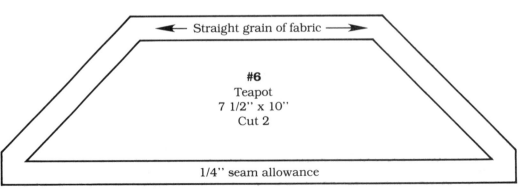

← Straight grain of fabric →

#6 Teapot 7 1/2" x 10" Cut 2

1/4" seam allowance

84

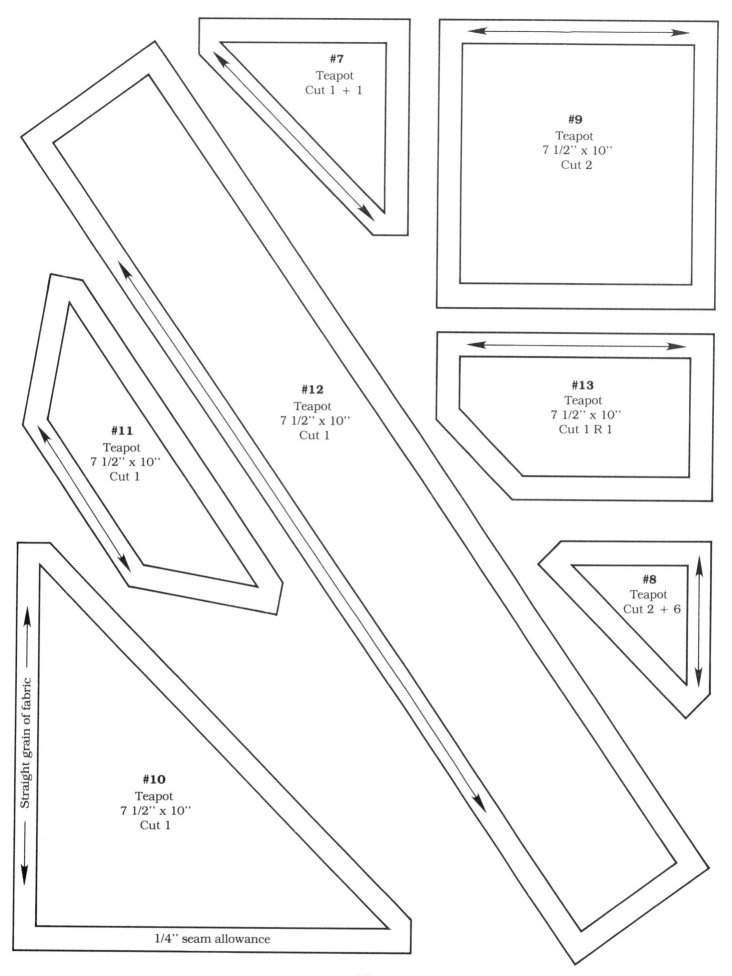

#7
Teapot
Cut 1 + 1

#9
Teapot
7 1/2'' x 10''
Cut 2

#12
Teapot
7 1/2'' x 10''
Cut 1

#13
Teapot
7 1/2'' x 10''
Cut 1 R 1

#11
Teapot
7 1/2'' x 10''
Cut 1

#8
Teapot
Cut 2 + 6

Straight grain of fabric

#10
Teapot
7 1/2'' x 10''
Cut 1

1/4'' seam allowance

3. Cut two of Template 9 from the background print and piece with remaining 2 1/2" Sawtooth Stars, as shown. Sew the resulting sections to the Teapot block.

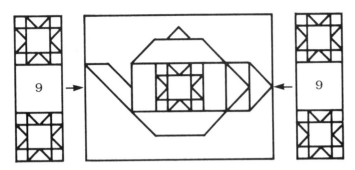

4. Make four Sawtooth border units consisting of 12 two-triangle units each. Use the Bias Strip Piecing method described on page 46 and the 1 1/4" template on page 47. If you have four different prints, make 12 repeats of each print and muslin. Join the repeats as shown.

5. Using all the dark prints, cut and piece six 5" Cup and Saucer blocks — three with handles on the right and three with handles on the left. Use Templates 14-20.

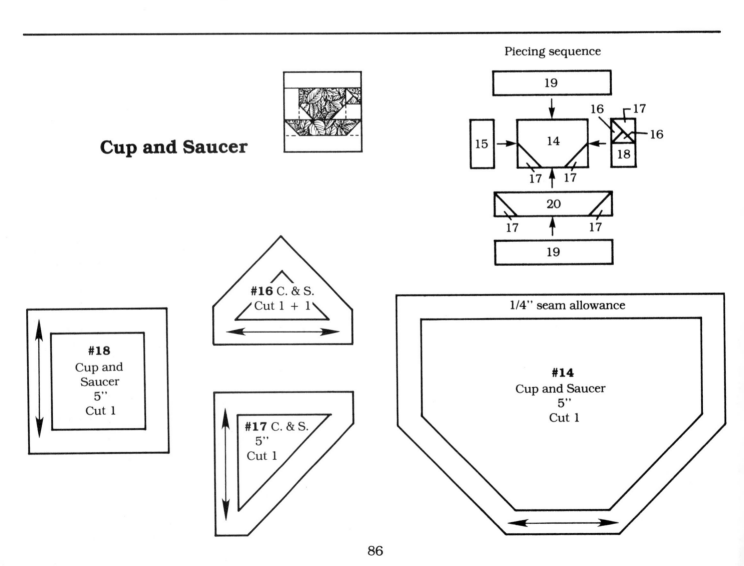

Cup and Saucer

Piecing sequence

#16 C. & S.
Cut 1 + 1

#18
Cup and Saucer
5"
Cut 1

#17 C. & S.
5"
Cut 1

1/4" seam allowance

#14
Cup and Saucer
5"
Cut 1

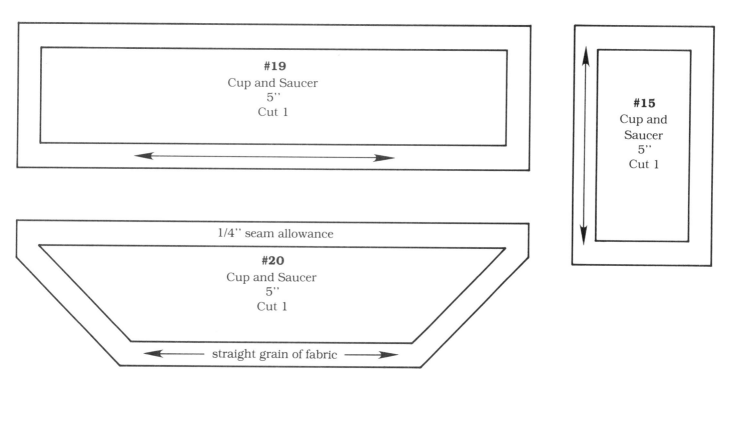

#19
Cup and Saucer
5"
Cut 1

#15
Cup and
Saucer
5"
Cut 1

1/4" seam allowance

#20
Cup and Saucer
5"
Cut 1

← straight grain of fabric →

6. Join the Cup and Saucer blocks in two rows of three blocks each, as shown.
7. Sew the Sawtooth border units to the rows of Cup and Saucer blocks.
8. Join the Cup and Saucer units to the Teapot and Sawtooth Stars unit.
9. The outside border treatment for this Wall Quilt may vary. You can choose single borders as in the line drawing or double borders, as shown in the example on page 54. For single borders, cut two 3" x 20 1/2" strips and two 3" x 27 1/2" strips. Sew to the center pieced section and miter the corners. See Mitering Corners on page 34.
10. Finish with hand quilting and binding. Hang with a rod pocket and dowel.

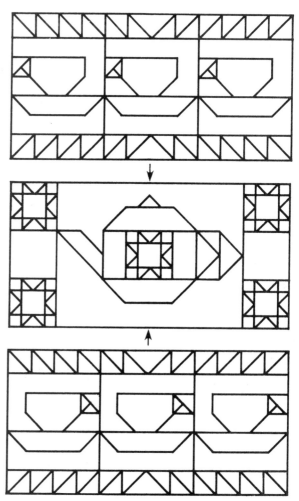

Techniques for Hanging Quilts

One of the greatest joys of completing a Wall Quilt is to hang it where it can complement your home's decor and become part of your life. There are several different methods for hanging quilts and I will discuss two of them here, Stretcher Bar Frames and Rod Pockets and Dowels (see page 90). I have found these two techniques to be the most satisfactory for displaying my fabric work to the best advantage while guarding against damage to the quilt or to the wall.

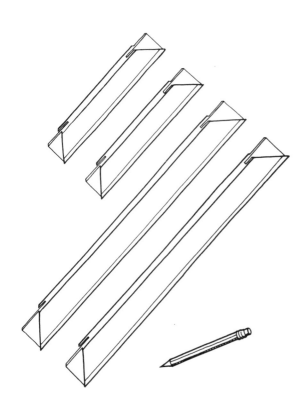

Stretcher Bar Frames

Many patchwork blocks and small quilts can be mounted as described here. If a piece is to be mounted unquilted, the piecing must be very flat. When making Wall Quilts, it might be wise to put off cutting borders and purchasing frames or dowels until the actual piecing is completed and an assessment can be made of the patchwork's "stretchability." If your piecing is a little wavy or if there are many triangles in the design, it can still be mounted on a stretcher bar frame, but it will probably need to be hand quilted first. Then the quilting, not the seams, will absorb the stress of "stretching."

Stretcher bar frames can be purchased at art supply stores, framing shops or at some fabric stores. Ready-made stretcher bars come in lengths that increase in 2" increments (12", 14", 16", etc.). Frame shops will cut them to any size, although there usually is a charge for this service.

Materials:

Wooden stretcher bar frame
Unbleached muslin for lining
Markers
Push pins
Household-weight staple gun with 5/16" sharp pointed staples

Directions:

1. Make the pieced design and add the desired borders (see Borders on page 33). Borders should extend 2 1/2" to 3" beyond the frame on all sides to allow enough fabric to be wrapped around the outside edge of the frame and to be stapled in place. Press the quilt top. Cut a piece of unbleached muslin lining the same size as the quilt top. If you are going to quilt your hanging and stretch it too, cut a piece of thin batting that extends only 1" beyond the frame edge, not to the edge of the borders. Quilt the piece before it is stretched (see Quilting on page 63). For an unquilted piece, press and pin baste the muslin lining to the wrong side of the quilt top.
2. Assemble the wooden stretcher bar frame. Squeeze the notched corners together to form a square or rectangle. Check the corners with a right angle. Put a staple across each joint.
3. Place the lined Wall Quilt face up on a large table or on the floor. Place the wooden frame on top and center the design through the "window" formed by the frame. When it is properly positioned, make a dot on the fabric with a marker at each outside corner of the frame.

4. After marking, place the Wall Quilt face up on top of the frame. Match the positioning dots with the corners of the frame. To hold the hanging in place for stapling, insert push pins through the fabric along the outside edge of the frame. Pull the fabric gently across the frame so it is flat and there is no slack. Don't try to stretch it tightly, as too much pulling will distort the seamlines.

5. With the Wall Quilt pinned to the frame, turn it face down. While folding the raw edges under, staple the border fabric to the frame on the side that will face the wall. Start with one staple in the middle of each side. Working from the center outward, place staples 2" to 3" apart on the first side. Stop 2" from each corner. Next, staple the opposite side, then the other two sides. To finish, trim away a little of the excess fabric at the corners, neatly fold what's left, and staple in place.

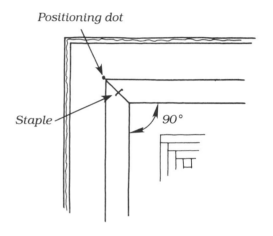

Positioning dot

Staple

90°

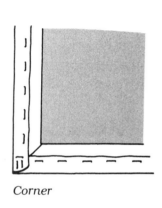

Corner

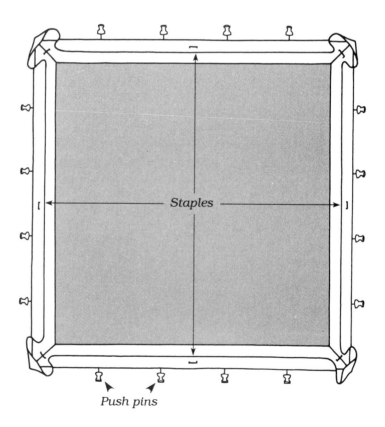

Staples

Push pins

Rod Pockets and Dowels

A rod pocket or "quilt sleeve" is an open-ended fabric tube that is hand stitched to the upper back edge of a quilt. A dowel, flat stick or curtain rod can be slipped through the fabric tube to evenly support weight of the quilt when it is hung. Depending on the size of the piece and the condition of the wall, the dowel, stick or rod is then secured to the wall with brackets, nails, hooks and fishing line, or whatever other support seems appropriate.

We live in an older home that has wooden molding on the wall about a foot from the ceiling. I hang my quilts from molding hooks with fishing line tied to the ends of dowels that have been inserted in the rod pockets. This system makes it easy to change the "quilt show" as I please. Quilt exhibitions often require displayed quilts to have rod pockets: for ease of hanging and to protect the quilts from the stress and possible tearing that pins, staples or tacks can cause.

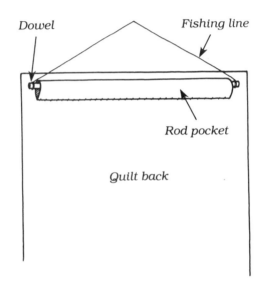

Dowel   Fishing line

Rod pocket

Quilt back

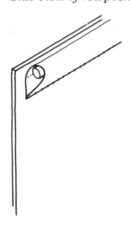

Side view of rod pocket

Materials:

8 1/2"-wide piece muslin or fabric to match quilt backing, cut as long as quilt's top edge
Dowel, flat stick or curtain rod
Hardware attachment for wall (bracket, hook, nail, etc.)
Fishing line (for invisible hanging in some situations)

Directions:

1. Cut a piece of muslin or fabric to match quilt backing 8 1/2" wide and as long as the quilt's top edge. Fold muslin piece lengthwise wrong side out. Sew the long raw edges together with a 1/2" seam. Leave the two ends open.

2. Turn the resulting fabric tube right side out and press. Hem the ends so the rod pocket extends only to 1" from each side of the quilt.

3. A side view of a rod pocket sewn to the top edge of a quilt is shown here. Notice that it is not flat. The side of the rod pocket that is away from the quilt has more fullness to accommodate the bulk of the dowel, allowing the quilt to hang flat. To attach a rod pocket, press the pocket with the seam at the bottom and a crease at the top. Press in another crease 3/4" to 1" from the first one.

4. Position the rod pocket on the quilt with the first crease along the top edge. Pin it in place so you can hand stitch the pocket to the back of the quilt, along the second crease and the bottom seam. Sew only through the quilt backing; no stitches should show on the quilt front.

NOTE: If a quilt is very wide and you are afraid its weight will cause the dowel to bow or break, make the rod pocket in two sections. Extra support can then be added in the middle of the quilt.

Hostess Apron

This Hostess Apron has a patchwork bodice and skirt border. The ties cross in the back, pass through loops at the waistband, and tie at the waist in a front or back bow.

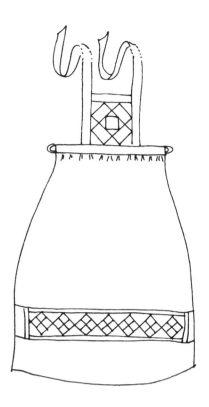

Finished Size: One size fits most people; full figure adjustments are noted below.

Materials:

1 5/8 yds. 45"-wide main color fabric
1/4 yd. each of two or three more fabrics for patchwork
9" x 9" square thin batting
Thread to match main color fabric for topstitching
NOTE: For full figures, add extra borders to the 8" unit block. If the 8" unit block is thus enlarged, lengthen piece B and cut larger backing and batting to accommodate the larger block size. If a longer waistband is desired, go ahead and make it longer, but remember that for every 1" added to the waistband, 1 1/2" must be added to the width of the skirt panel. If you add 4" or more to the width of the skirt, add one or more repeats to the patchwork border design, depending on the skirt width. In such a case, 1 5/8 yards of the main color fabric may not be enough; buy an extra 1/4 to 1/2 yard to accommodate size increases.

Directions:

1. Cutting Instructions. Cut from the main fabric:
    A. Four 3 1/2" x 45" (width of fabric) strips for ties
    B. One 3 1/2" x 8" strip (from the end of one of the other strips — see cutting diagram)
    C. Two 2 1/2" x 22" strips for waistband
    D. One 1 3/4" strip for loops
    E. One 32" x 45" panel (width of fabric)
    If the main fabric has stripes or a definite vertical design, and you want the stripes running up and down on the apron, buy two yards of the main fabric and follow cutting diagram 2.

Cutting diagram 2

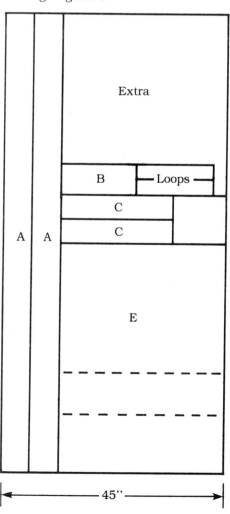

Cutting diagram 1

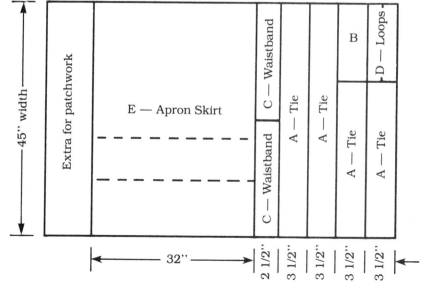

2. Patchwork and Quilting. Using the leftover main color fabric and the 1/4 yard pieces, piece an 8" unit block and a 28" border design section (seven 4" repeats). See Blocks on page 5 and Patchwork Border Designs on page 35. From the main color or another fabric, cut a 9" square to back the block. Place batting between the patchwork and the backing. Pin baste. Quilt by machine or by hand. (The border design in the skirt will be lined but left unquilted.) After quilting, trim excess batting and backing to match the raw edge of the pieced block.

3. Bodice Front. Place piece B and quilted design block with right sides together; sew together, using a 1/4" seam allowance. Press under 1/4" on the unsewn edge of piece B. Fold over the top of block and pin so that the topstitching on the front will catch the fabric edge on the back. Topstitch approximately 3/16" from the seamline. Trim excess length of piece B after topstitching.

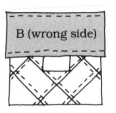

B (wrong side)

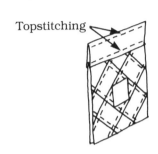

Topstitching

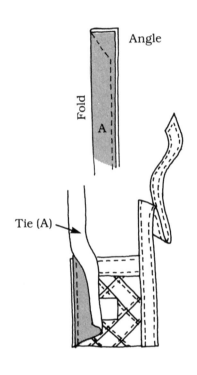

Angle

Fold

A

Tie (A)

4. Ties. Seam A strips together to make two long strips of equal length for the ties. (Note: The ties are extra long to accommodate larger figures. If you prefer not to deal with the length, 12" to 14" can be cut off the length for smaller sizes.) Fold the ties lengthwise, right sides together; pin. Beginning 10" from the end and using a 1/4" seam allowance, sew along the raw edge. When line of stitching is 1 1/2" from the end, angle the sewing line to a point at the end of the tie. Trim excess and turn tie right side out. Press. Sew ties to the bodice front in a 1/4" seam, as illustrated. Close the 10" opening with topstitching as in step 3. Topstitch along both sides of ties.

5. Waistband. To make two loops, fold raw edges of piece D (1 3/4" x 8 1/2" strip) to inside and topstitch. Cut piece in half. Baste two loops to the right side of the front waistband C, as illustrated. Place front and back waistband pieces right sides together, with the apron bodice centered in between. Using a 1/4" seam, sew on three sides as illustrated. Trim corners and turn. Press. At the bottom of the waistband, press in 1/2" seam allowance.

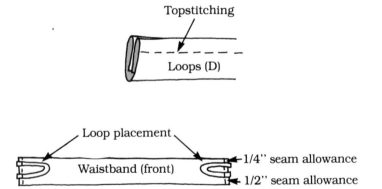

Topstitching

Loops (D)

Loop placement

Waistband (front)

1/4" seam allowance

1/2" seam allowance

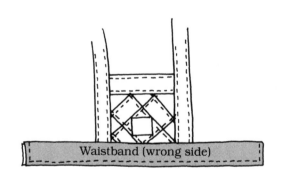

Waistband (wrong side)

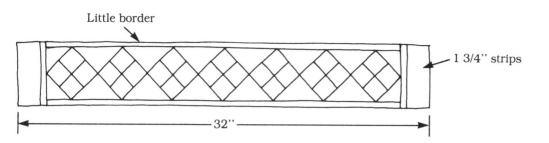

Little border

1 3/4" strips

32"

6. Skirt. Cut 1"-wide strips for the little border around the patchwork border design. Sew with 1/4" seams, as pictured. On
either end of this unit, add 1 3/4" strips to make a total length
of 32". From skirt panel E, cut the lining for the patchwork
border (6" x 32") and the hem section (8" x 32"). On the 8"
hem section, press under 1/4" on the bottom edge. Turn a 2"
hem. Press; topstitch in place (from wrong side). Sew patchwork border unit to the hem section with a 1/4" seam. Using a
1/4" seam, sew the patchwork/hemmed section to the main
skirt and 6" lining piece at the same time as shown. Press. By
hand, hem the lining piece along the bottom so the patchwork
is covered and no raw edges show. Hem both sides of the apron
front. Hold the apron skirt up to you to determine how long you
want it to be. Cut off excess fabric at the top unfinished edge.
Evenly gather along this edge and sew apron skirt to the waistband front with a 1/2" seam. Press. Enclose gathered top of
skirt with waistband so no raw edges show. Pin. Close with
topstitching as shown.

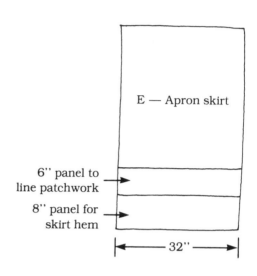

E — Apron skirt

6" panel to
line patchwork

8" panel for
skirt hem

32"

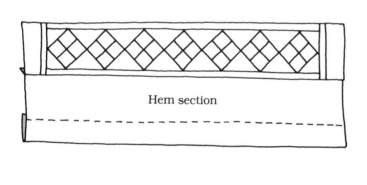

Hem section

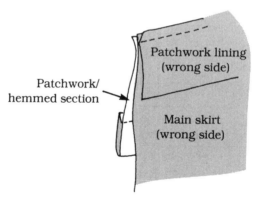

Patchwork/
hemmed section

Patchwork lining
(wrong side)

Main skirt
(wrong side)

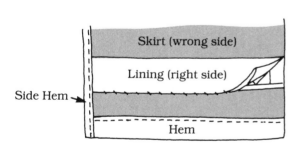

Skirt (wrong side)

Lining (right side)

Side Hem

Hem

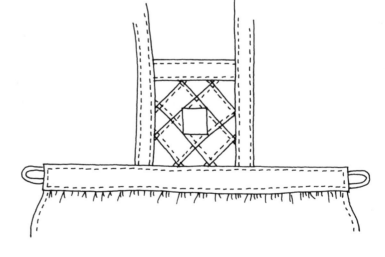

Style C

Tote

This patchwork Tote is large, but not too large — things don't get lost forever in it and you can still pick it up when it's full. The handles are long enough to fit over your shoulder with the bag tucked neatly under your arm.

Plans are given for three Tote styles. All utilize patchwork designs in this book. After the patchwork design is completed, basic construction for this sturdy Tote is the same for all three styles. Style A uses an 8" straight-set block (School House, Seattle Sails or Tall Pine Tree would be nifty here); Style B is planned for an 8" block set on the diagonal (Tulip or Flower Basket); Style C puts the 4" repeat borders found on page 35 to good use.

Finished Size: 16" x 15" tall

Materials:

1/2 yd. brushed denim or corduroy
1/2 yd. lining fabric (cotton print or main fabric)
Small amounts of several fabrics for patchwork
Thin batting and unbleached muslin to back patchwork

Directions:

1. Choose Style A, B or C. Make the patchwork block or borders as shown for the chosen style.

Note: Dimensions given are finished: for actual construction, add 1/4" seam allowances.

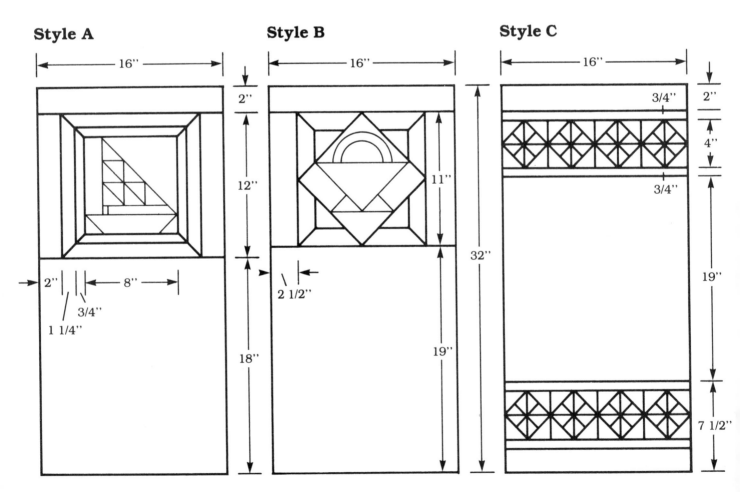

94

2. Cut lining and thin batting 1/2" larger all around than the patchwork. Baste layers together and quilt by hand (see page 68) or by machine (see page 67). After quilting, trim excess batting and lining even with raw edges of the patchwork.
3. From main fabric (denim or corduroy), cut two pieces 4" x 22" for the Tote handles. Cut the necessary pieces (A, C, D, etc.) to piece the rectangle that is the Tote body. The finished rectangle should measure 16" x 32" without seam allowances.
4. To make the handles, fold each handle strip in half lengthwise, wrong side out, matching the raw edges. Stitch long side in 1/4" seam. Turn right side out and topstitch 1/4" from each side. Position handles on long rectangle as shown. Machine baste in place.
5. Cut lining to match pieced rectangle.
6. If an inside pocket is desired, cut one from lining fabric, using pocket pattern piece. Fold in the middle with right sides together. Pin. Stitch 1/4" seams on each side, leaving a 2 1/2" opening at the bottom for turning. Turn pocket right side out. Press. Topstitch along top edge. Position pocket on lining, as shown, and attach with a double row of topstitching.

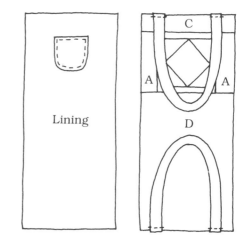

Lining

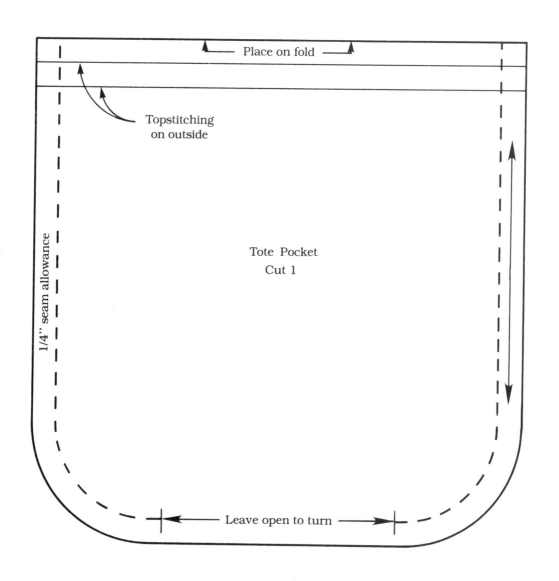

Place on fold

Topstitching on outside

1/4" seam allowance

Tote Pocket
Cut 1

Leave open to turn

7. Fold Tote body in half with right sides together. Sew side seams with 3/8" seam allowance. Box the bottom corners, as shown in the diagram.

8. Repeat the procedure in step 7 for the lining (sew 3/8" side seams and box corners).

9. You now have two "bags." With right sides together, place one inside the other, matching side seams and top edges. Leaving a 4" opening for turning, sew the Tote body and lining together along the top edge, using a 3/8" seam allowance.

10. Turn Tote right side out. Press. Topstitch around the top edge with one or two rows of stitching.

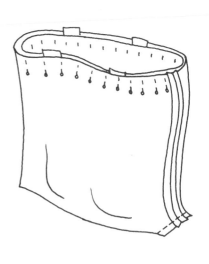

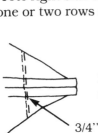

Box the corners. Double stitch for strength.

3/4"

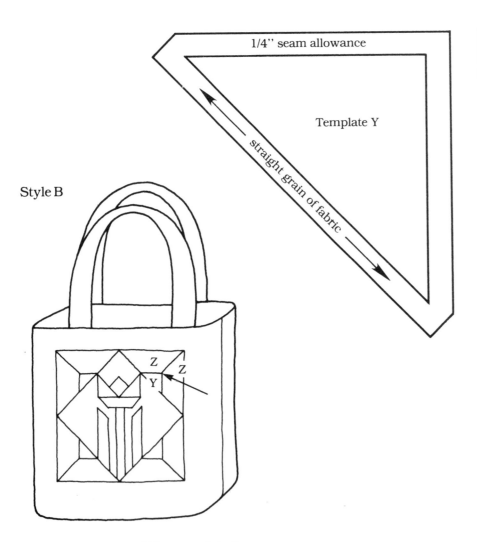

1/4" seam allowance

Template Y

straight grain of fabric

Style B

Template Z

Use Templates Y and Z to complete the pieced corner sections for Tote, Style B. Note the set-in seam. Sew only to seamline at this point and backtack.

96

Tea Cozy

I have an oversized earthenware Brown Betty teapot that requires an extra large Tea Cozy. A cozy should not fit the pot too tightly; if you have to struggle to get it on and off, spills are likely. The pattern for this Tea Cozy is pretty large: to accommodate my large teapot and so four 4" repeats of the border designs featured in this book will fit across it.

This Tea Cozy has two parts, a pad and a cover that can be washed separately. Use gentle setting or wash by hand. Dry pad in dryer; dry cover flat or in dryer. You can make one pad and use it with several different covers. Make them with different designs and fabric combinations to complement different sets of dishes, teapots or table linens.

Two basic styles of Tea Cozy covers are offered here. Style A is pieced and quilted and features the use of the 4" repeat border designs found on page 35. Style B has a simple unpieced cover that is decorated with appliqued or quilted motifs. An appliqued cover can be left unquilted if you wish. If you choose to make a quilted or appliqued cozy (Style B), you can reduce the size by cutting pattern pieces A and B down by as much as 1". Be sure to subtract the same amount all around each large pattern piece and adjust measurements in the instructions accordingly.

Finished Size: 14" x 16"

Materials:

Cover:

    1/2 yd. main fabric
    Fabric for appliqued or pieced design
    1/2 yd. unbleached muslin for lining
    1/2 yd. thin batting

Pad:

    1 yd. unbleached muslin
    1/2 yd. thick roll batting (If layers need to be doubled for thickness, buy twice as much.)

Templates:

To make the Tea Cozy, you will need two large templates: the pad shape (A) and the cover (B). On a large sheet of paper (17 1/2" x 22" graph paper is best), measure a 14" x 16" grid of 2" squares. Study the illustration provided. It shows the shape for Template A, the Tea Cozy pad shape. Copy the pad shape, square by square onto the larger grid. Template B, the cover shape, is made by duplicating the pad shape and adding 1/2" seam allowance all the way around. Glue the paper templates to posterboard to stiffen them. Cut the stiffening to match the paper shape.

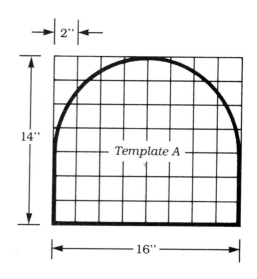

2"

14"

Template A

16"

Directions for Style A:

1. Cut and piece two 6" border design segments, using four 4" repeats each. Templates and instructions for Patchwork Border Designs are on page 35.
2. Cut four 1" x 16 1/2" fabric strips and sew to pieced border sections as shown.
3. Cut two 2" x 16 1/2" strips. Sew to bottoms of pieced sections.
4. Cut two large 9" x 16 1/2" rectangles from main fabric. Sew to tops of pieced sections.
5. Cut two 16" x 18" pieces of unbleached muslin for lining.
6. Cut two pieces thin batting to match lining.
7. Baste the three layers together and quilt by hand or machine (see page 68 for Hand Quilting; see page 67 for Machine Quilting). Hint: When I quilt Tea Cozy covers by hand, I use an 18" square adjustable quilt-as-you-go frame. Leave the cover section in its rectangular shape for quilting so it will fit on the frame. After quilting, trim to the rounded Tea Cozy shape.
8. Use Template B, the cover shape, and a fabric marking pencil to trace the curved cozy shape onto the quilted rectangles. Trim excess.
9. With right sides together, pin the two sides along the curve and stitch, using the even-feed foot (see page 67) and a 1/2" seam allowance.
10. Bind the bottom raw edge of cozy cover (see Binding on page 70). To join binding ends, leave 1/2" unsewn at the beginning of the binding strip; when stitching approaches the other end of the binding strip, fold the unsewn section back to hide the raw edge and finish sewing (see diagram).

Style A

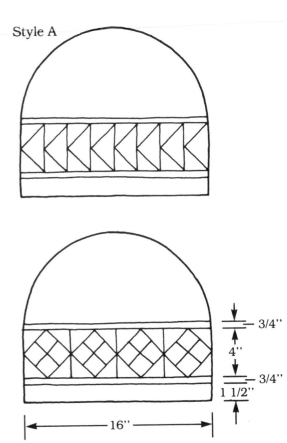

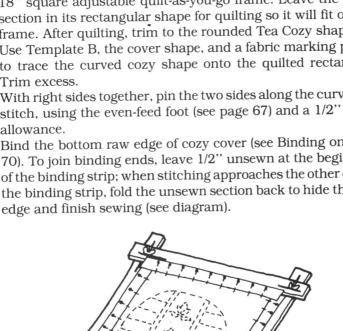

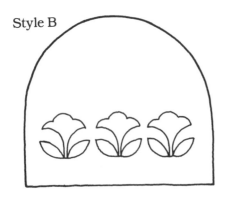

Style B

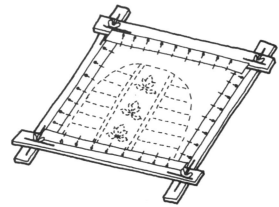

Directions for Style B:

1. Cut two large 16" x 18" rectangles from the main fabric. Lightly trace the Tea Cozy cover shape (Template B) onto the two rectangles, but do not cut them out at this time.
2. Position and applique chosen motifs within the pad shape, leaving room for seam allowances along outside edge. For applique patterns and design suggestions, see page 48. For applique technique, see page 21. An appliqued cover can be left unquilted if you choose, and instead of binding the bottom edge you can simply hem it. Another idea for an appliqued cover is to use a prequilted fabric in a solid color or a delicate print for the main background fabric.
3. For a quilted cover, as pictured on page 99, mark the quilting design within the pad shape on the rectangles (see Quilting on page 68) and follow steps 5-10 for Style A.

Directions for Pad:

1. Cut two pieces of unbleached muslin to measure 18" x 36" and two pieces of thick batting or several layers of thin batting to measure 18" x 18".

2. Fold the muslin rectangles in half, as shown, and press in creases. With the muslin pieces still folded, place Template A (pad shape) with the bottom of the template on the crease and trace the curved outline onto the fabric with a fabric marking pen. Only one side of each folded piece needs to be marked.

3. Unfold the muslin pieces and lay them flat with the marked side down. Place the batting with bottom edges along the crease in the muslin. Fold the muslin at the crease to cover the batting. Pin baste through all three layers along the curved marking line.

4. With a straight machine stitch, quilt through the three layers 1/4" inside the curved line. Make a second line of stitching on the line. After stitching the curves on each pad section, remove the pins from <u>one</u> pad and trim to 1/8" outside stitching. Do not trim the other pad.

5. Carefully pin baste the trimmed pad to the untrimmed pad, matching the sewn curves. Keep the trimmed pad on top. Stitch the pads together with a straight stitch along the curve that falls between the two previous rows of stitching.

6. Remove pins and trim remaining excess muslin and batting to the outside line of stitching. Take care not to cut the stitches or clip the muslin. The resulting raw edge will remain on the outside of the pad and be hidden by the decorative cover.

Muslin rectangle: folded, creased and marked

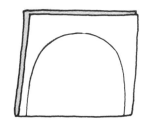

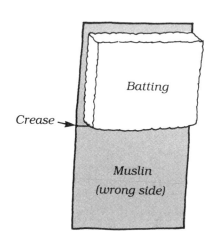

Pin baste curve.

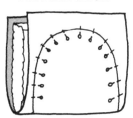

After stitching, trim excess on one pad only.

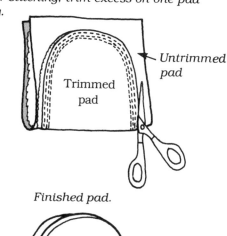

Style B

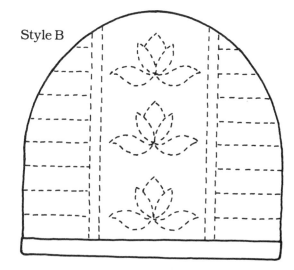

Finished pad.

Appendix

Templates for Set Pieces

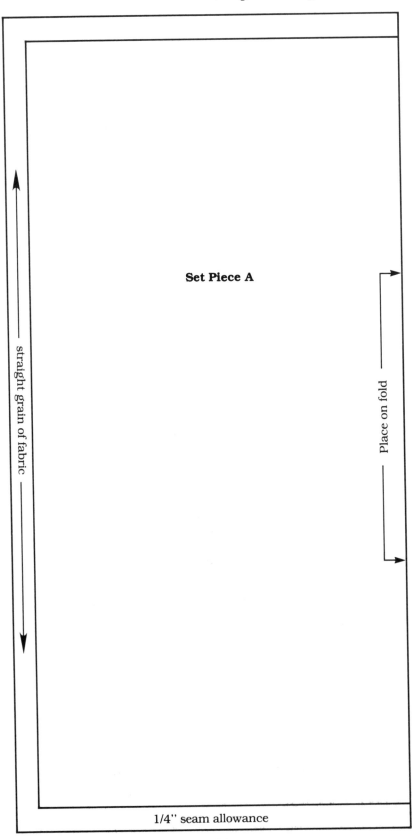

8" Alternate unpieced block, for straight and diagonal sets.

Set Piece A

straight grain of fabric

Place on fold

1/4" seam allowance

Use for diagonally set designs as shown in Quilt Plan C on page 60 and for cornering out diagonally set blocks for Totes, Pillows, etc.

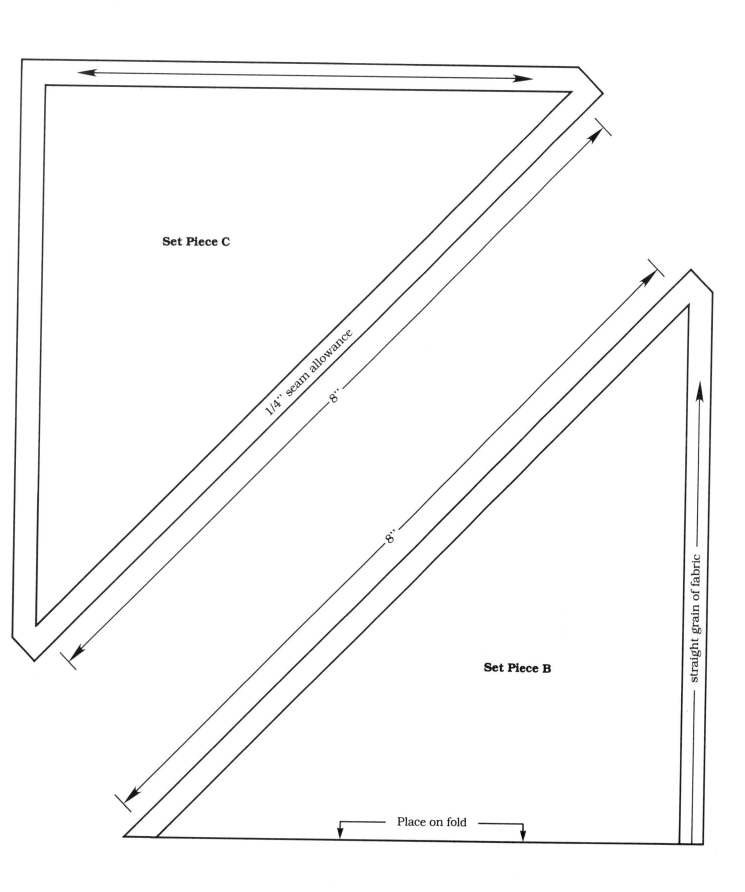

Set Piece C

1/4" seam allowance

8"

8"

Set Piece B

straight grain of fabric

Place on fold

Templates for Pieced Lattices

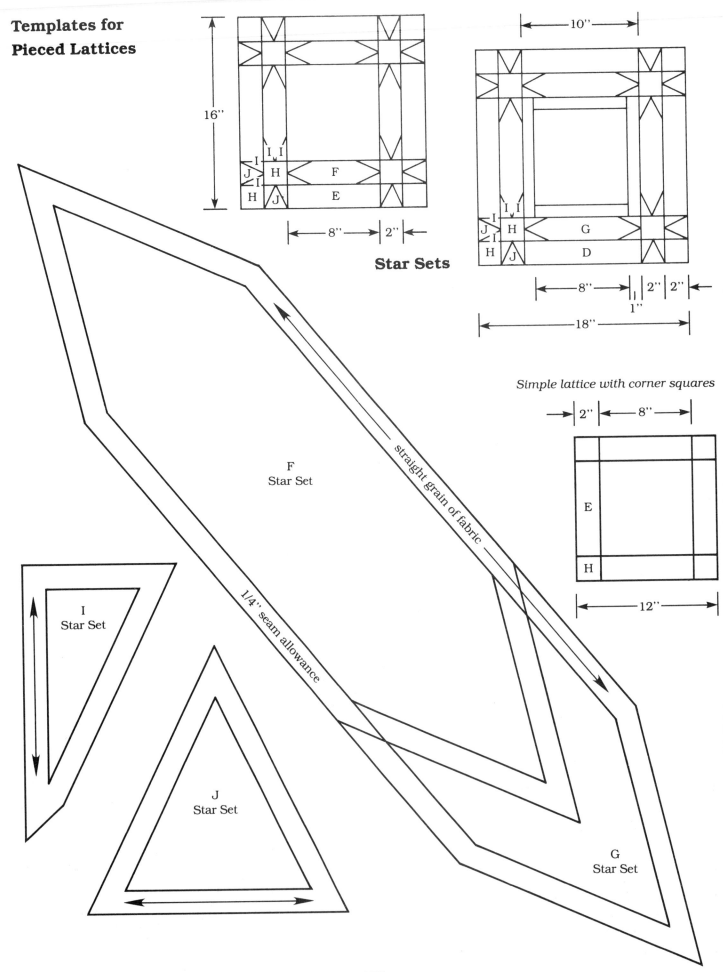

Star Sets

16''

8'' 2''

10''

8'' 2'' 2''

1''

18''

I I I

J

H

I

H J

F

E

I I I

J

H

I

H J

G

D

Simple lattice with corner squares

2'' 8''

E

H

12''

F
Star Set

straight grain of fabric

1/4'' seam allowance

I
Star Set

J
Star Set

G
Star Set

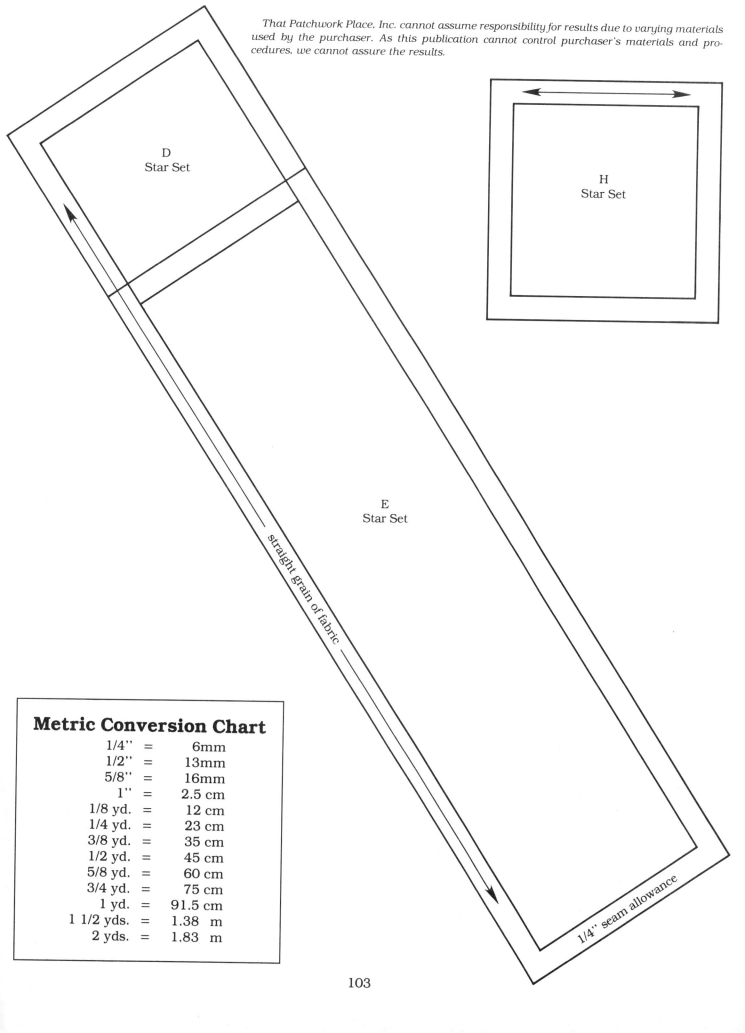

D
Star Set

H
Star Set

That Patchwork Place, Inc. cannot assume responsibility for results due to varying materials used by the purchaser. As this publication cannot control purchaser's materials and procedures, we cannot assure the results.

E
Star Set

straight grain of fabric

1/4" seam allowance

Metric Conversion Chart

1/4"	=	6mm
1/2"	=	13mm
5/8"	=	16mm
1"	=	2.5 cm
1/8 yd.	=	12 cm
1/4 yd.	=	23 cm
3/8 yd.	=	35 cm
1/2 yd.	=	45 cm
5/8 yd.	=	60 cm
3/4 yd.	=	75 cm
1 yd.	=	91.5 cm
1 1/2 yds.	=	1.38 m
2 yds.	=	1.83 m

Bibliography

Beyer, Jinny, *Patchwork Patterns*, McLean, Virginia: EPM Publications, Inc., 1979.

Gutcheon, Beth, *The Perfect Patchwork Primer*, Baltimore, Maryland: Penguin Books, Inc., 1974.

Halgrimson, Jan, *Patching Things Up*, Edmonds, Washington: Weaver-Finch Publications, 1983.

Hall, Carrie A. and Rose G. Krestinger, *The Romance of the Patchwork Quilt*, New York, New York: Bonanza Books, 1935.

Holstein, Jonathan, *The Pieced Quilt, An American Design Tradition*, Greenwich, Connecticut: New York Graphic Society Ltd., 1973.

Leman, Bonnie and Judy Martin, *Taking the Math Out of Making Patchwork Quilts*, Denver, Colorado: Moon Over the Mountain Publishing Co., 1981.

Martin, Judy, *The Patchworkbook*, New York, New York: Charles Scribner's Sons, 1983.

McCloskey, Marsha R., *Small Quilts*, Bothell, Washington: That Patchwork Place, Inc., 1982.

McCloskey, Marsha R., *Wall Quilts*, Bothell, Washington: That Patchwork Place, Inc., 1983.

Orlofsky, Patsy and Myron, *Quilts in America*, New York, New York: McGraw Hill Book Co., 1974.

Safford, Carleton L. and Robert Bishop, *America's Quilts and Coverlets*, New York, New York: Weathervane Books, 1974.

Sunset, *How to Make Pillows*, Menlo Park, California: Lane Publishing Co., 1980.

About the Author

A graphic arts major in college, Marsha McCloskey has been quilting since 1969. For many years, she sold the products of her talents as a seamstress and fabric artist, finding a ready market in gift shops and craft fairs.

Now living with her family in Seattle, Marsha shares her skills with others, teaching for quilting stores and special interest groups. This book is the third in a series of quilting books she has written, a sequel to **Small Quilts** (1982) and **Wall Quilts** (1983), published by That Patchwork Place, Inc.